Convergence Journalism

WRITING AND REPORTING ACROSS THE NEWS MEDIA

Janet Kolodzy

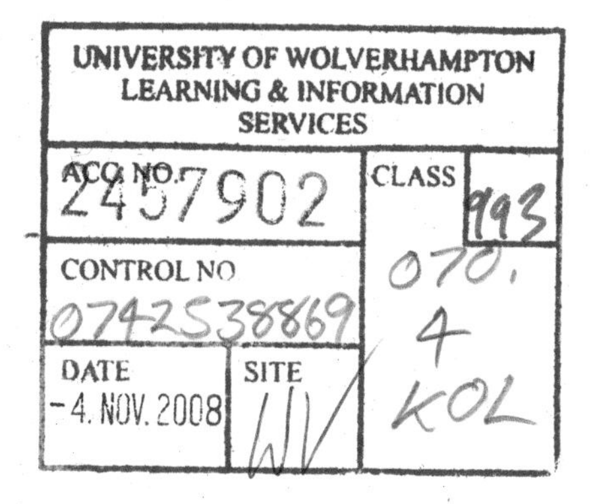

ROWMAN & LITTLEFIELD PUBLISHERS, INC.

Lanham • Boulder • New York • Toronto • Oxford

ROWMAN & LITTLEFIELD PUBLISHERS, INC.

Published in the United States of America
by Rowman & Littlefield Publishers, Inc.
A wholly owned subsidiary of The Rowman & Littlefield Publishing Group, Inc.
4501 Forbes Boulevard, Suite 200, Lanham, Maryland 20706
www.rowmanlittlefield.com

PO Box 317
Oxford
OX2 9RU, UK

British Library Cataloguing in Publication Information Available

Library of Congress Cataloging-in-Publication Data

Kolodzy, Janet, 1955–
Convergence journalism : writing and reporting across the news media / Janet Kolodzy.
p. cm.
Includes bibliographical references and index.
ISBN-10 0-7425-3885-0 (cloth : alk. paper) — ISBN-10 0-7425-3886-9 (pbk. : alk. paper)
ISBN-13 978-0-7425-3885-6 — ISBN-13 978-0-7425-3886-3
1. Online journalism. 2. Broadcast journalism. 3. Convergence (Telecommunication) I. Title.
PN4784.O62K66 2006
070.4—dc22 2005031034

Printed in the United States of America

∞™ The paper used in this publication meets the minimum requirements of American National Standard for Information Sciences—Permanence of Paper for Printed Library Materials, ANSI/NISO Z39.48-1992.

Contents

Preface: Why a Textbook on Convergence in Journalism?

EVER SINCE I made the leap from journalism practitioner to journalism teacher in 1998, media prognosticators have been declaring the death of radio, daily newspapers, the network news, journalistic ethics, and even journalism itself. Old media will be replaced by new media. Bloggers will replace journalists. "We media" will replace mainstream media. Yet if anything can be discerned about journalism's future from what has been happening in the first few years of the twenty-first century, it is that this will be a century of change and choice. Journalism of the future will involve all sorts of media: old and new, niche and mass, the personal and the global. It will involve storytelling in every combination of words, pictures, and sound. And it will be propelled not just by journalists but by news audiences. That is already apparent today.

As news audiences' informational needs and wants change, and as they seek more choices in getting that information, journalists will be expected to adapt. So how should they? Convergence has emerged within the past decade as a strategy to respond to the rapid world of media change and choice. Convergence acknowledges that news consumers are gaining more control of the news process. That change in the controlling forces of news requires changes in the ways of doing news. Convergence is about being flexible enough to provide news and information to anyone and everyone, anytime and all the time, anywhere and often everywhere without abandoning key journalistic values. Convergence refocuses journalism to its core mission—to inform the public about its world in the best ways possible and available. Convergence aims to give news audiences choices by coordinating and cooperating in news-gathering and news presentation.

The emergence of convergence as a different way of thinking and doing journalism led me to seek out how it is being tried in newsrooms and how it could be applied in the classroom. As someone who worked half her professional life for newspapers and half her professional life in broadcast, and who was excited about online's development, I thought convergence had a great deal of potential in building connections and creating more journalism choices for news audiences. I understand the pluses and minuses of each medium, having worked in them. So applying them to the practice and the teaching of journalism should seem simple. It was not.

I quickly learned that convergence means different things to different people, and that convergence is a dynamic, evolutionary process. Initial press coverage of Tampa, Florida's, convergence efforts alongside stories about megamedia mergers in the late 1990s cemented rather simplistic notions about convergence and how it operates. It became a catchword without much substance or understanding. Convergence in journalism became synonymous with the idea of one person doing it all, and the evils of media consolidation. One purpose for this book is to clarify what convergence is, and is not, as it relates to the day-to-day world of writing, reporting, producing, and presenting news. That is why this book opens with a look at the various ways people think about convergence and how that translates to the daily work of journalism. It sets out to explain that convergence is as much a way of thinking as it is a way of doing.

In fact, convergence in journalism defies a one-size-fits-all set of practices. The way that convergence works in Lawrence, Kansas, may not work in Hartford, Connecticut, because their news communities are not the same. And the way convergence was operating in 1998 is different from how it worked in 2004 or 2005. What is common is the idea that newsrooms should try to work together to do a better job of informing people. That is convergence. It is about acknowledging that the way journalism has always been done needs to evolve, and continue to evolve, because news audiences are evolving. Convergence is not about turning newspaper reporters into television anchors and radio reporters into online graphics designers. It is about getting news people to understand and play to the strengths of each medium—print, online, and broadcast—to better inform a public who already chooses among a variety of media to get the news. It is about flexibility.

This book aims to prepare journalists for an industry that requires flexibility and adaptability in addition to the traditional critical thinking, strong writing, and insightful reporting skills. It is about getting tomorrow's journalists thinking in multiple media, since that is how their public already thinks.

This book can serve as a practical guide, a basic primer, to thinking, writing, and reporting stories in print, in broadcast, and on the Web. It is not a print or broadcast text with some convergence mixed in. Nor is it an online text that focuses on technology over content. Instead, it is a journalism text that treats print, online, and broadcast as equal outlets. It aims to bridge the gap between old media and new, between older ways of teaching and doing journalism and newer ways that are being devised and revised.

As such, this book is about a mindset and a skill set that relies on each medium's strengths and common values. Broadcast's strengths are immediacy, simplicity, and visuals. Print's strengths are providing context and exploring complexity. Online's strengths are interactivity, searchability, and multimedia. All of them—print, broadcast, online—strive for accuracy, fairness, truth, and impact. Convergence-oriented newsrooms aim to accentuate the strengths and common values in their daily operations. Many of them have been attempting a team approach toward news producing, relying on different people with different skills to create different ways of delivering stories to the public.

In visiting nearly a dozen newsrooms in 2003 and 2004, in search of the one answer for implementing convergence, I instead found several answers. Newsrooms as different as the *Christian Science Monitor* and ESPN were attempting to deliver news in more than one way to reach diffuse news consumers. They were attempting convergence but in ways that fit their newsroom thinking. Time and again, the biggest obstacle to any and all implementation was an attitude that newspaper, radio, television, and online journalists have nothing in common. The medium defined their journalism. Many believed that the values of newspaper journalism, broadcast journalism, and online news are far too different for coordination and cooperation to work. They believed the cultural divide was too wide to be bridged.

This book aims to begin to bridge that divide. That is why the first three chapters, comprising part I, examine the mindset of convergence. Before convergence can work in the newsroom, journalists in different media have to acknowledge that technology has placed more choice, and thus more power, in the hands of consumers. They have to understand that the economic and social forces in which they operate demand that they change and adapt. And they have to be willing to take control of that change by breaking down the cultural barriers that have made working in multiple media so difficult. Part I of this book looks at how to get one's head around the idea of convergence in journalism.

Chapter 1 explains what convergence is and is not, as it relates to the news industry. It gives an overview of the changing landscape in the news industry, thanks to new technologies, lifestyle habits, and media economics. It explains how the audiences for news have changed and why convergence is being tried in response to that change.

Chapter 2 looks at newsroom cultures, setups, and attitudes which have been hurdles that must be overcome in implementing a more team-oriented, multiple media, and convergent news operation. It points out the areas where newspaper, broadcast, and online operations have similar functions, and where they diverge. The chapter then looks at how some news operations have attempted to pool their efforts and overcome conflicting ideas about deadlines, management, work flow, and communication. Chapter 2 examines how different news organizations have adapted their convergence-oriented operations to fit their newsroom culture, staffs, and mission.

Chapter 3 wraps up the first section by addressing how to think about convergence, with a look at the common values and goals of news organizations. It outlines the values that newspapers, television and radio stations, and news websites share: fairness, accuracy, seeking truth, independence, and public service. The chapter explores how convergence-oriented news organizations seek to capitalize on those basic values and goals in striving to overcome the barriers to cooperative news ventures. Chapter 3 also presents the strengths and weaknesses of each news medium and explores how cross-media news-gathering and news presentation plays to the strengths in an effort to minimize the weaknesses. The chapter explores the benefits to the news public as well as news organizations in providing news on various platforms.

While the first section of this book addresses needed changes in organizing and coordinating journalism, the second section focuses on some of the basic skills needed to do daily journalism in a convergent, multiple-media news environment. The skills delineated in each of the four chapters of this section could easily warrant a separate text, and traditionally they have been presented that way. Anyone who has tried to teach convergence (as I have) by drawing on the strengths of each medium for a class in convergence has had to seek information from separate books. This section of the text sets out to put basic skills of news-gathering for broadcast, print, and online together in one place. Again, this serves as a bridge from traditional basic writing and reporting texts often grounded in either print or broadcast. It serves as a starting point in learning and applying basic skills to multiple media. The section looks at the writing, thinking, organization, and collecting of information required for basic journalism. It discusses tried-and-true reporting and story presentation methods, but from a convergence standpoint.

Chapter 4, "Approaching the Story," begins with the various news-gathering and reporting skills that every journalist needs to develop, regardless of the outlet in which their work ultimately appears. It outlines how to find story ideas, story angles, and story sources. The chapter explores observation, interviewing, and note-taking techniques that remain at the core of all news-gathering. It discusses how knowing the story, the audience, and the medium or media used in telling the story affects the backgrounding, planning, reporting, and execution of the story. Chapter 4 looks at the gathering of information, imagery, and insight needed for good storytelling, regardless of the medium in which it finally appears.

While chapter 4 looks at common news-gathering techniques, the next three chapters explore the writing and presentation strengths of broadcast, print, and online. Each chapter adds to the previous chapters in developing from simple to more complex story reporting and storytelling.

Broadcast writing leads off the medium-specific chapters because it forces the development of simple writing. Nothing brings home the need for simplicity more than hearing the written word spoken. Broadcast forces writers to hear their words as others, the audience, will hear them. Chapter 5 begins with broadcast writing in addressing the clear and simple presentation of information. It examines basic components of news leads and news stories. The chapter then moves from the simplicity of writing to the complexity of adding sound and visuals to the storytelling. It explores how to seek out good sound and telling visuals to enhance the storytelling. It introduces the idea of layering elements of news—words, pictures, and sound—as part of the process needed in organizing multiple-media storytelling.

Chapter 6 looks at developing nuance and context in reporting. It also addresses the layering of words, visuals (description), and sound (quotes) via the limitations of presenting the news in print. It expands on the simple writing and reporting outlined in basic broadcast stories. The chapter addresses the stylistic variations required of print, such as placement of attribution and the use of quotes and time references. And it explores ways to take the reporting of a story to a more detailed level. Chapter 6 examines some observation and number-crunching skills that can add detail and significance to news stories. It also addresses nuance by discussing the notion of a story's voice and tone in the written word.

The last chapter in part II examines writing, interactivity, and multimedia for news online. Chapter 7 explores the different ways news and information are being presented on the Web. Online news and the technologies available to produce it are changing dramatically and quickly. But some common notions about writing for the Web and ways of developing multimedia and interactivity have been established. Chapter 7 explains the organization of writing for the Web, using chunks, bullets, and blocks to allow browsers to navigate and explore a Web story. It outlines various interactive activities, from discussion boards to games. It also presents various types of multimedia storytelling, using animation, audio, video, and text to give news audiences different experiences in understanding news and information. Chapter 7 looks at the various ways that the Internet and the Web represent convergence in one place: the computer.

The final section of this book takes a look at what might be ahead for convergence in journalism by looking at what is already emerging. Thanks to new technologies, consumers can easily become producers of news, and today's young news consumers are learning multimedia habits alongside the alphabet and multiplication tables. These changes require journalism to adapt; convergence is one strategy that incorporates change as a way of doing business.

Chapter 8, on participatory journalism, addresses a trend that exploded onto the journalism scene between the time this book was proposed and the time it was put together, less three years. While blogs, webcasts, podcasts, and other forms of individual online writing and information-gathering have not attracted huge audiences (thousands of visitors to individual sites versus millions to network news for example), they have attracted a following. And that indicates that traditional journalism's audience will continue to be nibbled away by new forms of storytelling. Chapter 8 explores how some news organizations are trying to adjust to this new wave of consumer-producer interaction and how people are creating new forums for news.

The final chapter of the book briefly explores what the next wave of journalists can expect their audience to want by looking at what tomorrow's news audiences are getting today. Operations producing news for kids have been working with convergence—doing news in print, online, and for broadcast—as long as, if not longer, than their adult counterparts. Interactivity, multimedia, and participatory journalism are commonplace for a generation that is giving new meaning to the term "media multitasking." Chapter 9 looks at what may be in store for journalists in the near future to respond to audience needs and wants being developed today.

Throughout this book, I have weaved examples from my own experiences as a consecutive convergent, a journalist who has worked in print and broadcast and has had some exposure to online journalism, although not at the same time. I also have included perspectives, examples, and comments from a variety of newsrooms that are attempting to do journalism in more than one medium.

Yet a textbook on convergence in one sense is an oxymoron, as it presents information about journalism in just one form—text. And because of that, it reflects the weakness associated with the print format: It lacks immediacy. News operations and their staffs change from one year to the next; the information in this text represents what was happening with convergence in certain newsrooms from 2003 through mid-2005.

A text also lacks interactivity and multimedia. A book on convergence needs to provide information in more than one medium. And since online allows for aural, visual, text, and commentary, a Web log, or blog, accompanies this book. It includes exercises, additional interview information, newsroom pictures, links to the news sites and blogs mentioned in the book, and an area for updates on convergence efforts. It aims to play to the strengths of different media as well as to refer users to websites with more detailed expertise. The website explores how convergence is working to respond to the century of change and choice in the world of news today.

PART I

Mindset

ONE

Why Convergence? It's the Consumer, Stupid

IN OPENING HIS epic *A Tale of Two Cities*, Charles Dickens wrote that it was the best of times and the worst of times. Those words aptly describe the state of journalism at the beginning of the twenty-first century. It is the best of times because of the wide range of news outlets, news operations, and venues available for getting information about the rapidly changing world. A visit to a bookstore or newsstand finds a display of dozens of magazines and newspaper titles. Basic cable television opens up a hundred or more channels for news, entertainment, and information, and the Internet provides thousands of sites. The choices seem endless.

Yet it is also the worst of times for journalism. Audiences are becoming more fragmented, while news media ownership becomes more concentrated. Daily newspapers see a decline in readers, as well as a decline in advertising. The nightly network news sees its viewership decline, as the age of its audience rises. Journalism itself is being redefined. Anyone with a website and information can have access on a Web log (blog) to an audience greater than many daily newspapers or monthly magazines. Bloggers are challenging the traditional media's role as gatekeepers of news and information.

As a result, the news industry is in a state of flux and, some might say, a state of disarray. Technological, social, and economic changes are challenging traditional news organizations to develop innovative ways to attract new readers and viewers and to hold on to current ones. Convergence is one strategy being tried in several newsrooms across the United States. Yet convergence in journalism is ill-defined, misunderstood, and misrepresented. It has been used to explain everything from computer use in news to corporate consolidation.

When it comes to journalism, convergence means a new way of thinking about the news, producing the news, and delivering the news, using all media to their fullest potential to reach a diverse and increasingly distracted public. Convergence refocuses journalism to its core mission—to inform the public about its world in the best way possible. But nowadays, the best way is not just one way: newspaper or television or the Internet. The best way is a multiple media way, doing journalism for a public that sometimes gets news from newspapers, at other times gets news from television and radio, and at still other times seeks news online. To be successful at convergence, journalists need to understand the strengths of each news medium or outlet and work to develop and provide news stories that dovetail with those strengths. Convergence requires journalists to put the reading, viewing, and browsing public at the center of their work.

However, convergence in journalism has many interpretations and definitions. Most journalists "know it when they see it" but really cannot describe convergence or explain its application in the newsroom. Although a 2002 survey of journalists indicates that nearly 90 percent of the newsrooms in the United States claim they are practicing some form of convergence, those same survey respondents were unable to define just exactly what they are doing that is convergent.[1]

More often than not, journalists distrust convergence. They view it as a marketing ploy, a way to promote the news as a "product," emphasizing the business rather than the journalism in the news industry. They also view it as a management ploy, a way to get fewer journalists to do more work with fewer resources.

In the pages ahead, we examine the different definitions of convergence: technological, economic, and journalistic. We also look at what has happened technologically, socially, and economically that led to this buzzword for all that is new in the news media. Finally, we examine why convergence is being tried in journalism, in response both to changes in news audiences and changes within the news industry.

DEFINING CONVERGENCE

Dictionaries provide a simple definition of convergence: Convergence means the coming together of two or more things. In discussing convergence in the news media, however, the definition gets tricky because of disagreement over what exactly is coming together.

Massachusetts Institute of Technology professor Henry Jenkins provides a simple framework for defining convergence. "Media convergence is an ongoing process, occurring at various intersections of media technologies, industries, content and audiences; it's not an end state."[2] Applying Jenkins to the news business, convergence of technologies involves the coming together of different equipment and tools for producing and distributing news. Think about computers and software. Convergence of industries involves consolidation of businesses

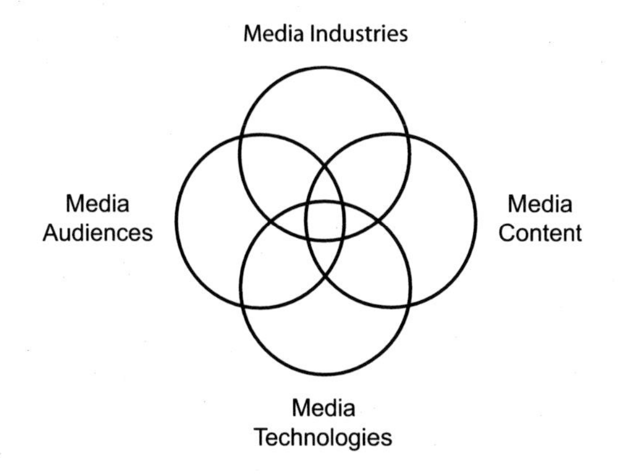

FIGURE 1.1. MIT's Henry Jenkins defines media convergence as an ongoing process in which content, technology, audience, and industries intersect.

and companies producing and distributing news. Think about Disney and News Corp. Convergence of journalistic content involves journalists working in different media coming together to provide different content for different audiences. Think about newspaper websites and news organizations text-messaging the latest sports scores or stock quotes.

TECHNOLOGICAL CONVERGENCE

The original discussions of media convergence focused on the technological: computers and digitization. Anyone who has sent an e-mail on a computer or used a cell phone that takes pictures and sends text messages is taking for granted technological convergence. But less than thirty years ago, the digitization of words, pictures, and sound for access by a variety of electronic devices seemed like science fiction.

The founder of MIT's Media Lab, Nicholas Negroponte, argued in the late 1970s that three industries that were separate at the time—computers, broadcast/film, and printing/publishing—would overlap and merge by the start of the twenty-first century.[3] In the late 1970s, technology was challenging the status quo in each of those areas, so the idea of those industries coming together seemed radical. Thirty years ago, the personal computer, which would revolutionize an industry, was being developed. IBM, the powerhouse of the time, would be upended by Microsoft. Broadcast and film were being challenged by the technology of videotape. Video would not only change the way television news, entertainment shows, and movies were seen and distributed but also how they were made. The printing/publishing industry was moving from "hot" or lead type to "cold" type, or computer-produced layouts and printing without heavy lead plates. Cold type brought color and revolutionized the look of printed news.

The development of digitization would set off a new debate about technological convergence. Ithiel de Sola Pool, a communications scholar, pointed out that this next wave of convergence would involve a merging of electronic devices, "the convergence of modes." In 1983, he noted that "electronic technology is bringing all modes of communications into one system."[4] Everything would come down to one device—computer + TV + telephone + stereo + movie player + organizer. This all-in-one megadevice has not yet become a household standard.

Although a single system that operates everything is just now emerging, on the consumer market, it is easy to see the rise of this new wave of technological convergence by digging into purses and backpacks and looking in our living rooms and dorm rooms at our information gadgets. The cell phone, personal digital assistant (PDA), and camera have become one device. Telephone companies have worked out deals with news organizations for sending news updates and headlines out to cell phone users.

Anyone can download a story, article, even a book off the Internet and read it on an electronic device, although it is still difficult viewing. In 1990, when Roger Fidler spoke about a portable electronic newspaper when he was new media director for the Knight-Ridder newspapers, that idea was considered crazy. He told groups of very skeptical journalists that, rather than buying a newspaper, subscribers would be able to plug their tablets into cable or phone lines, download newspaper content, and read it on portable electronic devices. Those devices are closer to reality now, as technology is making screens easier to read and easier to carry around without wires and heavy batteries.

Technological convergence of the stereo, CD player, and the computer, thanks to digitization, has brought about MP3 and on-demand music. The DVD is revolutionizing access to entertainment, first with players and now with recording devices, such as TiVO, that put the consumer in charge of determining content. Broadband cable service has merged the computer and the television into a viewing and interactive device. And the Internet, the World Wide Web, is the technological convergence of computers, satellites, and digital technology. It has opened up new ways of getting and exchanging information, destroying geographical and political boundaries in the process.

On one level, technological convergence means the coming together of formerly distinct electronic devices or media delivery systems, changing the equipment used to get information and to access it. But technological convergence has also opened up new ways of presenting that information. Technological convergence has led to multimedia information presentation. The Internet allows formerly separate and distinct storytelling media or platforms—the text of print, the audio of radio, pictures and graphics of visual design, and the moving pictures of animation, film, and television—to be combined into a new way of providing information.

Trying to pin down a name for this new, evolving type of journalism that comes together via the Internet has added confusion to the definition of convergence. Journalism distributed on the Internet has been called new media, online news, multimedia journalism, digital news. But it also has become known as convergence journalism, since it marks the coming together of different elements of storytelling. The merger of AOL and Time Warner in 2000 helped solidify the definition of convergence to mean electronic content delivery, because that merger was the coming together of a content company, Time Warner, with an online delivery company, AOL. Yet that merger also created confusion over the definition of convergence, because AOL Time Warner became the largest media conglomerate in the world. Thanks to AOL Time Warner, and the mergers of other media companies, convergence came to mean media consolidation.

ECONOMIC CONVERGENCE

Using the definitional framework of MIT's Henry Jenkins, AOL Time Warner represents economic convergence, or the coming together of media industries. When it was announced in 2000, the merger was the flashiest and most ambitious example to date of economic convergence. And it brought another buzzword to the fore, "synergies." AOL Time Warner executives talked about ways to work across the different media, taking advantage of all the company's different properties—online, television, magazines, films, and books.

Cross Promotion

A precursor of that synergy involved the handling in 1999 of the last movie directed by Stanley Kubrick before his death, *Eyes Wide Shut*. The Warner Bros. movie earned a big write-up in *Time* magazine; its stars, Tom Cruise and Nicole Kidman, appeared on the magazine's cover and conducted promotional interviews on shows such as *Larry King Live* on CNN, a Time Warner company.

The *Eyes Wide Shut* example demonstrates the most common and most visible aspect of economic convergence: cross-promotion of properties or brands. In the 1980s, at Turner Broadcasting, advertising that promoted CNN programs would appear on *Headline News*, TBS, and TNT. Ads for TNT and TBS programs would air on CNN commercial breaks. Additionally, an hour news special slated for the 8:00 p.m. CNN newscast would be cross-promoted in earlier newscasts throughout the day on the twenty-four-hour news channel.

These days, cross-promotion means cross-media promotion. At MSNBC, it not only means commercial advertising and promotions within MSNBC programs, but it includes promotion of NBC news programming as well as special slots on the MSNBC and MSN website for NBC news shows. Such extensive cross-promotion raises issues of independence, diversity, and control. These issues have bubbled over when news organizations of a media company end up reporting and cross-promoting properties of its entertainment divisions.

In the case of *Eyes Wide Shut*, the movie received considerable attention by a variety of news media, not just those associated with Time Warner. But media critics raised questions about the prominence of the Time Warner coverage—a cover story, promotional interviews—as to journalistic independence and control.

In the summer of 2000, CBS and CBS News's *The Early Show* drew criticism for reporting and cross-promoting the hit reality show *Survivor*. The show, which aims at winnowing down a group of people facing extreme circumstances and challenges, ends each installment with a contestant being voted out of the group and off the show. On the morning after each episode, *The Early Show* would interview the person voted off the show. Since the show was so popular, newspapers, magazines, and online news sites were carrying articles about the show as well as weekly polls and analyses. On the day of the *Survivor* season finale, all the network newscasts ran stories about the show or the reality TV phenomenon it had sparked. But the consistent use of *The Early Show* to promote the *Survivor* series came under the most frequent attack because it lowered the acceptable standard for the use of news programs to promote entertainment. "There seems to be no limit to what CBS News will do to shill for the network's prime time 'reality' entertainment shows in the vain hope that their popularity will rub off on its offerings," complained former NBC News president Lawrence K. Grossman.[5]

Four years later, that standard of acceptable cross-promotion in news was under attack again, as NBC News devoted two episodes of its prime-time newsmagazine, *Dateline*, to the finales of two long-running popular NBC comedies, *Frasier* and *Friends*. NBC's *Today Show* anchors Katie Couric and Matt Lauer hosted these two *Datelines*, further blurring the separation of news and entertainment. Associated Press television writer David Bauder questioned whether NBC News had "besmirched its reputation" with such blatant promotion on its prime-time newsmagazine.[6] *Washington Post* television critic Tom Shales referred to *Dateline* as "NBC's so-called news magazine,"[7] and NBC executives countered by saying the newsmagazine's audience understands that it offers a range of stories and that very little of it is promotional. They pointed to other hard-hitting journalistic reporting on the show, such as a look at racial profiling. Both the *Friends* and the *Frasier* shows on *Dateline* scored larger audiences than typical *Dateline* episodes, reinforcing the financial benefit of cross-promotion available through economic convergence, while undermining the journalistic value of untainted, independent news judgment.

Consolidation

This weakening of journalistic values in favor of marketing values has added fuel to the fire of protest against the other prominent aspect of economic convergence in the news media: media consolidation through corporate mergers. The 2000 merger of AOL and Time Warner created the world's largest media company and resurrected new fears about the lack of diversity of opinion and independent access to those opinions. But AOL Time Warner was created after a long line of mergers that mixed different media industries: film, music, television, cable, and news. The Time Warner half of the 2000 merger, in fact, was created in the wake of two previous mergers—the Time, Inc., publishing empire and the Warner Bros. entertainment empire in 1990, and the merger in 1995 with Turner Broadcasting, the cable news and entertainment company created by Ted Turner.

A few months before the January 2000 AOL and Time Warner merger announcement, Viacom, an entertainment and cable production and distribution company, bought CBS, creating yet another megamedia company. And before that, the Tribune Company, which owned several newspaper and television stations throughout the United States, merged with the Times-Mirror Company, a prominent newspaper chain. Don Hewitt, executive producer of the CBS *60 Minutes* program, joked to the *Wall Street Journal*, "I'm convinced that before I die, one person will own everything."[8] Hewitt was referring to CBS president Mel Karmazin and the Viacom deal. Yet his sentiment echoed criticism from media and political commentators Robert McChesney and Noam Chomsky that too much of the media were being controlled by too few companies. "We should deplore this concentration of media power," McChesney wrote in 2000. "It is dangerous when so few people control what we see and hear. And these giants have enormous power not only over the economy but the political system as well."[9]

Media companies, however, argued that the economic realities of a multimedia world required mergers. Consolidation would allow them to respond to the demands of audiences using different media, seeking different information. As the competition became bigger and more diverse, media companies argued that they had to get bigger and more diverse to keep up. "Owning television, radio, and newspapers in a single market is a way to lower costs, increase efficiencies, and provide higher-quality news in times of economic duress," said Jack Fuller, former *Chicago Tribune* publisher.[10]

JOURNALISTIC CONVERGENCE

News organizations that are experimenting with the notion of convergence aim to achieve Fuller's goal of "higher-quality news" in all the formats available: print, online, and on radio and television. The problem comes when convergence is seen as a benefit for media company stockholders and not as a benefit for journalists or for readers, viewers, or browsers.

Convergence in journalism requires changes in how news organizations think about the news and news coverage, how they produce the news, and how they deliver the news. Most convergence in journalism today focuses on the last of those areas, delivering the news. It involves a newspaper's daily edition or a newscast's scripts being placed online, a newspaper reporter appearing on television for a "talk-back" or interview on his or her story, the television weathercaster developing the weather page for the newspaper.

FIGURE 1.2. Journalism convergence efforts can come across as odd to audiences, as this cartoon illustrates. (By permission of Dave Coverly and Creators Syndicate, Inc.)

However, dozens of news organizations are trying to also think about and produce news differently. They are trying to ensure that the news they are providing is best suited for the audiences of each medium or format being used to distribute the news. These organizations realize that newspaper readers want more context and detail to their stories, while online browsers are looking for quick hits of information, interactivity, and the ability to seek out other information, and broadcast listeners and viewers are looking for the latest information that puts them at the scene. Convergence in journalism means the coming together of journalists and certain types of journalism that have been operating in separate spheres—newspapers, magazines, radio, television, and online—to provide quality news in all those different formats. That coming together can involve shared resources and information. It can involve joint reporting and production on projects. It can involve "one-man bands" or "backpack" journalists—one person doing the reporting and producing of news for all the different formats. It can involve multimedia storytelling online or what could be called "converged presentation." It can involve some or all of these variations.

Convergence journalism is happening in a variety of newsrooms, in a variety of manners. No one form of convergence journalism has risen to be the best template for doing convergence. What has emerged among news organizations aggressively pursuing convergence is a mind-set. In operations as disparate as the *Lawrence (KS) Journal-World*, the *Providence Journal*, the Ohio News Network, MSNBC, and ESPN, convergence is as much a way of thinking as it is a way of working. The *Journal-World*'s former director of New Media/Convergence, Rob Curley, says simply that convergence is just good journalism. Executives at ESPN say that doing journalism for a magazine, television, and website just makes sense and is the way they approach sports news.

While economic convergence has often pushed journalistic convergence, like at the Tribune Company, at Media General's *Tampa Tribune*, tbo.com and WFLA, and Time Warner's NY1, journalists are defining what convergence means for them. Journalist Chindu Sreedharan calls it "layering." Journalists "understand the possibilities of other mediums, contribute across platform when called upon, and begin to layer their stories."[11] Convergence is "new journalism" that is evolving to keep up with the times.

Convergence is one answer to the question of where journalism should be headed in the twenty-first century. It is a response to the convergence of lifestyle, business, and technological trends that are forcing a change in the relationship between the people who make the news—journalists—and the people who use it—the public. Convergence is a response to two seemingly dichotomous trends—the fragmentation of the news audience and the consolidation of news ownership.

WHY CONVERGENCE? BECAUSE OF NEWS AUDIENCE FRAGMENTATION

Changes in lifestyle and advances in technology have been working in tandem to affect the kind of news people want and the way they want to get it. American news consumers are individualistic, and their news interests are scattered. They use different types of media at different times of the day to get news and information. The single mass audience is giving way to multiple niche audiences.

Lifestyle

The audiences for news are becoming fragmented because their lifestyles are fragmented. People today talk about multitasking, doing more than one thing at one time. They talk about being time-starved, not having enough time to do everything they want to in a day. People discuss compartmentalizing their lives, trying to separate work, leisure, family, and other aspects of their world. And they complain about information overload, having to digest too much information at one time. All these issues impact the way people choose news and the way news should be presented. Convergence, putting news out to audiences in different formats, at different times of the day, attempts to respond to the lifestyle changes of the news audience.

Americans are also working longer and taking more time to get to and from their jobs. The U.S. Census Bureau reports that more than a quarter (28 percent) of all workers over the age of sixteen put in more than forty hours a week.[12] And 8 percent work sixty or more hours. The Organization for Economic Cooperation and Development has noted that while workweek hours in many European countries has decreased in the past twenty-five years, the average hours worked per person in the United States has increased 20 percent. The OECD study of nineteen countries found that more Americans are working, and they are working longer.[13]

And not only are Americans spending more time working, they are spending more time getting to work, driving alone in their cars. The Census Bureau found that 77 percent of all workers drive to work by themselves these days, up from nearly 65 percent in 1980. And it is taking them longer to get to work. While the national average for the work commute is about twenty-five minutes, about 7 percent of Americans take more than an hour to get to work. And about a fifth of all workers are heading out to work between midnight and 6:30 a.m.

Journalists need to understand that this increased time at work and getting to work affects how much time people spend catching up on the news and how they go about it. People do not have time in the morning before they head out the door to read a ninety-six-page morning paper. Many get their local news, particularly weather and traffic reports, from the car radio or by checking a morning newscast on television. Some are leaving for work before the morning newscasts begin or before the newspaper is delivered to their doors. At work, they are not reading the newspaper or watching television, but they are checking the latest news online. By the time their workday is over and they get home, they may have missed the evening news on network television, and they may fall asleep before the late-night local wrap-up at 10:00 or 11:00 p.m. The news cycle has become 24/7—nonstop, twenty-four hours a day, seven days a week—because American lives have become 24/7.

The biannual survey of news habits by the Pew Research Center for the People and the Press finds that people go after news morning, noon, and night. And thanks to the Internet, more and more of them are following it during the day. The 2004 survey found that nearly three-quarters of Americans keep track of news during the day.[14] However, the average amount of time Americans spend with the news media each day has dropped about seven minutes in the past ten years, the result of time-starved, busy schedules.

Increasingly, people under the age of twenty-five maintain that they are the most time-starved in terms of keeping up with the news. As a result, they spend the least amount of time getting news. They do not watch the network news, read a daily newspaper, or spend as much time getting the news compared to every other age group. Older Americans spend more time with the news (eighty-five minutes for the over-sixty-five crowd) than younger Americans (thirty-five minutes for the under-twenty-five crowd). And younger news audiences are not regular news consumers. More than two-thirds of the Pew respondents under the age of twenty-five said they check the news from time to time. When the Pew survey asked why they do not follow the news regularly, half of the under-twenty-five respondents said they are too busy. When people do not have enough time for news, or only have time for it at irregular hours and intervals, it affects when and how the news media interact with their audiences. Convergence—providing news in more than one medium, when it is convenient for people to get it—responds to the need for a different paradigm of interaction.

That interaction is also being transformed by the lifestyle trend of multitasking. Although its official definition involves a computer running more than one program at a time, Americans have taken over the word to describe doing several tasks at once. From driving while talking on a cell phone, to listening to music while making dinner, to checking e-mail while grabbing a bite to eat or even talking to the office while watching a child's soccer game, Americans are doing more things at one time.

More and more, news audiences are multitasking when they are getting information. A 2003 study of media use by researchers at Ball State University found that while people think they multitask with media about 12 percent of the time, when those people were watched throughout a day, they were using more than one medium close to a quarter of the time. The study found that "the most common media multitasked with reading were TV (well ahead of all others) then radio and music."[15] People who were using more than one medium were most often reading while watching TV.

Additionally, Americans are multimedia, getting news and information from not just broadcast television or daily newspapers or a news website, but from various sources. This is especially true for young audiences, who are shying away from traditional news media (like newspapers and network newscasts) and are more comfortable with new media. The Online Publishers Association found that eighteen-to-thirty-four-year-olds consistently own more new media gadgets, from video games to Blackberry wireless PDA/e-mail devices.[16] The study also found that young news consumers use television and the Internet in tandem when there is breaking news. These consumers also prefer news in a more visual format. Nearly two-thirds of those in the 2004 Pew survey say their best understanding of the news comes from pictures or video. Surveys of the next generation of news audiences show they are even more likely to be multimedia multitaskers. For example, the Kaiser Family Foundation examinations of media use in both 1999 and 2003 found that computer and television use is common in the under-age-six set, and many youngsters are using more than one medium at a time sometime during their typical day.[17]

Multitasking and communicating with visuals as well as with words has a profound impact on how news is presented, especially if news organizations want to maintain an audience for their news or expand on their audience. Convergence, trying to take advantage of various formats to reach various audiences, allows traditional media to adapt to these new audience preferences.

Convergence is also a strategy that could allow traditional news media to adapt to how news audiences are reworking the notion of community. Common interests are often topical rather than geographical. Currently, the traditional news media respond to local audiences and local interests. But increasingly, the news audience is fragmenting into special areas of interest that are not limited by geographical boundaries.

For example, an audience interested in all things Rhode Island can come together on projo.com, the website for the *Providence Journal* newspaper. CNETNews.com, a website dedicated to new technology news, attracts an audience from around the world with an interest in everything digital.

But this phenomenon is not just a result of the Internet. Audience interests have been fragmenting for years, as is evident by the plethora of special-interest magazines, from *MacWorld* for Macintosh computer aficionados to *Popular Mechanics* for do-it-yourself mechanics. In broadcast, audiences are dividing along special interest lines by tuning into niche cable channels like OLN, the Outdoor Life Network, or the SciFi Channel, which is devoted to science fiction entertainment. Satellite radio allows audiences to choose music formats from hip-hop to country, regardless of geographical location.

Technology

The rise of the Internet, satellite global connections, and wireless communications has hastened audience fragmentation and has raised expectations about how and when people can get news and information.

Today, no one thinks twice about being able to get information and news at any time of the day or night. But a generation ago, that was not possible. If you wanted to get the up-to-the-minute score of your favorite Major League Baseball team thirty years ago, you had few options: You could listen to the game on the one local AM radio station allowed to carry it (if it carried it), you could wait until the news wrap-up at the top of the hour at another station, or you could hope for an update of game score during the one televised game of the week, which often did not feature your team. Today, you can check sports scores online, have them text-messaged to you on your cell phone or PDA, check the graphic crawl of scores on numerous cable and broadcast channels on television, and listen for scores on the radio. Sports fans today rarely have to wait more than a few minutes to find out a score, and they have numerous places to go to find it. The technological advances in communications equipment have allowed news and information to be delivered instantly. As a result, news audiences expect instant news.

The use of satellites for transmitting information and images brought about the first wave of instant, specialized news in the late 1970s and early 1980s. Networks such as ESPN for sports and CNN for news could not have developed without satellite technology. That technology allowed those networks to get video (also a new technology in the 1970s) and send it out to audiences. The true measure of the impact of that technology came during the Gulf War in 1991. Audiences around the world heard and watched bombs falling on Baghdad in real time. They did not have to wait for the evening news; they could watch it, unfiltered, as it was happening.

Within the decade, the technology of the Internet provided another outlet for satisfying a demand for news at any time of the day or night. The only limitations on up-to-the-minute news online are the speed with which news organizations can update their information and user overload, when too many people try to go to one site. Wireless technology and cell phones have taken instant news to yet another level by allowing it to be accessible anywhere. Cell phones were used by a group of college-age journalists to report on the 2004 Democratic and Republican political conventions and to send those reports—both text and images—to cell phone users. Technology has not only broken down time limitations to getting news and information, it has broken down geographical and cultural ones.

During the military offensive in Iraq in the spring of 2003, American news audiences who wanted perspectives other than those offered by U.S. newspapers and television networks went to non-U.S. news media websites such as english.aljazzeera.net, the website for the Arab news network Al Jazeera, and guardian.co.uk, the website for Great Britain's *Guardian* newspaper. A poll by the Pew Internet and American Life Project in the spring 2003 found that 10 percent of Internet users checking out war news went to sites by "foreign news organizations."[18] Another 8 percent checked on nontraditional news or alternative commentary, such as Salon.com.

The Internet also broke down barriers to the display of graphic images of war and terrorist violence in Iraq. While newspapers and television stations declined, for example, to show the beheading of an American contractor or the charred remains of ambushed U.S. contractors in the spring of 2004, audiences who wanted to see those images could find them on Internet sites. Technology once again created a niche interest in particular information not available from mainstream media.

The technological transformation of the ways to get news and the rapid pace of the work world and family life are bringing about the transformation of the audience for news. People are not looking for news at the same time, from the same place, with the same outlook, in the same format, or on the same communications device. The audience for news is shifting away from one-size-fits-all. News organizations trying convergence see it as a strategy to respond to this shift by news consumers.

WHY CONVERGENCE? BECAUSE OF NEWS MEDIA CONSOLIDATION

The economic landscape for news organizations is shifting as well. That shift has profound implications for how journalism is produced and distributed. Consolidation has become commonplace within the news industry. So has vertical integration, which in business means having control of different companies along the production line between supplier and consumer. In the news media, vertical integration can mean a company like Viacom has control of the supply of raw materials (reports, stories, scripts), products (newscasts, movies), and distribution (outlets or platforms—television, cable, movie theaters).

When media critic Ben Bagdikian published his book *Media Monopoly* in the 1980s, he warned of ownership consolidated among about fifty companies.[19] At that time, the fear focused on the demise of independent voices in newspapers. By the 1980s, hundreds of afternoon newspapers had folded or merged with their morning counterparts in joint operating agreements allowed by the 1970 Newspaper Preservation Act. Newspaper chains such as Gannett bought out smaller, individual- or family-owned newspapers, moving control of those papers out of town and into a corporate boardroom. Radio and television stations were gobbled up just like newspapers, and in 1975 the Federal Communications Commission (FCC) initiated the Newspaper/Broadcast Cross-Ownership Rule which prohibited one owner from having both media in any one market.

Despite such limitations, media consolidation kept rolling along. At the beginning of the twenty-first century, the majority of the media in the United States are owned by a half dozen major international media corporations. Yet media companies have been arguing for more consolidation to remain profitable in an era of scattered audiences, outlets, and interests. Their arguments have focused on rewriting federal legislation and regulation to allow them greater flexibility in handling the economic challenges of a world of instant messaging, wireless and satellite technology, and the Internet.

As the nation headed into the booming dot-com era in the mid-1990s, the Telecommunications Act of 1996 opened up all sorts of possibilities of mergers and consolidation. The act required the FCC to review its regulations every two years, to ensure that the rules were keeping pace with the technological advances in telephones, broadcast, and telecommunications. It was a much-needed update to a 1934 law, a law drawn up at a time when telephones, radio, and film were the new media technologies. In the meantime, federal courts ruled that the FCC needed to develop a modern-day justification for its ownership limits that were anywhere from twenty-five to fifty years old. Media businesses pushed for the FCC to loosen if not eliminate those rules. Then FCC chairman Michael K. Powell told senators in 2003 that keeping the rules as they were was not an option, but that the FCC would make rule changes that would fulfill the FCC mandate to protect diversity, promote competition, and foster localism.[20]

Consumer, antitrust, and civil liberties proponents, however, felt that the Telecommunications Act and further relaxation of FCC ownership rules would give corporations too much license to swallow up small competitors at the expense of diversity and local control. As evidence of "merger mania," anticonsolidation forces point to what has happened within the radio industry. Hundreds of independent radio stations and small radio station ownership groups have disappeared following the February 1996 enactment of the new telecommunications law. Within months, newspapers in cities like Pittsburgh; Minneapolis; Columbus, Ohio; Boston; and Washington reported on local stations being bought up and big radio chains like Westinghouse merging with other big radio chains like Infinity. An FCC study of the radio industry from 1996 to 2002 noted a 34 percent decline in the number of commercial radio owners, creating more group-owned stations and bigger radio chains. That consolidation has led to smaller radio news staffs and the elimination of radio news at many commercial stations. Music formats are limited and are no longer programmed locally or with local on-air talent.

The largest owner of U.S. radio stations, Clear Channel Communications, has been at the forefront of criticism over consolidation. One oft-cited example of central control of music came in the wake of the September 11, 2001, terrorist attacks. The nearly 1,200 Clear Channel stations received a memo suggesting a list of songs that should not be played. Songs on the list included R.E.M's "It's the End of the World as We Know It" and "Crash Into Me" by Dave Matthews. While the list was offered as a guide and not a corporate mandate, journalists on several newspapers suggested that the guide was an example of corporate censorship. Two years later, Clear Channel organized and promoted Rallies for America, in support of the Bush administration's war in Iraq, in more than a dozen Clear Channel markets. With more than 110 million listeners, Clear Channel was attacked by media critics for supporting the rallies, and antiwar activists decried Clear Channel's use of the airwaves to promote a political position.

The demise of much independently owned radio through consolidation became the leading argument against further efforts to allow more consolidation in ownership throughout all media. A second wave of media consolidation had been anticipated if and when federal regulations are loosened. In June 2003, the FCC approved new rules allowing more concentrated ownership of the news media nationally and more cross-media ownership locally. But those rule changes were preempted by legislative and legal challenges.

In 2004, five companies dominated most broadcast media nationally and some of those companies exceeded the FCC limit as to the amount of the national television market they could control. Before 2004, FCC rules said that no one broadcaster could reach more 35 percent of the national audience. A new law passed by Congress and implemented in 2004 changed that to 39 percent, bringing News Corp. and Viacom into compliance. The media conglomerates and the FCC were pushing for a 45 percent cap. A federal appeals court rejected that higher limit, and the 39 percent limit is now the law of the land.

BOX 1.1

Major Media Companies

1. Viacom, which owns CBS, UPN, Nickelodeon, MTV, Simon & Schuster Publishing, Paramount Pictures.
2. Time Warner, which owns HBO, CNN, TNT, WB, Time Publishing, Warner Bros.
3. Disney, which owns ESPN, ABC, Lifetime, E! Entertainment.
4. News Corp., which owns Fox, Fox News Channel, 20th Century Fox, HarperCollins Publishers, and television stations in New York, Los Angeles, Chicago, Boston, Houston, Phoenix.
5. General Electric, which owns NBC, MSNBC, Telemundo, Vivendi Universal.

Source: "Who Owns What," *Columbia Journalism Review*, www.cjr.org/tools/owners.

The appeals court also rejected a planned FCC rules change eliminating the 1975 ban on cross-ownership of newspapers and television stations in a local market. The ban on cross-ownership has been eroding for years, following several national media mergers. Media companies such as the Tribune, Gannett, and Media General own television and radio stations and newspapers in major cities such as Los Angeles, Chicago, Dallas, Tampa, Hartford, and Phoenix. Many of these companies anticipated the end of the newspaper/broadcast ban after the Telecommunications Act became law in 1996. The FCC has been told by the courts to review this cross-ownership ban.

Journalists, civil liberties activists, and consumer groups have been fighting these ownership rule changes, fearing they will lead to fewer jobs, fewer voices, less local news and programming, and thus less public service. A review of recent history following media mergers and corporate consolidation lends credence to some of those fears:

- Within months after the AOL Time Warner merger, CNN eliminated 10 percent of its employees from news operations, the largest staff cut in the cable news network's history. Part of the job cuts came amid consolidation of CNN Interactive, the award-winning, trend-setting CNN website, with the AOL interactive operations.
- One study found that children's television programming in Los Angeles, the second largest TV market in the country, became less diverse in the wake of consolidated ownership of local stations. The study by Children Now, a children's research and advocacy group, reported that local, original children's programming was cut almost in half between 1998 and 2003 and that "the number of the same shows repeated

between cable and broadcast channels increased almost fourfold between 1998 and 2003."[21]

- Sinclair Communications, which owns more than sixty television stations around the country, has implemented News Central, a newscast production format in which weather, national and international news, and sports segments are put together in a central production facility in Hunt Valley, Maryland, near Baltimore. In several Sinclair markets, local newsroom jobs or unprofitable news operations were eliminated. *Television Week* reported that two-thirds of Sinclair's stations were not doing local news when this "central casting" format began in 2002.[22] Sinclair officials maintain that News Central allows for more local news at its stations that cannot afford full-blown local news operations. And they point out that the format allows for longer reports on local news stories during the one hour-long News Central newscast of the day. News Central critics argue that the format takes away local control and local voices from the news, noting that the News Central newscast includes a nationally aired Sinclair political commentary.

Cross-ownership and cooperative relationships within local markets has raised concerns about the lack of diversity of opinion. If the newspaper's movie critic also serves as a TV station's movie critic, the local audience is getting only one opinion on whether the latest offering at the box office is worth seeing. Or the television critic for the local newspaper might think twice about criticizing the news team of the television station owned by the same company he or she works for.

Proponents of cross-ownership, particularly former FCC chairman Michael Powell, dismiss the diversity argument by noting the wide variety of outlets now available to anyone online, on television, and at newsstands and bookstores.

BOX 1.2

Diversity Dilemna

Retha Hill, vice president of content development at BET.com in 2002, champions diversity and wonders if convergence works against it. "I'm concerned that you might decrease the number of divergent voices in a community covering the news," she said at a 2002 conference on converged journalism. "I'm really concerned that when you have newspapers doing theater reviews, movie reviews, restaurant reviews, commentary, and business reports for television, all of a sudden you just have this one viewpoint."

Source: www.jou.ufl.edu/converge/webcast/

> Today, news and public affairs programming—the fuel of our democratic society—is overflowing. There used to be three broadcast networks, each with thirty minutes of news daily. Today, there are three twenty-four-hour all-news networks, seven broadcast networks, and over three hundred cable networks. Local networks are bringing the American public more local news than at any point in history, and new tools such as the Internet are becoming an increasing and diverse source of news and information for our citizens. There has been a 200 percent increase in outlets. But, more importantly for diversity, there has been a 139 percent increase in independent owners. In sum, citizens have more choice and more control over what they see, hear, or read than at any other time in history.[23]

In the city of Boston alone, news audiences can choose from six local news stations, including a regional cable news network, New England Cable News, for newscasts in the mornings and evenings. They can pick up the *Boston Herald* and *Boston Globe* newspapers, the free *Metro* newspaper on Mondays through Fridays, alternative papers such as the *Boston Phoenix* and the *Improper Bostonian*, suburban and neighborhood newspapers such as the *Daily News Tribune* in Waltham and the *Beacon Hill Times*, ethnic papers such as the *Boston Irish Reporter*, specialty papers such as the *Boston Business Journal* and *Boston Law Journal*, and dozens of other publications. Web logs of local interest, such as the H2Otown-info.bryght.net about the city of Watertown, Massachusetts, have also expanded the marketplace for news and information.

Ethnic press, such as magazines, newspapers, radio, and television outlets in Spanish, Chinese, and other languages are "growing rapidly," according to the State of the News Media 2004 report.[24] The report noted that the number of Hispanic daily newspapers grew from fourteen in 1990 to thirty-five in 2002. The Latino Press Network lists nearly 150 newspaper publications nationwide. The Magazine Publishers Association annual handbook reports that more than 17,000 periodicals were available for public consumption in 2003, or an addition of 3,000 magazines in a ten-year period. The big leap came in 2003 with 440 new titles.

News websites are so plentiful that Google, AOL, Yahoo! and others are providing news site indexes and compilations. More than 90 percent of most newspapers and television stations in the United States have websites, and hundreds of publications and broadcast outlets around the world; from regional Arabic broadcasters like Al Jazeera to national newspapers like the *Manila Times*, put their news online. Additionally, millions of Americans are using the Internet to publish their own content online. A March 2003 survey by the Pew Internet and American Life Project determined that 44 percent of adult American Internet users put some type of material online. That material ranged from e-mail to personal Web pages to Web diaries. A November 2004 Pew survey found that 7 percent of Internet users say they have a Web diary or Web log online, and more than a quarter of Internet users were reading blogs.[25]

Audiences have more sources than ever for news and information, yet at the same time, financial control of those sources is being concentrated in fewer entities. The news industry is evolving in two seemingly contradictory directions—the mass media are getting more massive, while niche media are developing even smaller niches. Both have profound ramifications for the practice of journalism that news organizations cannot ignore or avoid. Being too small, being too limited a niche, causes the journalism to get lost in a sea of information. Being too big causes the journalism to get diluted. Journalism convergence, doing news in more than one medium, attempts to ride these waves of change in the news business.

CONVERGENCE: TAKING JOURNALISM BACK TO THE FUTURE

Convergence journalism is providing news and information in more than one format, using the strengths of each format to best serve news audiences. It aims to respond to the fragmentation of the news audience while acknowledging the economic reality of consolidation of media ownership. The fear in newsrooms about convergence journalism centers on the notion that convergence may make sense from a corporate standpoint but not from a journalistic one. The concern is that convergence is responding more to the profit-making, cost-saving reality of consolidated ownership of news and less to the public-interest aspect of addressing audience needs and demands for news and information.

News organizations that are trying convergence journalism, however, argue that for convergence to work well, audience needs must supersede corporate strategies. They see the public as the ultimate winner of their efforts. A 2003 survey of journalists in four convergence-oriented newsrooms found that those reporters, editors, producers, and managers believed that the people reading, listening, watching, and using their news were better served by their convergence efforts.[26] Newsroom managers, that is, editors and producers, of many convergence-oriented operations such as MSNBC, ESPN, Ohio News Network, and the *Lawrence (KS) Journal-World* acknowledge the corporate aspects of convergence, but they are unwilling to concede to being overtaken by them. Instead, they are seeking opportunities to redirect attention to public service. As a result, they have had to redefine how they think about their work and how they do it. They have had to develop a different mindset about journalism.

"We have to get away from this notion that we put stuff out there and news consumers can take it or leave it," said Dean Wright, editor in chief of MSNBC.com until mid-2005. "We have to serve the public but we can't give them just the candy they want . . . we have to tell them things they don't know and things they already know but in different ways. And we have to make it accessible."[27]

The two current news media audience leaders—television and newspapers—have developed mindsets about audiences that need updating. Over the years, newspapers have developed a reputation of being detached and arrogant. Many reporters and midlevel editors at newspapers had little exposure to, and perhaps even little use for, readership surveys and other audience information. That is changing. For example, many papers now list e-mail addresses along with reporter bylines. Less than a decade ago, many journalists opposed such

FIGURE 1.3. Dean Wright: "We have to get away from this notion that we put stuff out there and news consumers can take it or leave it." (Photo by the author)

an opportunity for direct reader feedback. Still, while many newspapers' marketing and advertising departments collect readership information, that information about the people reporters and editors are serving—or not serving—often does not make it to their desks. Newspapers can seem a bit patronizing or condescending toward their public. Newspapers can come across as out of touch with regular people.

Television, on the other hand, could be considered on the other end of that spectrum, fretting too much about giving the audience what it wants so the viewers will keep watching and keep stations' ratings high. Television journalists know all too well their audience's likes and dislikes as the Nielsen ratings' estimates of viewers' interest is broken down minute to minute. Television news uses focus groups and other marketing research to determine everything from the likeability of an anchor to the types of stories to conduct during key ratings weeks (known as sweeps weeks). Television can seem to pander to news audiences, seeking ways to manipulate them to be interested.

With all the fragmentation of news audiences today, journalists need to strike a better balance. They cannot be so arrogant about their work that they forget who they are doing journalism for, or so driven to be popular that they forget their responsibility to provide useful journalism. In that sense, convergence, in which journalists are working in different media to address the changing information needs of the public, is an opportunity for traditional media who have strayed from their basic focus and purpose. By adopting a new approach, convergence, they can return to their traditional values of serving the public.

"The reasons for convergence have to be based on true journalistic collaboration," says Jon Schwantes, corporate director for news convergence for the Dispatch Group in Columbus, Ohio. "The reasons for convergence have to be rooted in good journalism and in serving the news consumers."[28] Schwantes argues that if convergence is aimed at responding just to corporate concerns, such as cross-promotion of stories and efficiencies in staffing, then it will fall short. Cross-promotion has its limits with audiences, as Lawrence, Kansas, 6News television learned in its convergence efforts.[29] A credibility roundtable in the city found disagreement over the use of cross-promotion references in the news, so its news director decided to cut back on them. Managers at other convergence-oriented operations consistently point out that convergence requires a commitment to more staff, better training, and management flexibility.

MSNBC.com's Wright has argued that the online news medium is in the best position to take advantage of emerging technologies to develop a new way of doing journalism. He sees convergence with television and print partners, such as the NBC and MSNBC cable networks and *Newsweek* magazine, as a way to use new technologies to develop "new ways of looking at things," new ways of providing information and telling stories to better inform the public. "It *is* going back to the future," contends Wright.[30]

Newsroom leaders at ESPN, which has proven to be successful in broadcast (ESPN cable channels, ESPN radio), online (ESPN.com), and in print (*ESPN the Magazine*) profess a goal of serving and satisfying sports fans in whatever format those fans want sports news. John Walsh, ESPN executive vice president and executive editor, explained that "convergence is just another 'how can we do it better?'" He added that he believes in the "everybody is in" theory, which means that he believes journalism thrives by trying to reach as many people in as many different ways as possible. "There are people who prefer the little screen to the big screen. There are people who still read the daily newspaper, still read magazines, still listen to the radio." Add them together, he said, and journalism gets an audience that he calls "astonishing."[31]

ESPN, which is owned by Disney, one of the Big Five media conglomerates, has used the notion of journalistic convergence to respond to the fragmentation of media audiences and the consolidation of media ownership. It has come closest to a convergence goal in which all media partners view each other as equals, share their information and ideas, and work together to find the best way to present stories to their audiences using the strengths of any and all outlets available to them. Other organizations are achieving a lesser level of convergence, one that could be called content sharing, in which stories and ideas are freely exchanged among the different news outlets.[32] By using convergence, news organizations are innovating, taking risks in trying to scope out a new role for journalism in the digital age.

Nicholas Negroponte, who as a founder of MIT's Media Lab is an expert on the digital age, has argued that "without innovation we are doomed—by boredom and monotony—to decline."[33] New ideas, he has written, need diversity, risk, openness, and idea sharing to thrive.

FIGURE 1.4. John Walsh, ESPN: "Convergence is just another 'how can we do it better?'" (Courtesy ESPN)

Convergence is a new idea in journalism that relies on the diversity, openness, and idea sharing among different media and that takes a risk on that mix to better serve news audiences.

SUMMARY

Convergence journalism is a new way of thinking about the news, producing the news, and delivering the news, using all media to their fullest potential to reach a diverse and increasingly distracted public. It aims to address the growing fragmentation of the news audience, while working with the growing consolidation of news ownership.

Changes in lifestyle habits affect how and when people get and want news, the types of news they will look for, and the way they look for it. The nine-to-five, forty-hour workweek does not exist for most Americans. They are developing shorter attention spans and contending with increased demands for their time and interests. Fewer people under the age of thirty are watching network evening newscasts or reading daily newspapers.

Technological changes, such as the rise of the Internet, global connections, and wireless communication, have raised expectations about how people can get news and information. Those changes mean news audiences are limited by time and geography in getting news.

Convergence refocuses journalism to its core mission—to inform the public about its world in the best way possible. But nowadays, the best way is not just one way: newspaper or television or the Internet. The best way is a multiple media way.

LEARNING THE LINGO

- Blackberry
- Consolidation
- Cross promotion
- Economic convergence
- Multitasking
- News central
- PDA
- Technological convergence
- Time-starved
- Vertical integration

NOTES

1. Carrie Anna Criado and Camille Kraeplin, "Convergence Journalism: Landmark U.S. Media & University Study, 2003," April 4, 2003, at www.convergencejournalism.com (accessed November 29, 2005).
2. Henry Jenkins, "Converge? I Diverge," *Technology Review*, June 2001, 93.
3. Stewart Brand, *The Media Lab* (New York: Viking Penguin, 1987), 10.
4. Ithiel de Sola Pool, *Technologies of Freedom* (Cambridge, MA: Belknap Press of Harvard University Press, 1983), 28.
5. Lawrence K. Grossman, "Shilling for Prime Time: Can CBS News Survive Survivor?" *Columbia Journalism Review*, September/October 2000, 70–71.
6. David Bauder, "Dateline NBC: How Is 'News' Defined?," June 1, 2004, at www.cnn.com (accessed June 19, 2004).
7. Tom Shales, "A Big Hug Goodbye to 'Friends' and Maybe to the Sitcom," *Washington Post*, May 7, 2004, C1.
8. Kyle Pope and Martin Peers, "Merging Moguls: Redstone, Karmazin Both Like to Be Boss; Now, They Must Share," *Wall Street Journal*, September 8, 1999, A1.
9. Robert McChesney, "A Media Deal with Plenty of Bad News," *San Diego Tribune*, January 19, 2000, B7.
10. Rich Gordon, "Convergence Defined," in *Digital Journalism: Emerging Media and the Changing Horizons of Journalism*, ed. Kevin Kawamoto (Lanham, MD: Rowman & Littlefield, 2003), 64.
11. Chindu Sreedharan, "The 'C' Word," May 11, 2004, at www.poynter.org/content/content_view.asp?id=65471 (accessed November 29, 2005).

12. www.census.gov/Press-Release/www/releases/archives/facts (March 2004, accessed November 29, 2005).

13. "Striking Facts," *OECD Employment Outlook 2004*, at www.oecd.org/document/62/0,2340,en_2649_201185_31935102_1_1_1_1,00.html (accessed December 5, 2005).

14. "News Audiences Increasingly Politicized, Where Americans Go for News," June 8, 2004, at people-press.org/reports/display.php3?PageID=834 (accessed November 29, 2005).

15. Robert A. Papper et al., "Middletown Media Studies," *International Digital Media and Arts Assn. Journal* 1, no. 1 (Spring 2004): 25.

16. www.online-publishers.org/?pg=press&dt=042004 (April 20, 2004, accessed December 5, 2005).

17. Victoria Rideout, Elizabeth A. Vandewater, and Ellen Wartella, "Zero to Six: Electronic Media in the Lives of Infants, Toddlers and Preschoolers," October 28, 2003, and Victoria Rideout, Ulla Foehr, Donald Roberts, and Maryann Brodie, "Kids & Media @ The New Millennium," November 17, 1999, at www.kff.org/entmedia/upload/Zero-to-Six-Electronic-Media-in-the-Lives-of-Infants-Toddlers-and-Preschoolers-PDF.pdf (accessed December 1, 2005).

18. www.pewInternet.org/pdfs/PIP_Iraq_War_Report.pdf (page 5, June 3, 2005, accessed November 29, 2005).

19. Ben Bagdikian, *Media Monopoly* (Boston: Beacon Press, 1997), xiii.

20. Michael K. Powell, statement before the Committee on Commerce, Science, and Transportation, United States Senate, June 4, 2003.

21. www.childrennow.org/newsroom/news-03/pr-05-21-03.cfm (May 21, 2003, accessed April 2004).

22. Aaron Barnhart, "Sinclair Fortifies Station Newscast; Local-National Hybrid 'News Central' to Counter 'Biased' Reports," *Television Week*, January 5, 2004, 4.

23. Powell, statement.

24. Project for Excellence in Journalism, "State of the News Media 2004," at www.stateofthenewsmedia.org/2004/narrative_ethnicalternative_ethnic.asp (accessed November 30, 2005).

25. www.pewinternet.org/pdfs/PIP_blogging_data.pdf (January 2005, accessed November 29, 2005).

26. Jane Singer, "The Sociology of Convergence," paper presented at the meeting of the Association for Education in Journalism and Mass Communication, Kansas City, Missouri, August 2003.

27. Dean Wright, interview by author, April 12, 2004.

28. John Schwantes, interview by author, July 5, 2003.

29. www.apme-credibility.org/members/2003/6NewsReport.html (April 19, 2004, accessed November 29, 2005).

30. Wright, interview.

31. John Walsh, interview by author, May 6, 2004.

32. Larry Dailey, Lori Demo, and Mary Spillman, "The Convergence Continuum: A Model for Studying Collaborations between Media Newsrooms," paper presented at the meeting of the Association for Education in Journalism and Mass Communication, Kansas City, Missouri, July 2003.

33. Nicholas Negroponte, "Creating a Culture of Ideas," *Technology Review*, February 2003, 34.

TWO

Consorting with the Enemy

ON JANUARY 26, 1990, the Persian Gulf War delivered a wake-up call about a new era of journalism—technology-driven, twenty-four-hour, seven-day-a-week news. When the Gulf War started in Kuwait and Iraq, people around the world did not have to wait until the next morning to read about it in a newspaper or to watch it on the evening news roundup. They could see it on CNN in real time, thanks to satellite transmissions and satellite phones. New technology opened up new opportunities and new dangers for journalism. And it was just the first of many new technological developments that would challenge and confuse journalists who were used to a less complicated media landscape.

In the late 1970s and early 1980s, when today's generation of news executives started out in journalism, the Internet, cable television programming, satellite radio, cell phones, personal computers, digital music, digital video, digital photography, scanners, wireless networks, even the remote control did not exist. Back then, most cities had two competing, independently owned newspapers. Just about every city had three local TV stations affiliated with the three national networks—NBC, ABC, and CBS. Even rock music radio stations had news staffs.

A generation later, millions of Americans say they cannot live without a cell phone, do not know how to change the channel on their television without a remote, will not read a newspaper unless it is online, and never watch a nightly network newscast. Their basic cable subscription offers them a choice of at least fifty different channels, including three all-news channels. Most Americans live in cities with just one daily newspaper, usually owned by a media chain, and they have never seen an afternoon newspaper.

And when those Americans wanted to find out about the second U.S-led war in the Persian Gulf—the War in Iraq—they could check the latest developments online, on a cell phone, or on a PDA. They could go to non-American, nontraditional sources of information, such as

BOX 2.1

Journalism: The Old Days

I started my first full-time newspaper job in 1978 in Little Rock, Arkansas, where two reporters shared a telephone line, stories were written on a typewriter, and news copy was sent via vacuum tube to a scanner to be put into the computer. My photographer shot in black-and-white on a single-lens reflex camera. The television stations in town were in the midst of moving from film to video. None of them did live reports because none of them had a microwave or satellite truck.

Britain's *Guardian* newspaper's website and the Arab-oriented news network Al-Jazeera, as well as read the personal online journals or Web logs of soldiers and reporters in the combat zones.

The rise of instantaneous news and the use of new technologies that allow consumers to get news anytime and anywhere present huge challenges to traditional news media. Daily U.S. newspapers and nightly network and local station newscasts are constrained by specific times and specific production requirements for delivering the news. This rise of multiple media, 24/7 news means that newspapers can no longer just report on what happened, and print journalists have begun to rethink what kind of news they should be presenting. As a result, several newspapers are working at being more analytical, examining ways to provide more context on events. Networks and local television stations are doing more live news reports. Online news is developing ways to provide interactivity about the news as well as depth of content. Newsrooms, in other words, are trying to figure out a balance between reacting to news and events and being proactive in planning and seeking out news stories. They are struggling to keep up with and respond to the profound changes of a 24/7, multiple-media world. They are looking at new ways of doing journalism because their news audiences demand it.

Today's readers and viewers go to different media for different content and for different reasons. The events of September 11, 2001, demonstrated how news consumers expected different information from different sources. They turned to television for its immediate and emotional storytelling and to newspapers for context and extensive detail. They overwhelmed the Web that day, seeking instant news on their desktop computer. Millions tried to find out the latest about the attack in the same way they check their stocks, sports scores, or political race. They later turned to the Web to review, reflect, and research different perspectives and to comment and interact with others about the ramifications of the terrorist attacks on the United States.

A 2004 report on the state of the American media indicates that audiences are seeking "tailored content . . . on demand."[1] Newspapers, television, radio, and online may no longer be competing for the same audience but for any audience. Journalists today not only compete with other news organizations for the public's attention; more and more they are battling with nontraditional sources of news, such as entertainment shows, specialty websites, and blogs. A 2004 project survey by Pew Internet and American Life found that one-fifth of those polled under the age of thirty get political news from comedy shows such as *Saturday Night Live* and *The Daily Show*. "For Americans under thirty, these comedy shows are now mentioned almost as frequently as newspapers and evening network news programs as regular sources for election news," according to the poll's summary.[2]

But most journalists view the competition as other journalists, not alternative outlets. That has been the prevailing attitude in journalism for most of the twentieth century. It may not be a good approach for the twenty-first, when the most vigorous competition is in getting audiences interested in news in the first place. The best strategy for delivering news in the twenty-first century is to take advantage of the strengths of every outlet available. It means being more creative, flexible, and committed to telling stories in multiple media so that more stories can reach more people. So far, that is not happening much.

The 2004 State of the News Media report says news organizations have failed to put resources into newsgathering of stories, the one area where news organizations can and should compete with each other. And even when resources *are* being dedicated, they are devoted to just a few big stories. As a result, traditional news outlets are competing among themselves for people interested in just those big stories. In the meantime, they are failing to compete for diverse audiences seeking "tailored content." Journalism may need to shift from competing for a mass audience to competing for many smaller niche audiences.

Convergence is one approach to making that shift. It calls for coordination and cooperation rather than constant competition among print, broadcast, and online media. And that cooperation means changing what might be called the culture of news.

That culture of news does not change easily, however. Studies show that news organizations are among the institutions most resistant to change. One analysis of an American Readership Institute report in 2001 about newspapers noted that the news organizations' culture resembles the culture of the U.S. military.[3] That means journalists working in today's newsrooms, and their bosses, are working with old assumptions about not only their competition and audience but also about the way they work and the way they are organized.

Convergence is requiring newsrooms to reshape the way they think about and do journalism; it aims at taking advantage of the strengths of each medium, at a time when journalists refuse to acknowledge the strengths of competing news media. In addition, the ways television, newspapers, and online journalists work—how they plan their workday and the stories they produce—often do not dovetail. Convergence invites journalists to develop new habits toward doing their jobs so they can work together. But old habits die hard.

Journalists' disdain for those doing news in other media has proven to be a big hurdle to convergence. John Burr of the *Florida Times-Union* noted at a 2004 convergence symposium that newspaper journalists stereotypically view television reporters as superficial, while broadcast journalists contend that newspaper journalists are arrogant and out of touch with their audience.[4] When it comes to online reporting, the debate still rages as to whether it is "real" journalism. Convergence opponents argue that newspaper, television, and online journalism cannot work together because the journalistic culture of news competition will not allow it. Convergence advocates argue that the consumer culture of news on demand requires that they do so.

Newspapers, radio, television, and online take different approaches to deadlines, newsroom organization, workflow, and communication. Deadlines can range from one or two a day to one or two an hour. Newsrooms can either be centralized, with a handful of people overseeing all operations, or decentralized, with different people overseeing small work teams. Reporters can be organized by covering beats, special areas of interest, or they can work general assignment, covering stories as they emerge. They can be one-man bands, working alone, or teams that work together to gather words, pictures, and sound.

News organizations that want to be more convergent have had to make changes in how they are organized and operated. Technological advances and changing consumer demands require shaking up the organizational status quo and the journalistic mindset.

In the pages ahead, we first look at the setup and work flow of newspapers, television, radio, and online news organizations. We examine the traditional editorial production and news-gathering tasks of newspapers. And we see how those tasks compare and contrast with what is being done in broadcast and online news operations. Finally, we explore the changes in the organization, operations, and thinking of journalists providing news in more than one media outlet.

HOW NEWSROOMS ARE ORGANIZED: THE LAY OF THE LAND

The size and type of news operation often determines the organization of the newsroom. The bigger the newsroom, the more decentralized it is; this is especially true for newspapers. Conversely, radio and television are more centralized, because the staffs are small and news-gathering and production operations require a central communications post. Online news operations often depend on where they fit with their parent news organization—if they are a separate entity or part of the general news operation.

Putting news out in several formats requires a different way of organizing and managing news. It challenges the status quo in terms of who controls the decisions needing to be made. Each news organization that is trying to be more convergent has developed its own newsroom management organization to accommodate that change. But that first requires understanding how the news organizations that are being asked to work together operate on their own, and then figuring out the best way to bridge the differences.

Most newsroom operations can be divided into "outside" work and "inside" work. Generally, outside work is news-gathering—talking to people and getting information, visuals and sound. Some news-gathering can be done over the telephone, or with e-mail, Internet searches, and database analysis. Often the best news-gathering is done in person, out in the field. That is true of any type of journalism—newspaper, radio, television, or online.

Inside work is most often production work, putting together the pieces of a story so it can be presented to the public in the best possible way. It also means putting together different stories for a cohesive newspaper, newscast, or home page. In newspapers, it involves copyediting, layout, and design. In broadcast, it involves editing as well as audio, video, and graphics presentation. In online, it involves editing, layout, design, audio and video presentation, and interactivity.

Newsroom organization and management aim to coordinate the so-called inside and outside work. In operations that are trying to be convergent, that coordination is tricky because inside and outside work is changing.

Newspapers

Every newspaper in the country would argue that its newsroom operation is unique and tailored to fit the needs of its community. Despite local influences, every newspaper follows a similar division of labor, involving editors, reporters, photographers or graphic artists, and people on the desk—copyeditors and layout designers. Over the past fifteen years, some of those jobs have merged and duties have shifted. Ways of working together have changed, but the news and editorial division of a newspaper, large or small, still has those four major job categories.

Newspaper editors generally are of two types: those whose job it is to work with reporters, make assignments, and review reporter work and those, such as copyeditors, whose job it is to review reporters' work for writing and reporting errors and for the placement of copy in the newspaper. Both jobs have undergone changes over the past fifteen years.

EDITORS AND DEPARTMENTS Editors, as opposed to copyeditors, oversee the reporting and writing process in a newsroom and are usually in charge of a team of reporters. Traditionally, newspapers have had editors supervising departments for sports, features, business, editorial or opinion, and metro or city news. Some small newspapers, such as the *Pensacola News Journal*, in Florida, with a daily circulation of 60,000, list about a dozen editors, including one executive editor and one managing editor.

Larger papers have more reporters, and more reporters mean more editors, departments, and editorial subdivisions. The *Los Angeles Times*, with an average daily circulation of nearly one million, has three deputy managing editors and six assistant managing editors, as well as

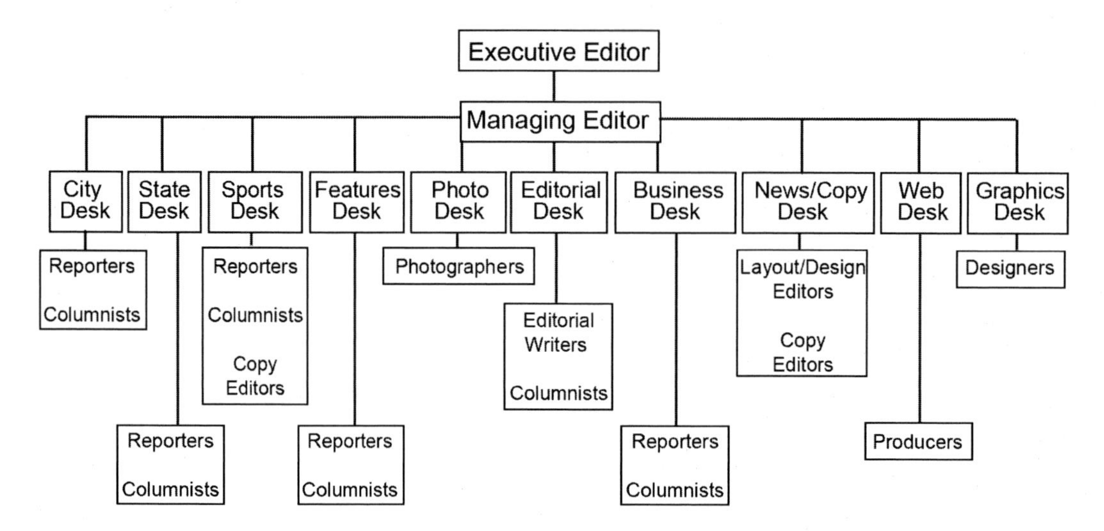

FIGURE 2.1. An example of a typical newspaper organizational chart.

several editors for each of its seven weekday sections.[5] Newspapers have also established polling or investigative teams headed by editors to work on special projects.

COPYEDITORS Thanks to computers and "pagination," the electronic process of page design and layout, many of the production jobs that once belonged to typesetters and composers were eliminated from newspapers in the 1980s and turned over to the copydesk. At the *Memphis Commercial Appeal*, copyeditors now work in the editorial production department, while at the *Atlanta Journal-Constitution*, the job is known as editing and presentation. Generally, the news editor serves as the leader of these divisions.

Some newspapers operate what is called a universal desk, where stories from all sections of news are handled by a main desk. Many other papers, such as the *Pensacola News Journal* and the Scripps-Howard papers in Stuart, Vero Beach, and Fort Pierce in Florida, have a universal copydesk for everything but sports. The sports department has its own copydesk to do editing and layout design. Some papers split the desk between editors who handle wire service news and those who handle staff-generated stories.

While some newspapers still have what could be considered "pure" copyeditors who are the final reviewers of copy and who write headlines but do not do page layout and design, most expect copyeditors to do some page layout design. A check of classified ads in newspaper trade publications these days will often list a combination of editing and design skills for copyediting openings.

REPORTERS Reporters are organized within each department of a newspaper, and most are assigned a beat, or special area of reporting expertise. In sports, for example, high school sports or the city's professional football team might be a beat. Features departments are subdivided, with reporters and writers in specialty areas from film to food.

News departments often have established institution beats, such as city hall, the school board, the police, federal court, and the statehouse. In recent years, some have organized topical beats, such as money, growth and planning, education, and environment. The *Los Angeles Times* has a deputy editor for religion and immigration who guides and supervises the reporters for Asian affairs, ethnic communities, immigration, and religion.[6] In the 1990s, the team concept of organizing reporter-editor teams took hold at several newspapers, putting a subeditor, such as an assistant city editor, in charge of a group of reporters with beats that might overlap. For example, beat reporters for city government, the police, and the courts might be coordinated by one team editor.

Most newspapers also have general assignment reporters, who are called upon to do stories that do not fall into a particular beat. General assignment reporters also provide relief and backup to beat reporters. Photographers for newspapers are also either specialists, assigned to a particular area like sports, or general assignment, called upon to shoot pictures to illustrate planned news stories or special news events.

Television

Broadcast newsroom operations vary dramatically from those of newspapers. Copyeditors exist in few local television newsrooms; most television editors edit videotape, not written copy. The vast majority of television reporters work general assignment, although some larger stations have beat reporters for consumer, health, and political news specialties. Often, television reporters develop expertise on a specific story or topic in addition to their general assignment work.

ASSIGNMENT EDITORS A television newsroom is much more centralized than a newspaper newsroom, with the assignment desk at that center for both logistics and communication. The assignment desk is responsible for knowing which stories are being pursued, who is working the stories, and when the stories might be ready for air. Assignment editors also coordinate with producers, who oversee the organization and development of the parts of a newscast. Producers need to know about the availability of video, sound, live reporter

FIGURE 2.2. MSNBC and MSNBC.com newsroom in Secaucus, New Jersey, March 2004. (Photo by the author)

capabilities, and completed reporter stories or packages for their newscasts. That information comes from the assignment desk.

Assignment editors supervise the gathering of not just information but also pictures and sound. They also may have to work the phones, calling news sources for information and for the logistics of scheduling interviews. Unlike newspapers, in which every story has a reporter assigned to it, some broadcast stories begin with a cameraperson (called a videographer or shooter) being sent out alone for an interview or for footage. Information gathered on the phone by the assignment editor, coupled with video and sound from a shooter, may be handed to a producer, anchor, reporter, or writer, who then puts it together for a story for air. The assignment desk operates as the bridge between the inside and the outside work in broadcast news, often doing a little of both to get the elements of a newscast together.

PRODUCERS For the inside work in television, show or line producers operate as the main coordinators. In some ways, they are like an editor at a newspaper, because they determine the space and the place of a story in the final news product for delivery to their audience. While newspaper editors work with the number of words in a story (space) and on which page in the paper a story should go (placement), producers determine the number of seconds for a story (space) and in which block of a newscast a story should go (placement). While the front page of each section of a newspaper is a prized spot, so is the first story of every block or section of a newscast. Commercial breaks separate each newscast block or section. The broadcast equivalent of the front page is the A block, or first section of a newscast before the first commercial break.

Producers put together a rundown, or list, of stories they want to air. Because television requires use of words, pictures, and sound, or what are called story elements, this list has to specify the mix of those elements. Also, producers have to work with anchors, who present the news and often write news scripts, and with skilled technicians in the studio and control room, where that mix of elements comes together for transmission to the audience. Producers serve as copyeditors in checking the writing and the reporting of newscast scripts.

Just as newspapers are broken up into sections, so too are newscasts. Most newscasts cover news, weather, and sports. A producer's rundown or game plan for a newscast requires a director, videotape playback operator, and audio, graphics, and camera technicians to carry out the plan. Advances in technology, from robotic cameras to server-based digitized video, have eliminated or revised control room jobs and have opened up new techniques in television storytelling. The producer is expected to worry about every detail in the newscast, ensuring that it is a complete telling of the main stories of the day.

REPORTER TEAMS While newspaper reporters can and often do work on a story alone, television stories require more teamwork. If available, a reporter will be assigned to go out with a cameraperson to work on a significant story to be put together in a package—a detailed report featuring interviews and video. At the network level, a reporter may be sent out on a story with a shooter, an audio technician, and even a field producer, who has done preliminary reporting work and logistical setup of interviews and site visits for shooting video. A field producer coordinates all the people and elements for a reporter package. This person often gathers information for reporters who are doing live reports and are sometimes unable to do extensive reporting because of their on-air demands.

Network reporters also are more likely to have beats, or specialty areas of coverage, such as the Pentagon, Capitol Hill, the Midwest, health and medicine, or financial markets. In many instances, a network reporter, a field producer, and a photographer might work together as a team exclusively on many assignments, developing a certain style of reporting and storytelling.

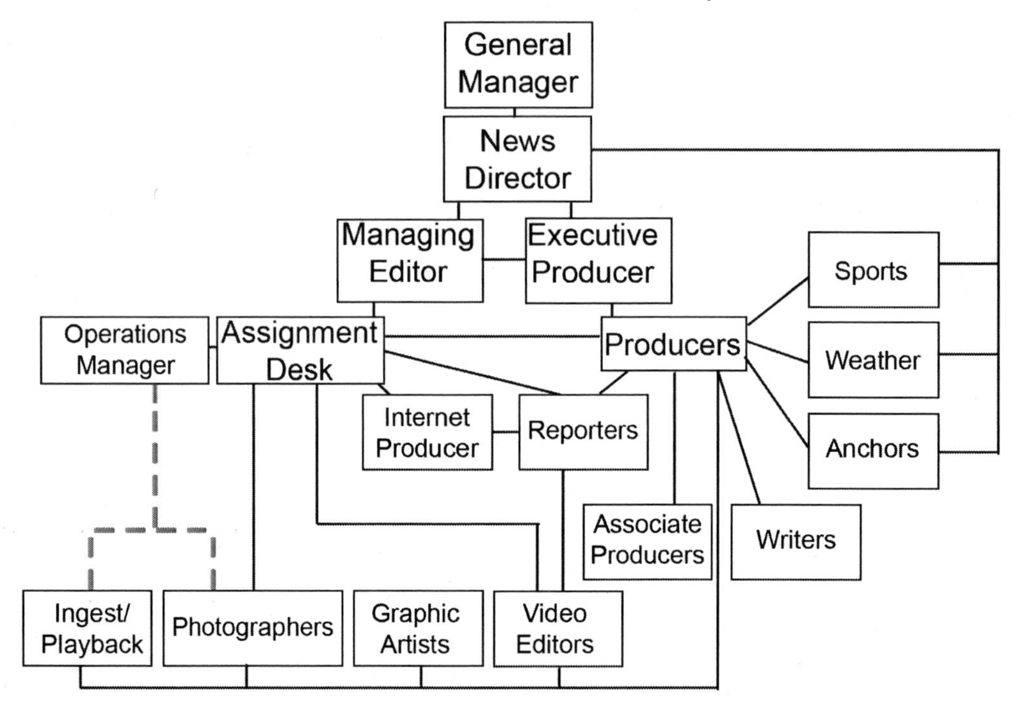

FIGURE 2.3. An example of a typical television station's organizational chart.

At local television news stations, beats are less likely, as reporters could be called upon to cover a fire, a city council meeting, and a new health study on any given day. At smaller news stations, and for stories in hard-to-reach locales, one-man bands are used for news-gathering. In a one-man band, a reporter shoots the pictures, edits the pictures, writes the script, voices the report, and makes it a cohesive story. As technology makes camera and editing equipment smaller and less expensive, news stations and networks entertain greater use of one-man bands.

Radio

Radio news operations are even more centralized than television newsrooms, because they have much smaller staffs. The 2003 Radio-Television News Directors Association (RTNDA) survey of news operations in radio and television found that the average full-time staff size of a radio news department is 3.5 persons.[7] More than 96 percent of all radio news departments handle news for more than one station, translating to about one person for each radio station doing news.

All-news radio stations have it slightly better, with more reporters and editors. For example, WBZ Radio 1030 AM in Boston has combined the duties of the assignment editors with newscast producers. These news editors are in charge of finding the news, planning the news, and putting together the rundown or story plan for the newscasts during an eight-hour time period.

When Jill Madigan worked as midday editor at WBZ, she would come in at 6:30 a.m. to make assignments for the station's three field reporters. She also coordinated with two anchors and two writers, who worked on the fifteen-minute news segments that run continuously throughout the day. The anchors alternate their on-air time. Each is on air for fifteen minutes, then off air for fifteen minutes, writing and reviewing scripts.

Radio reporters operate as one-man bands. They report the story by gathering information, interviews, and sound. They produce the story, writing the script, voicing the narration, and editing the narrations with sound. Radio reporters also transmit their stories—the scripts and the final edited audio report—via telephone, satellite phone, and now wireless technology.

In addition to news, many twenty-four-hour commercial news radio stations fill out their programming schedule with talk shows. Some also provide live broadcasts of professional or collegiate sports games. For example, WBZ in Boston carries the Boston Bruins' professional hockey games, and WSB in Atlanta airs the University of Georgia Bulldogs football games.

Online

Online staffs are often divided into content and production jobs, but with some blurring of tasks, and titles. Most editors and producers in online operations have some responsibility for the technical production aspects of the website, even if that means merely knowing HTML for coding of text and layout. In general, online news staffs consist of editors, producers, and reporters. But like television, online enlists technical experts in certain aspects of computerized, digitized production work, such as video streaming.

EDITORS Online editors function like newspaper editors; they review the work of producers and reporters and determine style, policies, projects, and work assignments. The top two news executives for MSNBC.com, like most online news executives, bear the title of editor and develop the policies, projects, and style for their websites.

Andrea Panciera, editor of projo.com, the website of the *Providence Journal* in Rhode Island, works with one online news reporter but oversees all the news content that gets put on the website. Panciera says her job is not only to ensure accuracy in the news online but to raise editorial policy issues, often before they are raised or decided by the print edition's editors. In some sense, she notes, she is "the default monitoring editor for the organization."[8] So although online editors control website content, they also make decisions about stories that affect stories for their newspaper or television partner.

Lucy Mohl is Panciera's counterpart at the *Seattle Times*. She coordinates the online staff, serves as liaison with newspaper reporters and editors, and plots out special features for seattletimes.com. But her title is senior news producer, which illustrates the differences between news organizations in naming and defining online jobs.

Editors at MSNBC.com and MSN.com oversee specific news sections, such as business, arts and entertainment, technology, and health. Jane Weaver, a writer and editor at MSNBC.com, keeps track of wire service stories related to health throughout the day.

PRODUCERS Newspapers such as the *Seattle Times* and the *Providence Journal* have online producers assigned to different departments and working at desks within those departments, rather than a separate online news section. These producers bear responsibility for repurposing or reworking stories from each department for sections on the Web. Bob Payne, a Web producer for seattletimes.com, has been working in the sports department, while Sheila Lennon serves as the features department producer for projo.com. They write teases (one or two sentence enticements about stories) and photo captions and headlines, and they format stories for their respective section's home page. They also work to determine which story from their department (sports for Payne and features for Lennon) should be featured on the paper's home page. They can be called upon to put together a poll or an idea for a graphic or further links to a story. Some producers, like Lennon, also write a Web log.

MSNBC.com works with two types of producers—multimedia producers who work with graphics, photos, and video and audio streaming, and content producers, who work either on the cover or on home page content. These producers work together to determine picture placement, captions, headlines, and graphics on the home page. They may debate whether a picture that is visually powerful is also journalistically true. Both content and multimedia producers also help develop multimedia projects or graphics for NBC or MSNBC news shows, such as a special database relating to a *Dateline* segment about saving money on income taxes.

Mark Pawlosky, who has worked at both MSN.com and MSNBC.com, notes that the notion of a producer, developed in television as someone who puts together all the elements into a whole, jibes better with online and the technology culture. Online, like television, might be considered "more communal" in its approach than has traditionally been the case on newspapers.

REPORTERS Some websites have reporters solely dedicated to providing news for the websites; others use producers to do reporting designed for the site. Most websites associated with daily newspapers or local broadcast stations rely on reporters from those papers and stations to supply stories. MSNBC.com has dozens of reporters working specialties or beats such as homeland security. Some work out of Washington in the NBC network bureau.

At csmonitor.com, the website for the *Christian Science Monitor* newspaper, producers also serve as reporters; they are expected to gather information or rework information to fit the Web. They could be asked to enhance a story originating for the print edition or put together a new story for the Web. Sometimes that could be a simple question-and-answer interview with an expert on a story that was developed for the *Monitor*'s newspaper edition. While the newspaper would not have the space to run such an interview, the website would.

Convergence

Convergence affects how people put together the news (production, or inside work) as well as how people gather the news (reporting, or outside work). People are at the heart of making convergence successful. And since each newsroom doing convergence journalism has a different mix of people, no one model of organization or operation has arisen. A few patterns, however, have emerged: Convergence is encouraged but not mandated, convergence requires more and better communication, and convergence is more team-oriented.

COORDINATORS News organizations committed to multiple media journalism have reorganized some managerial tasks, newsroom setups, and newsroom communications to ensure cooperation.

Many newsrooms working with convergence, like the *Orlando Sentinel* and *Baltimore Sun*, have established a multimedia editor, who acts as a coordinator and liaison between convergence partners. The Tribune Company, which owns dozens of metropolitan newspapers like the *Sentinel* and the *Sun* as well as the *Chicago Tribune*, advocates convergence. Most Tribune Company newspapers have a multimedia editor, who oversees online operations while serving as a liaison between newspaper editors, online producers, and/or broadcast producers. David Underhill, who served as Tribune Company's vice president for convergence, adds that each Tribune news operation devises its own response to doing news in multiple media, with the coordinating editor serving as a bridge. "Using the multimedia tools rests in the local markets," he says. "Each local market sets its own multimedia strategy, and that strategy is tailored to the station and the newspaper."[9]

Another Tribune paper, the *Hartford Courant*, in Connecticut, has a multimedia editor who works with the online operation, CTnow.com, and with a television reporter-producer, Ellen Burns. Burns puts together news reports for the *Courant*'s convergence partner, WTIC-TV Fox 61, a television station that is owned by the Tribune but that airs Fox network entertainment and sports programming. This is the only Tribune partnership that has a television reporter-producer working for a newspaper. News managers decided to try this approach because of the *Courant*'s long journalism history. The *Courant* prides itself as the oldest continuously published daily newspaper in the United States. So news managers decided that the best way to get convergence accepted in such a tradition-entrenched culture was to make the television reporter a part of the newspaper's newsroom. Burns works for the *Courant*, not for its long-perceived television competitor.

That relationship proved crucial when the *Courant* uncovered documents on how New York's Cardinal Edward Egan handled priest sex-abuse cases when he was bishop in Bridgeport, Connecticut. While the newspaper's reporters wrote their stories, Burns put together a well-documented, quality television report that aired the night before the paper's presentation. It brought more readers to the newspaper's in-depth examination and gained national prominence for the reporting.

In Columbus, Ohio, the convergence coordinator for the Dispatch Media Group, Jon Schwantes, not only coordinates the stories and reporting projects for the paper, website, and television and radio stations, he works with reporters to help write and produce stories or reworks them himself. Schwantes makes a concerted effort to put good television stories in the newspaper and not just newspaper stories on air. For example, an Ohio News Network reporter's piece on the family of an Iraqi émigré facing deportation was converted to a story on the front page of the second section of the *Dispatch* newspaper.

Some news organizations, like the *Tampa Tribune* and the *Lawrence (KS) Journal-World,* have put television, newspaper, and online staff together in a central location to make coordina-

BOX 2.2

Columbus Convergence Lesson

Columbus Dispatch columnist Mike Hardin found that convergence reinvigorated his writing and his reporting. A dream assignment—to roll down Route 66 from beginning to end in 2003—gave him a new perspective on storytelling. He had to report his trip not only in print but on television.

Now he says that when he gets an idea for a column, he starts thinking about whether it might work better as a visual piece. For example, Hardin got excited about doing a story on a café in which customers can play a song or two on the piano as payment for their coffee. He realized it would make for fascinating television. "It was a matter of sorting out what story is best for what medium. It opens up a lot of possibilities."

Hardin admits he had to unlearn certain stereotypes about television, such as that it is not as easy as it looks. Other tips he learned: write tighter, crisper more direct sentences, and do not describe what is being shown on the video.

Source: Mike Hardin, interview by author, summer 2003.

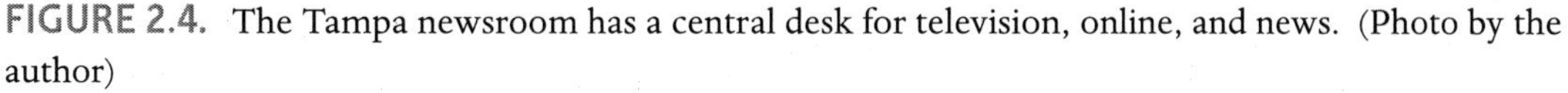

FIGURE 2.4. The Tampa newsroom has a central desk for television, online, and news. (Photo by the author)

tion easier. The Lawrence news operations are situated in a restored post office, and the people who oversee news assignments sit at a main news desk. The assigning editors and reporters are grouped by beat or coverage topic rather than by medium. When it is time for a regularly scheduled meeting to discuss what is being covered that day, the editors at the news desk come together to review the story list. Throughout the day, they can update each other about any new information coming from reporters out in the field.

In Tampa, Florida, editors for the *Tribune* newspaper, WFLA television, and tbo.com website also sit around a central desk, while the staff of each operation is on a floor that opens up to that central desk area. By being located in the same building, editors and producers have more chances to coordinate coverage.

REPORTERS Convergence for reporters takes on multiple forms—from talking about their beat on television, to calling in latest developments to an online producer, to planning special projects for multiple media.

One of the simplest forms of convergence involves newspaper reporters appearing on television as experts on a news story or development. These are called talk-backs. At New England Cable News, reporters for the *Boston Globe* and the *Hartford Courant* appear on the station to discuss developments in major stories. Michelle Johnson, a personal technology columnist for the *Globe*, appeared on NECN on December 2, 2003, to talk about high-tech Christmas gifts, the focus of her column that day. For Darren Rovell, the sports business reporter for ESPN.com, hardly a day goes by when he isn't doing talk-backs on television or radio. On May 6, 2004, when his online story appeared about Major League Baseball allowing the promotion of the *Spider-Man 2* movie via logos on the bases, Rovell was on ESPN radio that morning, talking about the story. He estimates that in a year he does about 350 talk-backs on radio and about 100 television segments. Sports and entertainment reporters and reviewers commonly do talk-backs.

Special projects also open up convergence opportunities for reporters. Newspapers are getting more comfortable in planning projects for both online and print. Tracy Cutchlow, of Seattletimes.com, says the website proved invaluable when the newspaper launched an expose on a revered cancer research institute in town. The website enabled the paper to make available online documents about two failed clinical trials at the Hutchinson Cancer Research Center, lending the project, and the paper, greater credibility. The website included dozens of documents showing researchers' financial interests in a cancer drug they were testing, letters of concern about the trials, and even audio files of reporters' interviews for the series entitled, "Uninformed consent: When cancer patients at 'The Hutch' weren't told about the experiments in which they died."

Reporters and photographers are also taking advantage of new technologies in newsgathering to distribute pictures and information in more than one medium. Newspaper still photographers are carrying video cameras as well as digital still cameras. Reporters and producers covering the 2004 Democratic primaries, such as *Boston Globe* reporter Glen Johnson, carried digital recording devices that helped them archive candidates' speeches and download audio files to their website.[10]

A few journalists are asked to write and produce reports for newspaper, television, and online. In both Lawrence and Tampa, reporters are called upon to produce stories for all three media. Peter Howard, of tbo.com in Tampa, recalls that convergence proved to be a big plus in late 2001, when a student pilot flew his plane into a bank tower in Tampa, just months after the September 11 attacks. A Web designer saw the plane hit the building. Armed with a digital camera and a cell phone, the young man got the story out to both television and the Web for news audiences in the Tampa Bay area.

As the consumer reporter for WFLA-TV in Tampa, Victoria Lim worked with a photographer to produce a television consumer report and then converted the pictures, audio, and script for a multimedia presentation online. She also writes a consumer column for the *Tampa Tribune* newspaper. She notes that new technologies are making conversion from television to online easier, but she admits it is a lot of hard work.

WFLA-TV reporter Jackie Barron had an intense convergence experience, covering a murder-for-hire trial that required her to produce a journal for the website, live reports and packages for television, and a story for the newspaper. "My brain was mush by the end," Barron says.[11]

Rob Curley, formerly of the Lawrence convergence operation, says convergence has become so commonplace that reporters and photographers do not think twice about journalism in more than one medium. A photographer for the newspaper visiting an egg farm recorded the sounds of the farm during his photo shoot and put together a slide show with audio for the paper's website. A television reporter's look at the impact of the Columbine High School shootings on local schools five years later was reworked for the front page of the newspaper.

A handful of other journalists have taken convergence reporting to a higher level, doing the work of reporting and producing in all media by themselves. Jane Stevens, a freelance multimedia journalist and journalism educator, calls it "backpack journalism." The idea evolved from a program called Video News International, developed in the 1990s in hopes of expanding international news reporting.[12] These truly multimedia reporters are not common in the news industry. However, some have put together reporting projects in places like Afghanistan and Iraq, where access to news stories is severely restricted. They are using new technologies to get information for stories and produce them for different audiences.

Kevin Sites, who worked for CNN and NBC News covering the war in Iraq and writing a blog about it, has been working as a freelance convergence journalist, first in Iraq and then in Indonesia in the aftermath of the December 2004 tsunami. Sites is now reporting from world hot zones for Yahoo!

Doing convergence journalism now covers a range of reporting and producing activities. It can mean that newspaper reporters provide timely updates of stories on the Internet, or appear on television to explain those latest developments. It can mean recording the sounds of an interview to accompany a photo gallery. It can mean a television reporter gathering documents from a police investigation and downloading them on the Web. Or it can mean testing the flammability of sound insulation in an investigative follow-up to a deadly nightclub fire and videotaping those tests so they can be replayed on television and online. That's what the *Providence Journal* did when it investigated the causes of the February 2003 Station nightclub fire.

Convergence provides journalists with an opportunity to expand the way they tell stories, the way they get information out to people. But with that opportunity come challenges in dealing with the demand for instantaneous news, delivered any time and any place.

HOW NEWSROOMS WORK: THE DAILY RHYTHM OF NEWS

On election night, November 3, 2000, the American public got a firsthand look at the challenges facing print, broadcast, and online journalism in trying to remain accurate and timely in a 24/7 news world.

On television, network news anchors first declared Al Gore the winner of Florida's electoral votes and thus the presidency about 8:30 p.m. Eastern Time, before a few hours later saying it was too close to call. Later, after midnight, the networks reported that George W. Bush would be the next president of the United States, but by dawn they again backtracked, saying it was a toss-up. A battle between being first and being accurate was fought on television in November 2000, with the credibility of broadcast news being the ultimate loser.

Newspapers also scrambled to update headlines for each of their morning editions, as the results kept changing. The *Boston Herald* offered the following headlines in various editions of its Wednesday, November 4, 2000 paper: "White House Vote Goes Down to the Wire," "Bush Victorious in Battle to the Wire," "Cliffhanger," "Unbelievable Recount Looms as Florida Vote Throws Election into Chaos."

The last headline was on the cover of the paper's newsstand edition, which is the last edition to go to press. The third headline was on papers delivered to the doorsteps of subscribers in the city and adjacent suburbs. The earlier headlines came from state editions, which had to get to press earlier than all the rest because the delivery trucks had to travel several hours before the papers could be distributed.

All across the country, newspapers that rely on the Associated Press for their national news coverage waited well past 2:30 in the morning for a definitive wire story on the election outcome. And online news sites throughout the election night and the next morning were jammed with users who could not get to the websites because of the huge volume. Getting updated, accurate information to millions of Americans proved problematic for every news organization—from those with fixed, strict deadlines for distributing the news to their audiences, like newspapers, to those with fluid, continuous deadlines, like live television and online news sites.

Thanks to satellite technology and digitization, television, radio, and online organizations now have the capability of distributing the news at the same time the newsroom and production center get it. As a result, the deadline for a story in a twenty-four-hour news operation could be just minutes or seconds before air, when the news is sent out to an audience for viewing.

Deadlines

U.S. newspapers operate with late-evening deadlines so their readers have their papers on their doorsteps by 6:00 or 7:00 in the morning. Newspaper reporters often have hours, if not days, to work on stories and rework stories with editors before turning them over for printing. Generally, stories that are not completed by the paper's deadline do not get printed and are held until they are ready, when editors determine the story's accuracy, balance, clarity, and relevance.

Like newspapers, network and local newscasts establish a particular time they are distributed to the public. For most of their existence, traditional broadcast newscasts have operated under the notion of "appointment viewing." Generally a term used for entertainment programming, it means the audience makes an appointment in their daily activities to watch a program. For news, it means people set aside a specific time in their day to get the news of the day.

Network news operations focus on the 6:30 p.m. Eastern Time newscast, and the deadlines for most network news reporters are for that newscast. But the increasing popularity of morning news programming, such as NBC's *The Today Show*, ABC's *Good Morning America*, and CBS's *The Early Show*, which begin airing at 7:00 a.m. Eastern, has led to early morning deadlines as well, as those shows demand updates of the evening's news stories and new reports on stories from overnight.

For local television stations, appointment viewing used to come at either 6:00 p.m., in a half hour of news before the network newscast, and/or at 11:00 p.m. Eastern Time, 10:00 p.m. Central, when network entertainment programming wrapped up for the evening. Deadlines corresponded to each newscast's airtime. Within the past fifteen years, local news stations have expanded the number of newscasts they air, and the number of deadlines has increased as well. Local news operations in most major U.S. cities now stretch from 5:00 a.m. through 11:30 p.m., with newscasts in the morning, early evening, and late night.

Online news operations handle a mix of rolling deadlines, by putting breaking news on their sites whenever necessary, and fixed deadlines, by putting stories from either their newspaper or broadcast partner online. For example, the *Boston Globe*'s online edition is updated at specific times of the day, such as between 5:30 a.m. and 6:00 a.m. to coincide with the paper's printed edition hitting subscribers' doorsteps. The *Providence Journal*'s projo.com website gets updated with the newspaper's content online soon after the printed edition has gone to press. For major news stories and updates, the *Globe*'s and *Journal*'s online sites add new, brief reports throughout the day.

To coordinate convergence efforts, news organizations have to agree to share information about their planned story coverage and figure out how and when they do that. That requires adjustments to the work flow and communication protocols in newsrooms.

Story Budgets

A story budget is a list of stories being planned and worked on that day. In a competitive environment, news organizations guard their story budgets because they do not want other news organizations to learn what they are working on and steal their story ideas. In a convergence

BOX 2.3

Convergence Story Budgeting

Producers for MSNBC's evening shows meet at their headquarters in Secaucus, New Jersey, at 9:00 a.m., using a telephone conference calls to include producers in Washington state and elsewhere. An MSNBC.com executive sits in that meeting as well, outlining plans for the website for that day.

An hour later, representatives of website staffs in Secaucus and in Redmond, Washington, videoconference to discuss website plans for the day. The meetings focus on what stories should lead the cover or home page. The MSNBC.com editors also discuss what needs to be coordinated with the various NBC and MSNBC shows that have specific locations for links on the main MSNBC.com home page.

environment, news partners share their story lists to avoid redundancy and to find different angles for telling a story, depending on the medium. Sometimes the story budget is shared via e-mail, or the editors of each news operation—newspaper and online; paper, TV, and online; radio and TV—meet to go over the stories planned for the day. But the work schedules of newspapers, television stations, and online news operations often fail to coincide, and convergence operations have to negotiate a new way to share their story budgets.

The workday for most newspapers traditionally begins around 10:00 a.m., while broadcast operations often start before the crack of dawn. A newspaper budget meeting might be at 11:00 a.m. while the first budget meeting at a television station is usually no later than 9:00 or 9:30 in the morning. Newspaper editors usually meet again in the early evening, often around 5:00 p.m., to make a final determination on what is going on page 1.

Because newspapers have much larger staffs and do not have to rely on every reporter for each day's edition, they can plan ahead and develop stories, taking what might be called a proactive approach to news.

Newspaper reporters are expected to generate story ideas, although assigning editors will also provide input for stories to be covered, especially about unplanned events. Beat reporters are expected to keep track of trends or activities that could warrant news stories in their areas of expertise.

Bob Bryan, of the *Pensacola News Journal,* says reporters and editor teams are expected to put together by the Friday of each week a budget of stories they anticipate working on for the next week. Then, every weekday morning, the editors gather and discuss the stories for the day, including updates on those stories listed in the weekly budget. They also plot out new ideas or events that require coverage and determine what still needs to be done in the days ahead.

Because broadcast news places a greater emphasis on immediacy and timeliness for news stories, it often takes a more reactive approach to story planning. Story assignments often come from the assignment editors to reporters, since the assignment desk has to determine which stories demand the limited resources of a reporter and a photographer. The assignment desk puts together a calendar of upcoming news events, such as a key murder trial or a legislative vote, to keep track of main stories that will warrant coverage. Reporters are encouraged to "pitch" or suggest stories, especially on days of few major news events. But the assignment desk is the main command post for story coverage decisions on any given day.

When the *Providence Journal* news editors had their 9:30 a.m. session on February 25, 2004, reviewing coverage plans of the governor's state budget unveiling, the paper's online editor sat in and asked questions about availability of information and graphics. The metro news editors also forwarded a list of planned budget stories.

Paul Lewis of WTIC-TV Fox 61 in Hartford says talking on the phone and sending e-mail keeps his station and the *Hartford Courant* newspaper in tune with the other's story plans for the day. Since his station's morning meeting is earlier than the newspaper's, he sends a memo to the paper's editors about the station's 10:00 p.m. newscast plans. After the paper's 11:00 a.m. meeting, Lewis gets a similar memo. The paper's multimedia editor acts as the liaison to ensure that paper, online, and television partners are kept up to date about stories for the day.

In many newsrooms, the cooperation and coordination is done informally. Online editors at the *Providence Journal* and *Christian Science Monitor* say overhearing an impromptu meeting of editors by the coffee machine or running into an editor by the water fountain often leads to coordinated efforts. At the *Stockton Record* in California, Sacramento television reporters whose bureau is based in the paper's newsroom exchange information with the *Record*'s reporters and editors.

Breaking News

When the unexpected happens or when breaking news breaks, cooperative convergence operations are challenged to determine exactly how, when, and where that news gets presented first. Print journalists have been wary of putting their "scoops" or exclusive news reports either online or on television, ahead of when the public would see those stories in the newspaper. They fear "scooping" or beating themselves.

But that attitude is slowly changing. Many newspapers have become more accepting of putting breaking news online before the next day's paper hits doorsteps. They acknowledge that readers go online during the day, between editions of the paper, to learn the latest news.

Newspapers such as the *Orlando Sentinel* have reporters call into the multimedia editor with the latest information to update the paper's website. At the *Pensacola News Journal*,

BOX 2.4

Breaking News in Multiple Media

Bruce Cadwallader is the *Columbus Dispatch*'s police beat reporter, but he spends a lot of time doing breaking news from his beat for online and for television. He says he enjoys doing police beat reporting for the television-online-newspaper operation in the Ohio capital city because he views his job as getting the news out to people.

His convergence work paid off when he did a talk-back, or interview, for *The Today Show* when a months-long, nationwide search for a highway sniper suspect ended in March 2004. He and his reporting gained a national audience.

The convergence coordination at his newspaper allows him to report across traditional boundaries. His boss, Mike Curtin, says, "Our print reporters more and more appreciate the opportunity" to break news on television or online.

Source: Bruce Cadwaller and Mike Curtin, interviews by author.

reporters call into their immediate supervisor, the team editor, who alerts the online editor with the latest information.

At several newspapers, the rewrite desk, that staple of the 1930s and 1940s, is getting a modern-day makeover. In that era, newspapers had multiple deadlines throughout the day. A handful of writers would take information over the telephone from reporters in the field, rewrite that information into a story, and get it to the composing room so it could make the latest edition. Newspapers would run extra editions for major stories, the print equivalent of the breaking news report.

These days, the online news reporter at projo.com in Providence often serves as the rewrite person, taking information from the newspaper reporter on the scene of a news event and putting it together for an online story. At other times, the online reporter for projo.com will call sources for information for an online version of a news story ahead of the newspaper reporter, since projo.com wants the story immediately. In both cases, projo.com editor Andrea Panciera says that online and newspaper reporters and editors need to communicate how each is doing the story, to avoid duplication of work and confusion by news sources.

Television, where there is still competition among local stations, often puts a breaking news story on air first, before putting it online. Some stations, such as Boston's WCVB, will break news on air but will update their website with a few short sentences a short time later. Other stations may put original reporting on air and wait to place a wire service story out on their site.

Adjusting to the Clock

Broadcast and online can and do change their story emphasis depending on the time of day. That's why traffic and weather play prominently in local morning television and radio newscasts and why sports scores are big news in late evening newscasts. It is the reason NBC's *The Today Show* has more features in its two-hour newscast, and the *NBC Nightly News* has harder national and international news.

Newspapers, because of production and distribution limitations, do not have that flexibility with time. That is why final scores of extra-innings baseball games on the West Coast may not show up in East Coast newspapers. It is also the reason the *Christian Science Monitor*, which prints its paper by late afternoon to mail out to subscribers, stresses a more analytical approach to news stories rather than emphasizing the latest information. The *Monitor*'s print journalism adjusts to its distribution limitations.

Managing editor for electronic publishing at the *Monitor*, Karla Vallance, calls the approach "second-day stories on the first day." Former *Monitor* editor Paul van Slambrouck says the *Monitor* aims to add meaning to news events. "What did it mean? Why did it happen? Where does it seem to be taking things? Those elements remain the core content ideas behind good Web and print products for us."[13] As a result of that philosophy, csmonitor.com will use the Latest News section of its website to provide up-to-the-minute wire service stories. But it sticks to the *Monitor* mission of providing more analysis and detail on major stories that happen past its print deadline.

During the 2004 presidential primary season, *Monitor* reporters worked with Monitor.com producers to put stories on the meaning of the late-night primary results on the website, rather than just do stories on the primary results. And, when Democratic presidential candidate Howard Dean bowed out of the race on February 18, 2004, at 1:00 p.m., the *Monitor* website posted the wire story on the announcement, which included quotes from Dean's withdrawal speech. But it also posted a *Monitor* report that would appear in the next day's newspaper about the impact of his departure. Liz Marlantes's report "Kerry Rivals Down to One" made it to online audiences about the same time as news of Dean's official withdrawal. The *Monitor* organization was using convergence to extend its type of journalism to audiences looking for the latest news with some context to it.

Thanks to technology, online news sites are able to track usage, getting a clearer idea of when people go online for news and what they are looking for in terms of information when they are online. News sites are then using that data to determine how they should update their sites and with what information. This planning of online news content to coincide with audience use is called dayparting.

An analysis of online use in 2003 by Rusty Coats, director of new media for Minnesota Opinion Research, Inc. (MORI) found that people expect hard news and information during the day but move to seeking more sports and entertainment news and information by early evening and into the night.[14] Online sites for the *Lawrence (KS) Journal-World*, the *Arizona Republic*, and the *Seattle Post-Intelligencer* have begun using dayparting, posting different types of content at different times of the day to make their websites more amenable to what Web users are seeking.[15]

Rob Curley, who headed the Lawrence convergence efforts, explains that the Sundown Edition of the newspaper's regular site moves from traditional hard news to more sports and entertainment news and format. It coincides in tone with a hipper tabloid edition of the *World* that aims to appeal to the younger audience and student population at the University of Kansas. Curley says the content of the website does not change as much as the placement of the stories on the site. Movie reviews or a chat room about a key story of the day may lead the site, as opposed to a traditional, harder-edged news story. Online users who still want the more traditional headlines news are just a quick click away. Curley says that dayparting has brought more traffic to the site in the evening, when online news usage plummets.

Other websites do a less radical version of dayparting, in that they deliberately update and change their website throughout the day. Web studies have found most Web news use occurs when people are working, between 9:00 a.m. and 5:00 p.m. Many websites want to keep those viewers engaged by offering them something different on their site when they periodically check it.

Robert Hernandez of seattletimes.com is in charge of updating the cover, or home page, of the newspaper's website during the day. While the website may be news-heavy in the morning, filled with the print edition stories, toward the end of the workday the site may take on a looser personality. "By the end of the day you unbutton the top button and may want a good read," Hernandez says, so the website takes that into consideration. He notes that sometimes new content may be a reader poll on a television show or a clever picture and headline in the photo gallery.

Boston.com also updates its sites throughout the day. Editor Teresa Hanafin says the main photo on the home page changes every hour, and one of the top two main stories is revised every two hours. Because online content can be revised and because online audiences are looking for revisions, online news sites are developing more ways to respond to those consumer expectations.

HOW JOURNALISTS THINK: ATTITUDE ADJUSTMENT

Convergence is a response to consumer expectations. Faced with trying to meet those expectations, more news organizations are finding ways to make convergence work for them and the people they serve.

FIGURE 2.5. Robert Hernandez, a producer at seattletimes.com, works in the *Seattle Times* newsroom. (Photo by the author)

When the Pulitzer Prizes for print journalism were announced on April 6, 2004, a television producer (Lowell Bergman) and a network (PBS) won, along with the *New York Times* and its reporters, for public service. When the Peabody Awards for outstanding television were announced a week earlier, the *New York Times* won along with Times Television, the Public Broadcasting System, and the Canadian Broadcasting Corporation. The combined print and broadcast reporting on safety violations in U.S. factories that led to the death and injury of dozens of workers demonstrated how convergence—doing journalism in more than one medium—is gaining acceptance, credibility, and respect.

The *Times*-PBS combination was not the only example of convergence on the Pulitzer list in 2004. Two other finalists for the public service award had developed some of their work online as well as in print. The *Seattle Times* story on male coaches' abuse of female athletes included an online question-and-answer session with the reporters and an extensive database for the public to search for their schools and coaches. The *Providence Journal* created animated graphics and videos online in an effort to explain how a hundred people died in the Station nightclub fire, which was set off by pyrotechnics igniting soundproofing insulation. Chat rooms and online guest books allowed friends and family to come together to share shock and grief over the tragedy.

While those convergence presentations may not have been a factor in the judging of the awards, they do indicate that convergence can inspire good public service journalism. They also indicate how the culture of newsrooms, defined as "the set of shared attitudes, values, goals, and practices"[16] that characterizes a news operation, is evolving. Journalists in convergence-oriented newsrooms are thinking differently about their audience and their competition, developing new attitudes and practices in their approach to news and storytelling.

One of the hardest transitions in convergence journalism involves redefining the competition. In many newsrooms, reporters are competing with each other to see who has the best story of the day. They want the best place in the paper, newscast, or home page. Plus, they are competing with journalists in their city or town to see who has the best, most exciting story of the day.

"We're asking people to put aside some sense of competition that has been driven into them since the start of journalism school," says Jon Schwantes, the Columbus, Ohio, convergence director.[17] Journalists believe competition delivers better journalism as it provides an incentive to dig deeper on a story and to write and present it better. Competition pushes journalists to want to be first, to scoop everyone else. And, just like football or basketball players who psyche themselves up preparing for a big game, journalists do the same with their competition. Convergence, however, asks opposing teams to join forces and to trust the "enemy."

Schwantes recalls asking print and television journalists in Indianapolis to provide a list of terms describing each other. He heard words like "staid" and "boring" for newspapers and "sleazy" and "blow-dried" for television. One journalist in a survey of convergence newsrooms referred to television journalists as "a subspecies."[18] Robert Haiman of the Poynter Institute, in criticizing convergence, worries about what he considers opposing values of each medium. "When newspapers and television and the Internet converge, there is going to be a tremendous clash of values—the journalism values of newspapers, the entertainment values of television, and the no-holds-barred, raw, unedited, anarchic values of the Internet."[19]

But convergence advocates argue that each medium has values and strengths, and journalists need think about themselves less and their public more. Cory Bergman, digital media director for KING-TV in Seattle, writes on the Lost Remote website that journalists need to shift from thinking that they "own" a story and consider rather that they "share" a story, with news media partners, and with the public.[20]

In convergence operations, reporters can and do share story tips, source information, and sometimes video or photos with their partners. "We share resources, content, and information," says Ohio News Network news director Greg Fisher, "and it has allowed for better information and for different ways for people to read and hear and see it."[21]

It is not always easy to share, as Lawrence's Rob Curley notes, recalling when a newspaper reporter learned of a politician's flip-flop on a public smoking ban less than a half hour before the 6:00 p.m. newscast of his television convergence partner. The newspaper reporter would have the exclusive in the next day's paper and on the paper's website if he did not tell television. But he decided to pass the tip along to his TV counterpart. He had the exclusive on the website for a few minutes before television was able to update its newscast. The story reached a variety of audiences because the reporter felt it was more important to get the story out than to worry about who got it out first.

Paul Lewis of Hartford's WTIC-TV Fox 61 described how the *Hartford Courant* shared with his station an interview with a nurse who saved a life during a 2003 nursing home fire. Earlier, a WTIC reporter got a tip about a development in a court case and passed it on to the newspaper. Lewis says the reporters are "covering each other's backs," allowing for his viewers and the newspaper's readers to get stories that might get missed. However, Lewis adds, the paper and television stations are still independent and "still beating the bushes for stories" but they share resources when it serves a journalistic purpose.[22] The same holds true in Tampa, one of the earliest and most scrutinized convergence news operations. Rather than forcing journalists to work in a medium they may not feel comfortable with, more and more journalists are sharing information across different media, ensuring that each medium benefits.

Convergence works, according to those who have seen its successes, when it serves the purpose of informing the public, not merely promoting a story and its reporter. In a case study on the news operations in Lawrence, Kansas, on the Convergence Tracker website, author James Gentry notes that "editors and reporters must learn to put readers/viewers ahead of their own egos."[23] For years, newspaper editors and the public looked at readership surveys, but reporters were never trained to think about how their audiences perceived their stories. As a result, newspapers gained reputations of being patronizing, aloof to audiences. Television, at the same time, became obsessed with ratings of newscasts, down to the seconds, and gained a reputation of pandering to its audiences.

Convergence journalism shifts the focus of news from the producer, the journalist, to the consumer, the public. A 2003 survey of journalists doing multiple media journalism in four cities found that the respondents believe their readers and viewers benefit from convergence.[24] A smaller survey of regional cable news operations found similar results: Convergence strengthens public affairs reporting.

"Most people who are in journalism really are into it to make a difference," notes the Tribune Company's David Underhill, and convergence gives their work greater impact.[25] The real danger, he says, is when good journalism fails to reach people. As newspapers see their circulation numbers stagnate or decrease, print journalists are expected to be more open to expanding the reach of their stories. When they see how widespread an audience their story gets, thanks to television or online distribution, journalists are less leery about having their stories done in more than one platform.

Reporters and editors at the *Christian Science Monitor* note that millions of people read their unique brand of journalism online each month, while their print edition's circulation sits at around 70,000. Convergence has "raised our visibility," says managing editor Marshall Ingwerson, not only among readers but also among news sources. "The presumption is the audience is out there, and we should give them the *Monitor* in all the forms they can and will digest it," says former *Monitor* publisher Stephen Gray. [26]

The *Monitor*'s Van Slambrouck agrees, and says the debate over which medium will be the dominant choice for news consumers is a futile one. "The important thing is the content, and you want to provide it in a way and at a price that the reader wants," he says. "Readers' choice is a big part of that."[27] News consumers are making choices, and while television and newspapers are still the top two choices for getting national and international news according to survey respondents in polling done by the Pew Research Center for the People and the Press, online news is gaining wider acceptance.[28] Additionally, news consumers are using more than one medium at a time—reading a news magazine while watching TV or listening to the radio while online.

"Each entity has its strengths, and the viewers and the readers use each for its strengths," Ohio News Network's Greg Fisher says. "On a basic level, it's all journalism, and we're all working to provide information to viewers and readers." This philosophy sets convergence news organizations apart from the others.

SUMMARY

Print, broadcast, and online news operations have developed different cultures in which they do news. Newspaper newsrooms are more decentralized, rely more on the beat system, and have fewer deadlines throughout the workday than broadcast or online news. Broadcast and online newsroom staffs tend to be smaller and often operate as generalists, doing several stories in one day.

Each news organization has developed teams of people who do inside or production work—putting together story elements for a final news product—and outside or news-gathering work—collecting story elements and information for that news product.

Inside work in newspapers involves assigning editors, copy editors, and layout and graphic designers, while outside work usually involves reporters and photographers. In television and radio, anchors, assignment editors, and line or show producers carry the load of inside work, while reporters, photographers, audio technicians, and field producers conduct outside work. Online, editors and producers often do both production work and reporting work.

News organizations with strict deadlines, such as newspapers and network and local newscasts, have struggled with adjusting to the rise of the twenty-four-hour, seven-day news cycle.

Convergence has opened up new ways for news media tied down by strict production and distribution timelines to answer consumer demands for instant news.

Convergence has also required news organizations to work at creating new lines of communication and new attitudes about sharing story information and ideas. They are sharing story budgets—the list of reporting efforts being planned for any given day. Those daily story plans will include information on how reporters' work will be developed and used in different media. Convergence asks journalism to think about making the news consumer the focus of their approach to producing and distributing a story.

LEARNING THE LINGO

- Appointment viewing
- Assignment editor
- Beat
- Copyeditor
- Dayparting
- Field producer
- General assignment
- Line producer
- Pagination
- Platform
- Repurposing
- Rewrite desk
- Rundown
- Scoop
- Story budget
- Talk-backs

NOTES

1. Project for Excellence in Journalism, "State of the News Media 2004," at www.stateofthenewsmedia.org/2004/narrative_ethnicalternative_ethnic.asp (accessed December 2, 2005).
2. www.pewinternet.org/reports/reports.asp?Report=110&Section=ReportLevel1&Field=Level1ID&ID=475 (January 11, 2004, accessed November 29, 2005).
3. Mary Nesbitt, "The Power to Grow Leadership: Results from the Impact Study of Readership," presentation at Institute for Journalism Excellence, June 13, 2001.
4. www.cyberjournalist.net/news/Converge2004-session1.asx (April 8, 2004, accessed May 15, 2004).
5. www.latimes.com/services/newspaper/mediacenter/la-mediacenter-editorialstaffstory.html (October 2003, accessed February 16, 2004).
6. www.latimes.com/services/newspaper/mediacenter/la-mediacenter-editorialstaff.htmlstory (October 2003, accessed Feb. 16, 2004).
7. Bob Papper, "On the Road to Recovery," *The Communicator*, September 2003, 5.
8. Andrea Panciera, interview by author, March 4, 2004.
9. David Underhill, interview by author, October, 24, 2002.
10. Katherine Q. Seelye, "Making the Digital Press Corps," *New York Times*, January 29, 2004, G1.

11. Joe Strupp, "Three Point Play," *Editor and Publisher*, August 21, 2000, 18–23.

12. Jane Stevens, "Backpack Journalism is Here to Stay," April 4, 2002, at ojr.org/ojr/workplace/1017771575.php (accessed November 29, 2005).

13. Paul Van Slambrouck, interview by author, March 27, 2004.

14. Rusty Coats, "Programming for Dayparts: Online Users, Content, Commercial Habits Change throughout the Day," January 2003, at www.digitaledge.org/DigArtPage.cfm?AID=4712 (accessed December 5, 2005).

15. M. Trombly, "News Sites Experiment with 'Dayparting,'" June 2003, at ojr.org/ojr/aboutojr/1055792590.php (accessed June 2003).

16. *Merriam-Webster Dictionary*, s.v. "culture," at www.m-w.com/cgi-bin/dictionary?book=Dictionary&va=cultuyre&x=20&y=13 (accessed November 29, 2005).

17. Jon Schwantes, interview by author, July 5, 2003.

18. Schwantes, interview.

19. Terrence Smith, "Media Mergers," July 17, 2000, at www.pbs.org/newshour/bb/media/july-dec00/mergers_7-17.htm (accessed November 29, 2005).

20. www.lostremote.com/story/convergenceclash.html (February 18, 2002, accessed November 29, 2005).

21. Greg Fisher, interview by author, July 2003

22. Paul Lewis, interview by author, July 2003.

23. www.mediacenter.org/content/777.cfm (April 14, 2003, accessed November 29, 2005).

24. Jane Singer, "The Sociology of Convergence: Challenges and Change in Newspaper Work," paper presented at the meeting of the Association for Education in Journalism and Mass Communication, Kansas City, Missouri, August 2003.

25. Underhill, interview.

26. Stephen Gray, interview by author, February 27, 2004.

27. Van Slambrouck, interview.

28. people-press.org/reports/print.php3 (October 4, 2001, accessed November 29, 2005).

THREE

Common Values, Common Goals

DURING MUCH OF the second half of the twentieth century, journalists would define their work by the way audiences received it: Newspaper reporter. Television correspondent. Magazine editor. Radio anchor. Copyeditor. Videographer. In newspapers, the written word is supreme. In television, the moving image rules. Radio demands sound. Television, newspaper, radio, and magazine journalists began believing that they followed separate philosophies, separate paths in looking at the news. Rather than noting similarities, they highlighted differences in their approaches.

The emergence of multiple media and multimedia in the news landscape in the 1990s, however, challenges this "separate but equal" notion of news. Online is mixing text, graphics, video, and animation. Print is becoming more visual. Digital technology is shrinking the screen for video. Journalists now need to capitalize on the strengths of each, and sometimes every, news format, choosing the best ways to deliver to their audiences. But no matter how many new ways journalists can deliver news to audiences, journalism's core values remain unchanged.

No matter what medium a journalist works in, when asked how he or she decides whether a story is news, the answer will be roughly the same: proximity, relevance, impact, usefulness, prominence, and timeliness will be among the common answers. When asked about the basic values and ethics of journalists, the answers also will sound similar: accuracy, truth, fairness, and balance. When asked about the purpose of journalism, the answers are similar from practitioners, no matter the media: to keep people informed about their world.

Convergence in journalism relies on these similarities of values and goals. It builds new ways of informing the public by using these values as its foundation. These values are the common language of journalism, regardless of the medium or format.

However, journalists do have to think about differences in how the media operate in order to determine the best way to provide information. Is the format active or passive—that is, does the audience have to do something (read, browse, click) or can it sit back and just see and hear rather than actively watch and listen? Is there a set sequence or pattern that must be followed to get the information, or can the audience jump around—that is, is it linear or nonlinear? Is it reliant on text to get the message across, or does it use audio and visuals or a mix of media? The medium still has some impact on how we get the message; as journalists we have to start thinking about the best ways to use the media we have to get information out to audiences. The medium does determine what gets emphasized in our storytelling. We need to understand and accept the strengths and weaknesses of the different ways we can provide news so we can provide it in the most effective ways. In doing journalism in a convergent media world, we need to think about the diverse ways people get their news to figure out how we should be giving it to them.

In this chapter, we first look at how journalists think about news and common aspects of what is known as news judgment and news ethics. After looking at what is common among the news media, we look at the differences among the news media formats. By understanding those differences, we explore the best way to deliver journalism to the public. Then we examine the common values and goals for journalists who practice convergence, with the story and the audience serving as the main touchstones.

COMMON NEWS VALUES

News has a myriad of definitions, and journalists over the past two centuries have developed quite a few ways to describe it. One of the most common descriptions of news has been attributed to the late publisher of the *Washington Post*, Phil Graham. Graham is quoted as saying that news "is the first rough draft of history." Another classic is from Charles Dana, the late editor of the *New York Sun*: "When a dog bites a man, that's not news, but when a man bites a dog, that's news." And finally, David Brinkley, one of the pioneers of television news, has been quoted as providing a definition that probably most journalists believe but are hesitant to admit: "The news is whatever I say is the news."

In fact, Brinkley's definition is perhaps the most honest: For many people, news today is what the news media says it is. And often, the public has a problem with what mainstream, traditional journalists are calling news. Thanks to the Internet, the definition of news and the definition of journalists—that is, the people who put together the news—are undergoing rapid transformation. Traditionally, news has some or all of the following characteristics:

timeliness, proximity, relevance or usefulness, impact, prominence, unusualness or novelty, and conflict.

Consider the following stories that "made news" in the past few years, and think about why: Britney Spears and Madonna kiss at the MTV Music Video Awards. Democratic presidential candidate Howard Dean screams to exhort his followers after not winning the Iowa caucuses. John Kerry chooses John Edwards as his running mate. Medicare premiums rise to 17 percent. Criminal rape charges are dismissed against LA Laker star Kobe Bryant. A million Sudanese are forced out their homes by civil war. Hurricane Ivan leaves thousands homeless in the Florida Panhandle. Three hundred people die at the end of a hostage takeover of a Russian school. U.S. soldiers humiliate and torture Iraqi prisoners.

Each of those stories is newsworthy for a number of reasons. Each day, journalists weigh those reasons in determining whether to "play" or present the story and how to play it. With convergence, journalists have more than one option about what they will report and how they report it.

Timeliness

The news media value timeliness above just about any other criterion, and journalists often gauge their success by being the first, the most timely, in getting information out to the public. It is, after all, called the "news" business and not the "olds" business. The availability of news any time and any place has redefined the idea of timeliness.

For example, a morning traffic jam caused by a tractor-trailer that jackknifed is news in the morning and perhaps in the afternoon, but by the evening or the next morning, its timeliness has waned. Or if a man is shot at a drugstore in the morning and police are searching for a suspect, then that's news in the morning. But if by late afternoon, police have arrested a woman suspected in the shooting, then the arrest is more timely than the shooting in the 6:00 p.m. newscast.

The newer the information in a news story, the timelier it is. A tornado warning issued in the past five minutes is timelier than a report that a warning, issued six hours ago, has since past. Timeliness can also relate to when a story is being told. A new report on the dangers of firecrackers is timelier when it is presented around the Fourth of July.

But timeliness can be dangerous when journalists try to be the most timely, the first to report the latest information. They can get burned reporting the latest information before double-checking its accuracy. Sometimes that is unavoidable, as illustrated by the early reporting of the September 11, 2001, attacks on New York City's World Trade Center. Though the information was sketchy, the public's need to know was overwhelming. News organizations struggled to be timely and accurate and sometimes made mistakes. Under the circumstances, this was understandable.

When it came to the selection of John Kerry's running mate, the rush to be first led to embarrassment for the *New York Post*, which reported on its July 6, 2004, front page that Richard Gephardt had been picked. Throughout that morning, journalists worked to beat out competitors by minutes and the official announcement by a few hours. The *Post* got it wrong; NBC's Andrea Mitchell got it first and right—John Edwards would be the nominee. But few members of the public probably remember that or even cared about it.

With convergence, news organizations can decide to deliver specific breaking news items almost instantaneously to specific niche audiences. For example, the *Lawrence Journal-World* in Kansas text-messaged the signing of a key University of Kansas basketball recruit via cell phones as soon as it happened, then wrote more extensive stories for its website and newspaper.

Proximity

Thomas P. "Tip" O'Neill, former majority leader of the House of Representatives, used to say that "all politics is local," and that is often true of news. The closer you are to what is happening, the more likely it is to interest you. A morning traffic jam in New York City means very little to someone in Akron, Ohio, and that plant closing in Muncie, Indiana, means little to someone in Gainesville, Georgia. The person from Akron or Gainesville is nowhere near where the news is happening.

News audiences are seeking information about areas of special interests, or niches. Local newspapers and news stations have carved out a well-established niche—their community. Convergence, putting their news out in more than one format, allows people interested in a particular area to be kept informed about that area. The editors and reporters for the *Providence Journal*'s website, www.projo.com, suggest that projo.com should provide information to people about Rhode Island, no matter where they are. The online version of the newspaper is responding to a niche audience: people wanting to know about Rhode Island.

More dramatically, the *Pensacola News Journal*, in Florida, demonstrated the value of convergence, timeliness, and proximity during its coverage of Hurricane Ivan in mid-September 2004. Although the paper could not be delivered for at least two days, the *News Journal* staff kept its community informed on all aspects of the hurricane via its website. While Ivan was a huge national story, the *News Journal* focused on information most important to its niche audience: residents of Pensacola and surrounding communities. As the storm approached, pensacolanewsjournal.com provided constantly updated satellite radar video of the storm, information on evacuation plans, lists of stores selling plywood and gasoline, locations of shelters, and insurance company contacts. It also created community forums.

In the days after the storm, the website was often the place for residents of inaccessible shore communities, such as Perdido Key, to find out about damage to their property via extensive photo galleries, including a series of aerial photos supplied by the Escambia County sheriff's department. Information about school closings, road and bridge openings, and relief centers was available on the site. For people not living in Pensacola, people who lacked proximity to area, the variety and depth of storm aftermath stories provided by the *News Journal* would not be as newsworthy or interesting.

Impact and Relevance

However, some hurricane aftermath stories did attract the imagination and interest of national news media and thus national news audiences. The destruction of the storm, both in Florida and throughout the eastern half of the United States, proved newsworthy because of its impact on so many people and because of its novelty; a storm that big does not happen often. Newspapers and television stations ran stories about the flooding and tornadoes that affected thousands of people from Pennsylvania to Tennessee.

It is not just disaster stories that have impact. Stories about government action or inaction, business misconduct or innovation, and societal trends and issues can be relevant to various audiences, regardless of proximity or timeliness.

A few years ago, the city of Springfield, Massachusetts, in an effort to control its health costs, decided to purchase prescription drugs from Canada. That story, while relevant to the people in Springfield, also proved interesting and meaningful to leaders in other communities nationwide and to anyone interested in cutting the escalating costs of prescription drugs. Subsequent stories about various state and federal initiatives to make it easier to purchase drugs from Canada were equally newsworthy.

Unusual and Unexpected

The prescription drug story from Springfield was also newsworthy because the city was one of the first to use Canadian drug purchases as a cost-saving strategy. It was unusual and novel. Charles Dana's definition of news—it's news when a man bites a dog—exemplifies this notion. It explains why an upset in a football or basketball game is considered more newsworthy than when a highly ranked team solidly beats a team that is struggling to get a win.

Novelty can also obtain when a story is told from a different angle or perspective. In trying to look at the devastation of Hurricane Ivan in a different way, the *CBS Evening News* put together a report about the animal victims of the storm and efforts to round up stranded creatures, from alligators to ostriches, in its aftermath. This report could have been told in different formats, but it worked best for television because of the sights and sounds of the animals being rescued. Without pictures, this story about "unusual" victims of the hurricane would not have had the impact or newsworthiness. To ensure a wider audience for this story, CBS used video streaming to put the report on its website, one of a handful of its daily hurricane reports the network placed online. Although CBS's animal story was designed for broadcast, the network extended its audience for the story by using the Web, a tactic that is the most pervasive and most basic element of convergence.

Prominence and Celebrity

Some people are newsworthy by the very nature of who they are or what they do, like the pope, the president of the United States, and the secretary-general of the United Nations. While many people condemned the U.S. military action in Iraq, a declaration by U.N. Secretary-General Kofi Annan that the action was "illegal" made headlines because of Annan's prominence as a world political leader. Similarly, while presidents of several nations typically address the opening of the U.N. General Assembly each October, U.S. president George W. Bush's speech was considered most newsworthy, especially among American media, because of his prominence as a political leader and the impact and proximity of the news to a U.S. audience.

During the first few months of the Iraq war in 2003, U.S. secretary of defense Donald Rumsfeld's daily press briefings made headlines in part because of the prominence of his role as a military leader as well as because of the possible impact and relevance of information he presented to reporters and the public. The death of Pope John Paul II, the spiritual leader of more than a billion Catholics worldwide, also merited widespread coverage because of both the pope's prominence and the impact his death would have on a dominant world religion.

These days, celebrity is often equated with prominence. Well-known entertainment and sports figures sometimes make news by making a speech or a public appearance, whether or not their words or actions have any relevance or impact. Often they make news when they do something unusual or unexpected. Movie stars and professional sports figures who get arrested find that their celebrity brings them greater media attention and newsworthiness.

Sometimes, celebrity is thrust upon people whose actions or misfortunes make them newsworthy. National media focused on the Ramsey family of Boulder, Colorado, in 1996 when their six-year-old daughter was found dead in the family home. The murder of a six-year-old is unusual, and it captured national attention because it happened around the Christmas holiday, a time when not much news is being made. The parents went on television appealing for help and information about the death of their daughter, at the same time that police began questioning the family's possible role in the girl's death. JonBenet Ramsey and her family became celebrities, and their actions and words have made them newsworthy ever since.

Need versus Want

In determining which stories get reported and which stories get selected for air, print, or online, journalists weigh all the above factors, trying to balance what their audience, their consumers, want to know about and need to know about. News organizations pander to the public when they decide that people want to hear news only about celebrities or political attacks or murders or car wrecks. Television news organizations get accused of relying too heavily on timeliness, proximity, celebrity, and unusualness in determining the news they present.

Those standards often work against the reporting of international news. The farther away from the United States news is happening, the less likely it is to get reported. News from other countries often has to pass the criteria of unusualness to be considered noteworthy enough for reporting. Conflict tends to be what puts foreign news into newscasts and newspapers, which makes for a very limited and biased picture of other countries and other cultures.

The convergence mindset of news audiences has led people interested in international news to seek it on the Internet or from direct satellite feeds. Audiences search for outlets that provide them with the news they want, with the news values they prefer. Many immigrants from West Africa, for example, look for news about their homelands on www.allafrica.com, rather than try to find it in their local newspapers or on television.

At the other extreme, news organizations can seem equally nearsighted about news choices by deciding that only they can determine what the public needs to know. Too often, that public is too narrowly defined. Daniel Okrent, the former ombudsman at the *New York Times*, made that point in criticizing the paper's coverage of the 2004 presidential campaign.

He wrote: "The paper's obsessive attention to backroom maneuvers and spin-room speculation obscures, rather than enhances, my understanding of the candidates. Much seems directed not at readers but at the campaign staffs and other journalists."[1] But political insiders have different information needs than most people. When news organizations decide that the public needs to know what journalists and decision-makers need to know, they have lost sight of what they should be doing. They have lost sight of their audience and the stories their audience needs.

Some media critics urge journalists to practice more humility in practicing their craft. *New Yorker* media writer Ken Auletta has written that humility is "the acorn of good journalism . . . more essential than good writing and hard work."[2] He notes that humility helps journalists ask questions and listen for answers, that is, it helps journalists keep in touch with the people, their audience.

Convergence can open up the way journalists think about news; it can return them to their roots. The consumer and the story once again become the driving forces of news. For example, convergence has been serving the audience consisting of other journalists, campaign staffs, politicos, and political "junkies" with websites such as The Note, which compiles political news reports from a variety of news organizations. The explosion of Web logs and Websites catering to specific news audiences, such as nkzone.org/nkzone, highlight the disconnect between the stories mainstream and traditional news organizations provide and the news stories news consumers want. Nkzone caters to an audience interested in news and infor-

SYNDICATE

RSS 1.0 | RSS 2.0 | Atom

ABOUT NKZONE

Banner photo: Chan U Chan
Movable Type & redesign genius:Boris Anthony
This is a "blog-zone" on North Korea: an interactive site that helps you stay informed and also helps you share what YOU know about North Korea with other people around the world. Have you been to North Korea? Do you know people who have? Do you have information and insights about North Korea that you'd like to share? Please share your knowledge with NKzone.
Email NKzone

OUR AUTHORS

NKzone has several regular authors. The views and analysis of each author are his or her own. We do not all agree with each other. NKzone welcomes authors with different

August 28, 2005 - 12:21 PM

An NK market

Current Affairs, Economic policy, Food Aid, Lankov on N.Korea

by Andrei Lankov

165) Market Research

Once upon a time, North Korea prided itself on being the country that came the closest to the complete the eradication of markets, those notorious dens of private commerce and capitalist spirits. It seems that in the 1960s markets were indeed formally outlawed for a brief while. Later, they made a moderate comeback, but they remained marginal to the life of most North Koreans until around 1990.

And then things changed. The slow-motion collapse of the Stalinist economy began in the late 1980s, and in a few years this slide developed into a free fall. By 1996, the old economy of coal mines, mammoth plants, and chimney smokes was dead, rations were not forthcoming, and many North Koreans had to resort to commerce to survive. The markets began to grow.

There is a large volume of evidence about these markets, and now I would

HEADLINE FEED

del.icio.us/tag/nkorea XML

North Korea Halves Number of South Korean Tourists

U.S. Agrees to 2-Week Delay in North Korea Nuclear Discussions

China wants N. Korea talks as security forum-paper

China, Japan says North Korea talks set for next week

Bush Names Special Envoy for Rights in North Korea - New York Times

North Korea Six Party Talks: The Bad News May Actually Be the Good News

Journal from North Korea: Wishing for Chollima

Divided Koreas mark 1945 freedom

America's North Korean policy has been in hibernation

CSM | A formal end to the Korean War?

FIGURE 3.1. The blog nkzone.org provides news and information from one of the most closed societies on earth, North Korea, which severely restricts journalists' access.

mation about and from North Korea, one of the most tightly controlled Communist societies in the world. It is nearly impossible for traditional news media to get into the country and for non-government-controlled information to get out, so North Korean news is scarce. Nkzone relies on nontraditional means, such as blogs, to relay information.

The rise of websites such as moveon.org, and news networks such as Fox News Channel also highlight the concerns for news consumers who seek out news and commentary with a certain slant. Media critics and advocates for First Amendment rights of a free press and free speech fear increasing political and social polarization if different viewpoints are not widely disseminated and heard. Others argue that news consumers have plenty of access to diverse viewpoints; they just need to look for it.

The new sources for news and commentary challenge some of the commonly accepted practices of mainstream media regarding fairness, balance, and independence. Traditionally, print and broadcast media have separated news from commentary. But the two can get blurred in radio's liberal-leaning Air America and conservative Rush Limbaugh's show, as well as on Fox News Channel's *The O'Reilly Factor*.

The documentary film *Outfoxed* presents documents and testimony that the Fox News Channel dictated to reporters that they slant stories and present viewpoints to support a Republican agenda, thus raising questions about the fairness and independence of its news. Former CBS correspondent Bernard Goldberg, in his book *Bias*, charges that CBS News harbored a liberal bias in the stories it chose to do, such as reports on problems with day care. A 2004 survey found that more Republicans favor the Fox News Channel, while more Democrats favor CNN, thus raising the specter of partisan news organizations and agendas.[3] This comes at a time when the public's trust in the news media is dropping. A September 2004 Gallup poll, taken amid the furor over CBS reports about George Bush's National Guard record, found public confidence in the news media at a thirty-year low, with just 44 percent of Americans surveyed believing the news media can report information accurately and fairly.[4] Previous Gallup polls showed public confidence hovering around 55 percent.

CODES OF ETHICS

Considering scandals over the ethical lapses of journalists in the past few years, it might be easy to believe that journalists have no accepted standards of behavior. But news organizations and journalism associations, as well as journalism scholars and analysts, have developed common codes of practice that stress values and goals such as truth and independence. The problem comes when the ideal confronts the real and the rules get written, rewritten, or forgotten in the heat of daily competition.

Seeking Truth

In every journalistic code of ethics, in every book on journalistic practice, and in every news organization's policy guidelines, the most prevalent value mentioned is finding or seeking the truth. But truth is also probably the most elusive value. In the age of spin, one person's truth is another's propaganda.

In discussing the pursuit of truth, the codes of ethics of both the Society of Professional Journalists (SPJ) and the Radio-Television News Directors Association (RTNDA) say that journalists should seek truth and avoid distortion. The codes call on journalists to be accurate—to not make things up. Journalists inevitably get in trouble when they "don't let the truth get in the way of a good story." NBC News got in trouble in 1993 when it rigged the visual of a gas tank explosion to make a bigger blast for storytelling purposes. When Stephen Glass of the *New Republic* made up a hackers convention because it made a good story, he got fired for it in 1998. Taking quotes out of context, staging an event so it looks better, or disguising commentary as reporting all distort the truth.

Bill Kovach and Tom Rosenstiel, in discussing journalistic truth in *The Elements of Journalism*, note that journalists need to get the facts straight and make sense of the facts.[5] Truth is a goal, they write, adding, "In real life, people can tell when someone has come close to getting it right, when the sourcing is authoritative, when the research is exhaustive, when the method is transparent."[6]

The best way to avoid distorting the truth is to disclose the sources of the information, to allow the public to decide the credibility of the news sources for themselves. To do that, journalists need to make the effort to seek out a variety of sources—that is, they need to do their research. And journalists need to show the public that they have done their research—that their work is transparent, that anyone can see how they came to their conclusions. In the age of convergence, in which news organizations can publish documents online that support their reporting, they can show how they sought the truth. The *Seattle Times* published documents on seattletimes.com supporting concerns about a cancer center's operations, thus putting the power of the paper's reporting in the hands of its audience. Additionally, news organizations and aggregators through their websites can provide additional links and facets to news stories. A recent story cited by Yahoo!News about a boycott of Kentucky Fried Chicken called for by black activist Al Sharpton linked to the fast food chain's website as well as to the site kentuckyfriedcruelty.com.

Going a step further, a former director of the Pew Center for Civic Journalism, Jan Schaffer, talks about the age of convergence in journalism as really more the age of collaboration with the audience where, as she says, "the consumers become the creators" of news. Journalists need to engage their consumers by making them part of the storytelling process. What journalists can do, and the general public cannot because of lack of time and access, is go out and get information. Because technology has expanded the way people can get news, however, journalists need to diversify their ways of providing it. Journalists often tell the public to trust them to tell the truth. But these days, journalists need to show the public why they should be trusted. Mainstream journalism often fails the trust test by neglecting to show the public who they go to for information. They often use anonymous sources, giving news consumers no chance to decide for themselves if those sources are trustworthy or free of bias. And, when those sources prove to have an agenda, as was the case several times during the 2004 presidential campaign, traditional news organizations too often fail to let the public know of their sources' political bent.

For example, a CBS News *60 Minutes* story on George W. Bush's spotty National Guard service became tainted when the documents it used as supporting evidence could not be determined to be authentic. The documents had come from an anti-Bush source. Other news organizations and political groups with agendas and Web logs led the attack against CBS. Those attacks forced CBS to begin to reveal more about its sources to defend its credibility.

If, however, journalists engage the public more in the storytelling process in the first place, perhaps the public would have a better idea about the elusive goal of seeking truth. Convergence requires journalists to rethink their role and the role of the public in the process of getting to the truth.

Maintaining Independence

Journalism codes of ethics also advocate independence. During the past hundred years or so, independence has become synonymous with objectivity, which most working journalists find as elusive as the truth in doing daily journalism. Objectivity, or treating every position or voice equally, can handicap the seeking of truth. It turns journalists into stenographers. Journalists need to provide audiences with context as well as facts, and context requires knowledge and perspective.

Christiane Amanpour, who has covered many conflicts for more than a dozen years for CNN, once spoke about concerns of so-called advocacy journalism in a documentary. In covering wars, and often in covering wars that get ignored by mainstream news media, she says she feels an obligation to not always evenly report both sides, if one side is committing atrocities, or if neutrality is leading to carnage.[7] The key is for the news media to provide an independent view of what is happening, after taking in information from all sides.

As any photographer or videographer knows, the camera's position affects the image, so it is good to look for different places from which to view the action, different perspectives, to get a fuller picture. This is really the basic tenet of all journalism: be independent in order to get the fuller picture for the audience.

To pursue independence, news organizations' codes of ethics call on journalists to avoid conflicts of interests, both real and perceived. They should resist "spin," or efforts by one point of view to convince journalists that theirs is the only correct point of view. They should not let their company's business interests overrun their public's news interests. The goal, however, often conflicts with the reality of daily journalism. And when it comes to convergence, some journalism ethicists argue that independence is sacrificed.

Convergence in daily journalism calls for collaboration, and collaboration can open up possibilities of conflict of interests. The television critic for the local newspaper has a potential conflict of interest in providing commentary on the evening newscast of the station that shares staffing, information, and reports with the paper. The consumer affairs reporter for the television station may have a damning report on the practices of the car dealerships in town that advertise heavily in the local newspaper. The consumer reporter is acting against journalistic ethics if he or she decides to kill the story because of the convergence partnership between the newspaper and TV station.

Acting independently has also become more difficult for news organizations because of their consolidated ownership. Television stations owned by Sinclair Communications faced this problem when the national company put together a documentary unfavorable to Democratic presidential candidate John Kerry in the 2004 campaign. After some stockholder pressure and national media exposure, the documentary was changed. But opposition to the documentary from Sinclair's Washington bureau chief resulted in his firing.

Often the bigger battles over ethical independence are waged over what does not get covered by news organizations as opposed to what does—acts of omission rather than acts of commission. Investigative reporting requires an investment of time, people, and money. The economic pressures to make profits for large media corporations translates into less time, people, and money devoted to projects that may not give as great a return on investment and could even damage the bottom line by alienating advertisers. Each year, Project Censored puts out a list of stories that go unreported or underreported by mainstream news media. Among them: the connections between Vice President Dick Cheney's energy task force, his influence over energy and oil policies, and the destabilization of Haiti.

Convergence should allow the sharing of ideas and resources among different media and ideally should allow for more multiple media investigative efforts. For example, the *Columbus Dispatch* and WBNS-TV conducted a joint review of fire inspections of commercial buildings, finding that fire department inspectors had not been present for the inspections or had done a cursory job at more than three dozen sites. The story aired on the station and ran in the paper.

Fairness and Balance

The news media have undergone much soul searching about being fair and balanced since 1996, when those words became the slogan for the Fox News Channel. The RTNDA ethics code interprets "fair and balanced" to mean impartial, "placing primary value on significance and relevance," and using professional perspective, not personal bias, to provide diverse viewpoints. The SPJ code cautions against stereotypes and encourages "the open exchange of views" even views seen as repugnant.[8]

However, the speed of news and efforts to spin news to specific interpretations can create problems for journalists in their efforts to be fair and to provide balance. Kovach and Rosenstiel say the danger for journalists is in making fairness a goal rather than part of the process. "Fairness should mean the journalist is being fair to the facts, and the citizen's understanding of them."[9] It does not necessarily mean presenting both sides with the equal number of words, quotes, time, or space. Media critic Ken Auletta says news should not be presented as "ping-pong matches." Instead, journalists have the responsibility to examine and report when one side is telling the truth and the other is not.[10]

STRENGTHS AND WEAKNESSES

Convergence aims to use each medium to its fullest to inform the public about the world. But as anyone who picks up a newspaper or magazine, tunes in to television or radio, or logs on to the Internet can tell you, all media are not alike. You can get the same information from each medium, but you are getting it in different ways. News organizations that want to capitalize on convergence have to figure out how to play to the strengths of each medium, while minimizing their weaknesses.

News operations that are striving for convergence are at different points in learning the strengths and weaknesses and in using them to their audience's advantage. Those resistant to convergence focus only on the weaknesses of the media they neither know nor like. As a result, they are ignoring what their audiences already know: Newspapers provide context, broadcast provides immediacy and emotion, and online provides interactivity and individuality. They all provide a snapshot of the world.

Newspapers

In most towns, the daily newspaper has the largest reporting and producing staff of any news medium. As a result, the newspaper can tell more stories about its community and the people in it. In those stories, reporters can seek out the nuances, the background details, that can help audiences learn more about the news that interests them. A newspaper generally has more space in which to delve into a story. Its journalism aims to reflect this opportunity for depth, breadth, and context. The *New York Times* won the coveted public service Pulitzer Prize for its massive reporting on the September 11, 2001, World Trade Center attacks. For nearly four months, it devoted pages of the newspaper to personal profiles on each of the three thousand people killed in the attacks. It also examined fire and safety construction issues as well as homeland security debates.

But news audiences may not have the time to read a lot of long stories. In fact, a key 2001 study of 37,000 newspaper consumers by the Readership Institute found that one way for newspapers to keep their customers satisfied is to make the newspaper easier and faster to read. Newspapers are not read in one sitting; rather readers typically pick up and put down the same paper several times.[11] As a result, newspapers are designing their front pages to give readers "quick guides to news" as well as the opportunity to delve further into the stories they are most interested in.

The Readership Institute survey also looked at how audiences react to story length. It found that readers like longer stories that provide additional information and viewpoints but often find them "harder" to read. The key is to make newspaper stories "readable." The survey found that newspaper audiences look for stories that engage and connect with them, that have characters that tell the story and have a beginning, middle, and end.[12]

Newspapers also allow readers to reflect and review the news. Readers can go back and reread an item they did not understand, or they can skip ahead, catching only the key points that are important to them. Newspaper audiences have the ability to control what they read. By scanning a headline or glancing at a picture, newspaper readers can determine if they want to go further with a story.

Sometimes, thanks to a headline or picture, reader might discover a topic they did not think they were interested in. This kind of serendipity does not happen in broadcast or online news as easily as in newspapers, because newspapers allow their audiences to flip back and forth among the pages. But thanks to digital recording, this advantage of newspapers over broadcast and online could be disappearing. Digitization may also start to limit another advantage of newspapers: their portability. Newspapers can be read on the subway, in a living room, on a park bench, in bed, or at the kitchen table with no wires or antennas needed.

Newspapers and newspaper stories can be clipped and saved; they can provide a sense of permanence. When Neil Armstrong became the first man to walk on the moon, thousands of people saved the front page of their newspaper with the picture, headline, and story. People often pick up newspapers to mark a historic event.

All of these factors affect the way people look for news from newspapers and the way journalists should present the news in this medium. If people turn to newspapers to find a record of their world, a more varied and less hurried context, and a chance to review and reflect, then newspaper journalism needs to play to such strengths.

As news audiences turn to other media for information, newspapers have been forced to recognize inherent weaknesses, most notably their inability to provide news immediately. The writing and synthesizing of the written word with depth and context takes time. This handicaps newspapers. Newspapers cannot take their audience to the scene of a news event, the way radio can with the broadcast of the sounds of that event or the way television can with the broadcast of the sights and sounds. From Edward R. Murrow's radio broadcasts of the sounds of London being bombed in World War II to the nonstop television reporting of President John F. Kennedy's assassination in November 1963 to the live reporting of the U.S. bombing of Baghdad in 1990 and again in 2003, newspapers could not compete with broadcast news in providing immediate news to the public.

Newspapers have to rely on description to transmit the tone and feel of the news, putting them at a disadvantage to radio and television. A newspaper story can describe the roar of a crowd at a football game, or quote the chant of protesters during a march, but radio and television can help the audience experience what it might be like to be at the game or in the march.

Radio and Television

The strength of broadcast media lies in its use of sights and sounds to place an audience at the scene, giving the audience a sense of the immediacy and the emotion of a news event. But that strength also poses a danger. Broadcast news has been repeatedly and soundly criticized for relying too much on immediacy and emotion without providing context and information.

In television, especially, this overemphasis takes the form of using live shots simply because of the capacity to produce them, rather than because the story requires them. "Live coverage as a ratings getter can override more traditional journalistic matters," writes Philip Seib, in his examination of the phenomenon of getting news in "real time" on television and on the Internet. He notes that technology can push aside news judgment when it comes to live news. "The theory in many newsrooms seems to be that if it's happening now and we can get live pictures, then it's newsworthy." Speed is seen to compensate for superficiality.[13]

Critics of convergence worry that the focus on the visual in television journalism will dilute the detail and nuance required by print. The immediacy of live pictures and reports from the scene may overshadow the values of accuracy and credibility. Broadcast news reporters are often called upon to present information about a breaking news story before they have had the chance to thoroughly check out often conflicting and incomplete details.

The track record of broadcast news on major stories often bears this out. Speculation replaces confirmed facts, and repetition replaces depth, when immediacy becomes the main motivating factor for news. During the first few days of reporting on the scandal involving White House intern Monica Lewinsky and President Bill Clinton, many television news reporters had very little information to present, so what was broadcast was often mere speculation. Bill Kovach and Tom Rosenstiel, in their analysis of coverage of that scandal, found that all too often news organizations relied on one source or unnamed sources in their initial reports. Too little time was devoted to confirming information before it was aired. "More than half of the reportage in the first week (53 percent) of this story was either passing along other people's reporting or commenting on the news."[14]

To maintain credibility while responding to audiences' need for immediate information, former ABC News executive Av Westin developed a list of best practices for broadcast journalists in live news situations. "Start with the need for accuracy. Use the reporter on the scene of a breaking story to determine its importance and scope," Westin writes. He emphasizes that news organizations need to accept that it is fine to admit a lack of information about a breaking news situation.[15]

But when speed does count, such as when providing information about impending danger, broadcast can serve the news audience better than any other medium. The events of September 11, 2001, illustrate the value of the immediacy of broadcast. While the initial coverage of the airplane attacks on the World Trade Center and the Pentagon failed to provide detail about what was happening, they provided enough visual information for news audiences to determine that what was happening was dangerous and historic. Broadcast remained in a better position to provide immediate information than online outlets. Efforts to find more information about the terrorist attacks online were hampered by the overwhelming demand placed on Internet technology; servers and networks could not handle the volume of users.

By 2003, thanks to technological advances such as wider use of broadband, the Internet was able to use television pictures as part of its War in Iraq coverage. "We had this huge network who found it inconvenient to go to a television to find out what was going on," said Dean Wright, former MSNBC.com chief. So, like the transistor radio of the 1960s that people used to listen to real-time events, the Internet allowed audiences to do that during the war. "They needed a way to keep in touch in real time, on their time, with the story, and video provided a way to do that," Wright said.[16]

The terrorist attacks also demonstrated the power of aural and visual images for not only attracting people's attention but for holding it. The sounds of the emergency vehicles at Ground Zero, the sight of a jumbo jet slamming into a building, and the rumble and tumble of the North Tower as it collapsed provided a sense of credibility to a seemingly incomprehensible and unreal event. Those images transfixed not only people on the streets of New York but everyone watching worldwide. They required little explanation or description. The images of September 11 connected with people emotionally. Because of that connection, people remember not only the images but the information and news associated with the pictures, demonstrating the strength of broadcast news.

Like emotion, the simplicity of broadcast storytelling can be both a strength and a weakness. Make a story too simple by eliminating nuance and depth, and broadcast can be accused of "dumbing down" a news story. Critics of television news argue that too often complex stories are ignored or abandoned because they are neither visual nor simple enough to work in a television context. But if a story with too much complexity is aired, the audience might be unable to follow it and will not remember much about it.

Broadcast journalists can help their audiences comprehend and retain news by presenting stories in a simple, straightforward manner, using dramatic images as signposts for providing information. To do that, broadcast news should emphasize sharp contrasts and descriptive sights and sounds. Often that means using an individual's story to represent a larger, more complex trend or situation. For example, a story on mounting credit card debt nationwide might focus on the plight of one person with too many credit cards to illustrate a larger problem. Broadcast would rely on the sound of cash registers ringing up charges, the sight of a pile of bills, sound bites from credit experts and a person struggling to get out of debt to humanize the story, to help audiences relate to the topic.

But if audiences are not watching or listening when the news is broadcast, or if they are distracted during the telling of a news story, they will miss all or part of the information presented. If audiences do not catch it all the first time, often they do not hear the news at all. Unlike newspaper readers, audiences of broadcast news have little opportunity to rehear or resee a news story. Broadcast news is linear, requiring audiences to follow along from beginning to end. Recording and replaying broadcast news stories can allow audiences to go back and check information or enter a story anywhere along the story line. But that takes work on the part of audiences, and traditionally broadcast news audiences are passive.

Online

News on the Internet, however, requires audiences to do something. They search, browse, click, and read. Online news poses the greatest challenge and potential for journalism because the medium and its use are so new and open to experimentation. Its strengths lie in creating new ways of storytelling, by building on its capability to be interactive, searchable, updatable, and multimedia. Its weaknesses lie in its newness. Its credibility, ethics, and financial viability are still being formulated. As a result, working online has both fascinated and frustrated news organizations.

The major strengths of online news, like broadcast, also pose its biggest challenges. The ability of a news consumer to interact with the news and the people producing the news give online news an instantaneous connection to its audience that older media have not had.

Many news organizations, in putting a story on the Web, include an e-mail address for audience commentary. Several news organizations provide the e-mail address of the main author or producer of the Web story. Special projects editor Walter Robinson, who put together the *Boston Globe*'s Pulitzer-Prize-winning reports on abuse by priests in the Boston area, credited the ability of readers of the *Globe*'s first story to contact the reporting team via e-mail and phone with more information on the abuses, which led to more stories.

However, journalists and news organizations can get inundated with e-mail. While some of that e-mail can provide new information or perspectives on news stories, much of it does not. "The bulk of e-mails tend toward the opinionated, not the factual, and a depressingly high number of those are personal attacks" writes former *Miami Herald* assistant managing editor Mark Seibel.[17] One *Miami Herald* reporter received nearly 1,000 e-mails in one day in response to a story he did on the 2000 presidential election vote in Florida.[18]

Online news organizations also make discussion boards and chat rooms available for users to communicate comments on stories, story ideas, and related information. The *Providence Journal* website still maintains an online forum for discussion and comments relating to the February 2003 nightclub fire that killed 100 people. However, news organizations are faced with problems when the information might be deemed inappropriate due to language or content or when it does not meet standards of ethics and reliability. Some news organizations, such as the *Christian Science Monitor*, have had to curtail their discussion boards because the organizations could not serve as adequate gatekeepers for the discussion boards and chat rooms linked to their websites.

News organizations have had similar conflicts over Web logs, or blogs, written by their own employees. When CNN's Kevin Sites began blogging about news from the northern Iraq front during the beginning of the U.S. incursion into Iraq, he was asked to stop because it was outside the realm of CNN editorial review and because of concerns that blogging distracted from the main focus of his CNN work: producing for television. Sites left CNN and later worked producing for NBC News and blogging. Sites put his blog to work in November 2004 to explain how he came to shoot and then distribute controversial footage of Marines shooting arrested Iraqi insurgents. Sites's blog, at www.kevinsites.net, has been praised as an example of journalistic ethics in war reporting. Sites's reporting gives the reading, listening, and watching public insight, or what could be called transparency, into the journalistic process.

Blogs not only give journalists a chance to relate to news consumers, they also make news consumers into news producers. Bloggers first pointed out discrepancies with information in the documents CBS News was using as the basis of its later discredited story on President George W. Bush's National Guard service. Bloggers have also kept alive issues or stories that the mainstream media started to ignore, forcing journalists to rethink and adjust their standards of news judgment. Some public officials record interviews they have with journalists and post them on their blogs to provide another viewpoint on a story.

Rebecca MacKinnon, a former Beijing and Tokyo bureau chief for CNN, said she began seeing the value of blogs when she used them to find story ideas. Tom Regan, who blogs for the *Christian Science Monitor,* agrees. He notes that interactivity will force changes in the role of journalists. Mainstream news media will no longer be the only voice of authority for the news of the day. "You can't fake it anymore because it's too easy to be found out," Regan says. "The Internet will force us to be better, more careful journalists, and that's good for journalism."[19]

The Internet also provides interactivity by giving news consumers the capability of what Regan calls "drilling" into a story to search for additional information, using links to access background information, commentary, and previous reporting on a topic. Many sites build in links to recent archives to allow online users to quickly find additional information about the topic of a news story. And the success of aggregators on the Internet, such as GoogleNews, websites, or portals designed to link users to news and information, have spurred news sites to open more links to other news sites. In an article for Online Journalism Review, Mark Glaser notes that news organizations worried that a link meant tacit endorsement of a site. That fear is fading. "We leave it to the readers to make up their own mind whether it's valid or not," says Bill Grueskin of wsj.com, the *Wall Street Journal*'s website.[20]

Online news has also given newspapers the ability to compete with television and radio in providing news as soon as it happens. The Internet can allow newspapers and television to make breaking news available to audiences who use their computer during the workday. But both newspapers and broadcast news managers worry that putting news on their websites discourages Internet users from picking up the paper or turning on the TV station, thus cutting into their main sources of revenue.

"I'm happy as a journalist to provide information any way people can get it," says Tom Heslin, managing editor of the *Providence Journal*. But while the speed of the Internet can satisfy people's need for immediate news, he is worried about inaccuracy and its reflection on the paper's credibility. "The Web's dynamic is speed but you can't be reckless."[21]

Newspaper and television stations also worry about "scooping" themselves, putting their exclusives out for the public before they can be published or aired in their traditional outlet and alerting their competitors about their scoops. Convergence advocates maintain that scoops are a holdover from an old way of thinking about the news, and that most news audiences are not fixated about who gets a story first. The difference between being first and an also-ran is often measured in moments, a difference that means little to audiences. "So much of the information is available to everyone pretty much at the same time," Wright says, and that fact should lead to better journalism. "It forces us to do things that make a qualitative difference rather than reporting something that happened twenty seconds before someone else reported it."[22]

Online websites can give newspapers the chance to make the news immediately available to audiences, but many newspaper sites are not in the habit of updating their local news. A review of some thirty newspaper websites by researchers at the University of Texas in 2003–2004 found that while a dozen were diligent in updating their sites, the others either updated infrequently with breaking news stories or not at all.[23] Many news outlets update their websites by refreshing their wire service offerings or putting out new pictures on major national or international stories. But newspaper or television websites lag in updating their news during the workday, when most people go online.

The Internet also provides news organizations with the chance to develop new forms of storytelling since it is multimedia: using text, still pictures, video, animation, graphic illustrations, and sound. Multimedia, according to the *Christian Science Monitor*'s Tom Regan, is about giving choices to people looking for news.

"We're different in that we give people control," says Angela Clark, deputy editor of MSNBC.com. For Clark, that opens up the possibility of providing more public service initiatives that benefit a national audience. Clark and others note that one of the most successful multimedia projects at MSNBC.com was a searchable database on unclaimed property that drew in the largest amount of traffic for the website. Another project that received acclaim was a multimedia game designed for the Web to coincide with an NBC examination of airline security screenings. The game gave the online audience a chance to be a baggage screener

FIGURE 3.2. Neal Scarborough, ESPN: Online "allows us to exploit all of the media at once." (Photo by the author)

and understand the difficulty associated with the job. "We have the unique ability to create on the Web an experience for people," Clark says, one that goes beyond telling or showing audiences the problems baggage handlers routinely face.[24]

ESPN.com has also pushed multimedia. "The medium I'm in, dot-com, really allows us to exploit all of the media at once," says ESPN.com editor Neal Scarborough. ESPN.com can use print, with sports scores and game stories, audio from interviews, and commentary from ESPN radio and ESPN Motion, which includes video highlights of key plays of games and meets. Scarborough adds that ESPN has worked with what he calls "verge events," or live game coverage that allows for fan interactivity with commentators as well as video and audio game reports.[25]

Using all the strengths of online news takes a commitment of time, money, and people, all of which tend to be in short supply in many newsrooms. Of all the outlets for news, online news has seen the greatest growth during the past decade. But news organizations are still seeking ways to make money from that growth. While online news popularity soars, few news organizations are reaping much financial reward from high audience interest and use, because most information on the Web is still free. Ninety percent of all news organizations say they now put news on the Web, but few organizations are investing large amounts of personnel and financial resources in it because of the low rate of financial return.

One effort to tip the balance sheet from expenses to revenues involves online user registration. News websites are asking users to register by providing demographic information such as age and gender. That registration gives the online news provider a sales opportunity. With the demographic information from site visitors, the news organization can provide potential advertisers the ability to target their online pitches to certain consumers. In return for registering, users get access to the full versions of news stories. The *New York Times* (nytimes.com), *Los Angeles Times* (latimes.com), and the *Chicago Tribune* (tribune.com) are just a few of the organizations that require user registration.

Some news groups look for revenue by charging users for access to certain website features. CNN's site, www.cnn.com, used to charge for access to streaming video reports. The *Boston Herald* charges nonsubscribers for access to its columnists' articles. Many online newspaper sites charge for access to their archives of stories that are more than a week or a month old. The *Wall Street Journal* requires a subscription for access to all of its stories online. The *New York Times* has created Times Select, in which Web subscribers can pay extra for access to the paper's columnists and other Web features.

"I don't think we've sorted out yet what the Web is for," says Tom Heslin, *Providence Journal*'s managing editor. "The Web as an information provider cannot live for long as a free environment, and newspapers can't afford to put information in the market for free."[26]

CONVERGENCE AND COMMON GOALS

Newsrooms tackling convergence vary greatly in how they go about using the strengths of each medium to best get news and information out to an increasingly scattered and diverse public. Using all media available—print, broadcast, and online—convergence journalists believe they can inform more people, at more times, and in more places, about the world. They also believe that not every story works best in every medium. They say the key to making convergence work is to understand how to tell stories in newspapers, on television, and online and to allow the readers, viewers, and users to reap the benefits.

The success of convergence in many of these news organizations depends on how well the journalists work to coordinate and achieve the ultimate goal of doing better news stories to satisfy the needs of a variety of news audiences. No one newsroom has achieved complete convergence, but many are struggling to figure out the right mix of people and processes to be more convergent. No single news organization has developed the true path to total convergence, but several have traveled further than others.

BOX 3.1

Convergence Benefits

Here is a brief look at the benefits that each medium can gain by being more convergent:

Newspapers:

- Access to news consumers who never read newspapers but get news from television or the Web.
- More visual content to enhance storytelling.
- Ability to provide more timely news via the Web.
- New ideas for presenting news.

Television:

- Better content via access to newspaper reporting and research resources.
- Ability to provide better context to stories.
- Access to audience that does not watch newscasts or misses them.
- Credibility and community stature associated with media partners.

Web:

- Better content via access to newspaper reporting and research resources.
- More visual content to enhance storytelling.
- Access to audience that does not use the Internet.
- Credibility and community stature associated with media partners.

In convergence-oriented newsrooms, news executives, editors, reporters, and producers realize that their work is more valuable when it reaches more people. All journalists want their work to be seen or heard, but in this age of 24/7 news and instant messaging, the competition for news audiences is fierce. While every news organization wants bigger audiences, not every newsroom and not every journalist is willing to embrace new ways of doing the news to reach those new audiences. That is why some forms of convergence—the easiest ones—are more prevalent. The goal of reaching more people with the news is a common one; the amount of change and effort committed to meeting that goal is not so common.

Gains

When it comes to audience, newspapers have been big losers, seeing circulation decline by more than 10 percent in the last fifteen to twenty years and advertising revenue move to other media. Convergence offers an opportunity to stem the losses. "Newspapers are challenged because their readership is aging," says David Underhill, who headed the Tribune Company's convergence operations. A review of readership patterns shows that people used to establish daily newspaper reading habits in their early twenties, but today's twenty-somethings are not developing newspaper habits. To attract younger people and new readers, newspapers are looking to convergence. They hope to find an audience for their news online or on television that they are not getting with the printed word. "You're extending the reach of the story; you're extending the breadth of the newspaper as the community's premier news provider," Underhill says. "You're keeping newspapers a strong entity in the community."[27]

The easiest and most prevalent convergence efforts are those that do very little to threaten the newsroom status quo, such as cross-promoting stories or reproducing a newspaper story or a television report on a website. But cross-promotion can be seen as more of a marketing effort than a journalistic one. You can find cross-promotion every time you listen to a television newscast and the anchor says, "For more information, go to our website." You also might see cross-promotion during a television segment called "Tomorrow's Headlines Tonight," in which newspaper headlines from the next day's paper are reviewed on the late evening newscast. Cross-promotion fulfills the goal of trying to reach new audiences by encouraging them to seek out other sources, other media, for news. It does little to engage the audience in the news.

Simply using convergence to reach new audiences but not offering them something new in news ultimately defeats the purpose, according to Jon Schwantes, who oversees convergence for the Dispatch Group, a mix of daily and weekly newspapers and television in Columbus, Ohio. "Rather than serving brand extension or reaching an audience, it has the complete opposite effect of putting off news consumers," he says. "They're not getting any news or information or value added. They're just getting bombarded with marketing messages and ultimately you get pretty jaded by it."[28]

Convergence with television works better for newspapers and online news organizations when they bring something new to a story as part of their effort to reach new audiences. That happens to a limited extent when reporters go on television to discuss their reports. The *Christian Science Monitor* works with national networks by providing its reporters as guests on news shows, demonstrating their expertise in an area of foreign affairs or domestic policy. *Chicago Tribune* reporters go on CLTV cable news station from a news set in the center of the paper's newsroom to explain details of a local government or political story that they have delved into extensively. Technology beat reporters also are used for talk-backs. For example, in February 2004, the technology editor for the *Chicago Tribune*, Eric Bettendorf, appeared on CLTV to talk about Apple iPod accessories.

Both ESPN.com and MSNBC.com use their television partners to increase their audience for stories that first appear on their websites. Darren Rovell, who reports on the business of sports for ESPN.com, often goes on ESPN radio or appears on ESPN News to talk-back a story he has done for the website. MSNBC.com's technology reporter has become an expert on

BOX 3.2

Convergence Continuum

Ball State University researchers have created a "convergence continuum" that lists five forms or stages of doing convergence. News organizations often move from one aspect of convergence to another, sometimes working in several areas at once. The convergence continuum ranges from the simplest and easiest to the hardest and most complex:

Stage 1: Cross Promotion. This entails one partner, such as a newspaper, promoting content of another, such as a TV station or website.

Stage 2: Cloning. One partner, such as a website, republishes content or news from another.

Stage 3: Co-opetition. A combination of cooperation or competition between convergence partners, such as breaking a newspaper's story online, or television providing pictures of a news event to a newspaper or website.

Stage 4: Content Sharing. Television and newspapers work together on a project or a series of stories.

Stage 5: Convergence. Working together to use each medium's strengths to best tell stories that engage people seeking news.

Source: The Convergence Continuum: A Model for Studying Collaboration between Media Newsrooms, by Larry Dailey, Lori Demo, and Mary Spillman.

Internet security and is often called upon to bring that expertise to MSNBC's cable television news audiences.

When newspaper or online reporters appear on television as a part of a convergence effort, television audiences gain information and knowledge developed by beat reporters that television station newsrooms often lack. The television station gains the credibility or gravitas more often associated with print journalism. Newspapers and online news organizations reach an audience that they may not normally attract. While each news organization benefits, the news audience also benefits because they get a better insight into a story and a clearer idea of the reporter's thinking. This is prevalent in sports talk shows, both on local television stations using newspaper sports columnists and on ESPN, for shows such as *Around the Horn*.

Talk-backs require newspaper and online beat reporters to be knowledgeable about television and comfortable with appearing on camera. Not all reporters are, and some find that the nuanced details of their text-based stories cannot be translated into quick sound bites on television. Talk-backs, like cross-promotion, require limited effort and commitment by journalists but also provide limited benefit to news consumers.

Repurposing news content from one medium for another demands a reallocation of newsroom production resources and can deliver big benefits to news audiences and the news organizations. Putting a newspaper story on a website or streaming a video report is another easy way to take advantage of convergence. It is like taking a square peg and sanding off the edges to fit it into a round hole. Headlines and text are set up and laid out differently on a Web page, but they are still headlines and text. A video report does not get reshot or rewritten to fit the smaller computer screen; it airs on a different medium but in the same way. News organizations that gain the most benefits from repurposing news are those that devote resources to making the original news story adapt to the other, less-familiar medium.

One area that has flourished in this type of convergence is weather news. This is also an area in which television has excelled and where its expertise is enhancing the content of its newspaper convergence partner. Weather news provides the starkest example of how newspapers can deliver more visual storytelling. Television weather reporters and meteorologists put together maps, illustrations, and graphics for their forecasts. Using those same visuals, they are working with newspapers to provide weather pages. For example, WSB-TV meteorologist Glenn Burns is featured in the *Atlanta Journal-Constitution*'s full page of weather forecasts, maps, and information.

With the weather news, newspapers use their production resources like copyeditors and layout designers to put television's informational and visual resources to good use. In exchange, newspaper readers get a faster, more engaging report on the weather because television graphics add value to the story.

Many local television stations also have staff consumer news reporters, and newspapers have been able to add that content to their news pages. Victoria Lim works for WFLA-TV News 8 in Florida, where her story may appear first, but those reports are then reworked for tbo.com and the *Tampa Tribune*. Consumer news and medical news are two beats that are often staples of local newscasts. As such, consumer and medical news stories are often repurposed for television stations' websites.

The greatest convergence advantages emerge when the different media partners work to create special reports and projects that use each medium's reporting and production resources. ESPN's John Walsh conducts weekly meetings to discuss and organize projects that may involve contributions from all areas of ESPN—online, radio, television, and the magazine—or just some of them. In Chicago, Tribune Company executive David Underhill points to a special project on the deteriorating condition of local roads and sidewalks that combined the efforts of *Chicago Tribune* and WGN television reporters and producers.

At MSNBC.com, rarely a day goes by in which an NBC or MSNBC news show is not coordinating with the dot-com about a Web project. One day in late March of 2004, the website and the MSNBC show *Hardball with Chris Matthews* worked on a quick project on political ads, allowing the Web user to get inside the process of making of positive or negative ads. "We had the ads themselves, a story on how to put the ads together," says Michael Silberman, MSNBC.com's former managing editor.[29] And Web users could also watch the videos of the ads. By using a Web producer who worked with the television show team, anyone watching the TV show or going to the website got a news experience tailored to fit each medium.

"The trick is to take original reporting in one medium and make it effective in this medium," says Dean Wright, a former editor at MSNBC. The key is to take advantage of the interactive and immediate capabilities of storytelling on the Web, using the best assets from television, such as visuals, commentary, and expert explanation. Angela Clark notes that MSNBC.com, like ESPN, conducts weekly projects or enterprise meetings that involve a team of people planning and organizing special projects that coordinate television and the Web.[30]

Neal Scarborough of ESPN.com points to a series of reports that Tom Farrey did on baseball players in the Dominican Republic and their abuse by *buscones,* or recruiters. The report not only included Farrey's magazine text and video reports, but it added timelines, additional commentary, and reaction. Farrey notes that the project ultimately included three television pieces, a magazine article, and five or six online reports.

When a reporting project is developed out of the weekly enterprise meetings at ESPN, different staff members are assigned to work on different aspects of it. Farrey, a former newspaper sportswriter, says he will work with a television field producer for a story that is expected to run in the magazine, air on television, and go online. "It's a lot of coordination and strategy," Farrey says. "The key is everyone having respect for the other media."[31]

The biggest advantage to convergence involves pooling news-gathering resources to open up more reporting opportunities. The most common pooling of resources is the sharing of story ideas and reporting plans. Small-staffed broadcast news operations gain the most from sharing ideas because they gain the news-gathering depth and resources of print. As a result, television stories from convergence partnerships have an added element of context. Newspapers and television can provide greater sourcing and depth to stories that go online. Realigning reporting resources to open up the opportunity for other stories to be covered remains an ideal but not yet a workable reality for most convergence-oriented newsrooms.

A lack of understanding of the value of other media tends to thwart efforts to take advantage of pooled resources. For some convergence operations, the pooling of resources has translated into the sharing of journalism tasks: one person doing reports for several media or one photographer shooting both still pictures and video. Critics of convergence efforts in Tampa have argued that this type of convergence expects every person to be good in all aspects of all media. But this jack-of-all-trades version of convergence was an early prototype that does not reflect most current convergence efforts.

In visits to nearly a dozen newsrooms, in various stages of putting convergence into daily practice, some common values and attitudes emerged. In Lawrence, Kansas, and Columbus, Ohio, there was a sense that working together on certain projects and sharing resources leads to better service to their communities. In traditional newspaper newsrooms like those at the *Providence Journal* and the *Seattle Times*, the online version of the paper is viewed as having a role, although that role is still being defined. At the *Christian Science Monitor*, convergence via an online presence is seen as a lifeline that gives hope to keeping its unique brand of journalism alive.

News organizations affiliated with megamedia companies, such Disney's ESPN, Media General's Tampa operations, and the Tribune Company's Chicago properties, are working to coordinate separate news organizations into more cooperative ones, with the intention of extending stories into more places for more people.

Not every newsroom has the same commitment to convergence, but all are at least examining the possibility that it could benefit their audiences and their journalism.

Below are some key values expressed by reporters, producers, and editors in convergence newsrooms, ranging from the most common and easiest to attain to the least common and hardest to master:

1. Reach news audiences wherever and whenever they may be.
2. Communicate so that everyone shares ideas, information, and values.
3. Coordinate news production resources to capitalize on each medium's strengths.
4. Use teamwork to capitalize on individuals' strengths and alleviate individuals' risks.
5. Coordinate news-gathering resources to capitalize on each medium's strengths.
6. Take chances to give audiences better news experiences.

SUMMARY

All journalists, regardless of how their work is distributed to the public, share common values about what is news and how they should operate in gathering and producing news. Proximity, prominence, timeliness, novelty, impact, and relevance all help to define news and shape news judgment. Truth, accuracy, fairness, balance, and independence are goals all journalists and news organizations profess to seek. News judgment is often a balancing act in determining what the public needs to know with what the public wants to know.

Each medium has strengths and weaknesses in providing information. Newspapers can be scanned, leafed through, returned to, clipped, and saved. They have more space and thus have a greater ability to provide context and detail. However, they are at a disadvantage in providing immediate and interactive information. Broadcast media can provide immediacy and emotion and give audiences a sense that they are witnessing the news. Online news can

BOX 3.3

ESPN: The Convergence Habit

The people at ESPN, the sports news juggernaut, do not waste much time talking about convergence; they just do it. Every day the people who put together content for seven U.S. and two dozen international sports cable networks, online news sites, a radio network, and a biweekly magazine exchange ideas, share resources, and brainstorm new approaches, all to meet one goal: to get information out to the sports fan. Although it first gained prominence as a cable network, in less than a dozen years ESPN has branched out into other media, winning prestigious honors doing so. From Emmys in television to the National Magazine Award for General Excellence and the Online Journalism Association award for General Excellence, both in 2003, ESPN belies the notion that quality and convergence cannot mix. Convergence is a habit that works at ESPN (which stands for Entertainment & Sports Programming Network).

"It's the way we do business," says Norby Williamson , senior vice president and co-managing editor at ESPN television. "We've converged talent over the mediums, we've converged content as it relates to our news reporting, long-form storytelling pieces across the different platforms—radio, magazine, dot-com, television—forever here."

FIGURE 3.3. ESPN newsroom. (Courtesy of ESPN)

Williamson and others say the original ESPN, the television network, began as a convergence operation back in the 1980s. From day one, the network's shows have worked from a shared, universal assignment desk and have shared information and staff, a practice not common at the traditional news networks, such as CBS, NBC, and ABC. Even with just the TV network, people "crossed over" from different shows, says Vince Doria. "The network itself was already a model for convergence. So when all these other entities came on board, it was just a natural evolution."

Many of the people who work at the various ESPN operations, as well as many of the staff, are veterans of media crossover. Neal Scarborough, who now heads ESPN.com, was the pro football editor for *ESPN the Magazine*. John Walsh, the executive vice president, was a newspaper and magazine reporter and editor before helping launch ESPN cable network, then *ESPN the Magazine*. Doria was a sports editor for the *Boston Globe*. "If I felt that I could come here as a print person and make a contribution to television, why wouldn't I think about that for ESPN.com or the magazine," Doria said. "So for me, it means more people to the party."

Every morning the parties to the daily action at all the ESPN outlets hold what is called the global meeting. At this meeting, representatives from various shows and all the outlets discuss their plans for the day. On May 6, 2004, the SportsTicker representative notes that it is New York Giants new quarterback Eli Manning's first NFL training camp. A fiftieth anniversary piece about Roger Bannister breaking the four-minute mile is slated for the 6:00 p.m. SportsCenter. Online's representative mentions a poll on the top ten individual sports performances tied to the Bannister anniversary. Tennis great Andre Agassi is slated for an interview, and producers and editors discuss who might want some sound or quotes from him. Editors in charge of following major sports such as basketball and baseball, weigh in with what can be expected. Game coverage is a given, so the discussion focuses on sports news available outside of the games. The global meeting normally includes magazine representatives on Mondays only, since the magazine is not on a daily schedule.

But the daily coordination does not end with the meeting. The ESPN outlets circulate a "hot list," a list of the stories generated by the assignment desk that comes out every three or four hours. Stories on the hot list are required for the sports shows. Also on that list are stories the shows should consider doing but do not have to do. The ESPN news desk editors also send out bulletins via the computer to alert producers and editors about new developments, new quotes or sound bites, or new stories developed by ESPN staff or reported by the wire services or other sports operations. "It's like a full-time job here, telling everybody what's going on," says Chuck Salituro. He adds that people at ESPN Radio or ESPN.com e-mail the news desk if they have a guest that provides some news or a sound bite for another story.

continued

"Journalism is very much an autonomous enterprise," says Walsh, and the profession does not lend itself to cooperation. "Sharing the resources for a common good that may make your story better and everybody else's story better and get the story out to more people is a difficult notion to persuade people of, and it takes the right people giving the right cooperation to make that happen."

It also takes coordination, Walsh says, to ensure that convergence does not get in the way of the storytelling. At ESPN that means coordinating and assigning staff to meet and match the different outlets' needs. When Tom Farrey wanted to report on baseball scouts in the Dominican Republic, he pitched it at the weekly enterprise meeting, a meeting of ESPN outlets' officials to work on longer-term planning. When it was given the go-ahead, Farrey's project got an editor to oversee it for the magazine and a producer to do the same for television. "It's sort of a buy in and check off at the very front end," Farrey says. He adds that the story benefits from the additional resources of producers and editors from the different media, and he benefits from the additional perspectives of those resources to his story. "It's got to be a real cooperative venture from the get-go," Farrey says, noting that everyone respects the needs of the other media—online, television, and magazine.

And they acknowledge each medium's limitations. Sports business reporter Darren Rovell says that he finds writing and reporting for television challenging "because you feel you're never telling the whole story," within the time constraints of the medium. In writing for television, Rovell says he cannot include everything he has for a story, yet he knows he has to satisfy the audience in the end. Scarborough says that online provides a place for information and news that does not fit into the time constraints of television and the space constraints of the magazine.

It does not always work, and sometimes the communications break down. Once ESPN carried a report that discounted a report on ESPN.com, creating some headlines and some discussion within the various outlets on the ESPN "campus" in Bristol, Connecticut, to remedy the issue. But because most ESPN outlets are housed in Bristol, "relationships form because of the closeness of the place, and it begins to feed into the ability to gather news and get the most efficiency out of what you're doing," says Doria.

"They won't tolerate us being a bunch of islands," says ESPN radio's Bruce Gilbert. "Radio's not going to be an island, and dot-com is not going to be an island, and that's the right mentality. And if you recognize that there's no need to be insecure about that, and that we can help each other, then everybody wins, including the consumers."

Sources: Norby Williamson, Vincent Doria, Chuck Salituro, John Walsh, Tom Farrey, Darren Rovell, and Bruce Gilbert, interviews by author, May 2004.

provide interactivity and multimedia storytelling. It can also provide depth through its search capabilities.

Convergence news operations seek out common goals and try to exploit the strengths of different media to provide better news storytelling to their audiences. Each newsroom that is trying convergence is trying different strategies, from cross-promotion to simply replaying a story from one medium to another.

LEARNING THE LINGO

Blog	Interactivity
Co-opetition	Readability
Cloning	Verge event

NOTES

1. Daniel Okrent, "How Would Jackson Pollock Cover This Campaign?" *New York Times*, October 10, 2004.
2. Ken Auletta, *Backstory: Inside the Business of News* (New York: Penguin, 2003), xix.
3. people-press.org/reports/display.php3?ReportID=215 (June 8, 2004, accessed November 30, 2005).
4. www.gallup.com/poll/content/login.aspx?ci=13132.
5. Bill Kovach and Tom Rosenstiel, *The Elements of Journalism* (New York: Crown Press, 2001), 43.
6. Kovach and Rosenstiel, *Elements*, 45
7. *Dying to Tell the Story*, CNN, September 14, 1998, directed by Kyra Thompson.
8. Society of Professional Journalists, Code of Ethics, at www.spj.org/ethics_code.asp (accessed December 6, 2005).
9. Kovach and Rosenstiel, *Elements*, 77.
10. Scott W. Libin, "Auletta to Journalists: Walk Humbly, Adjudicate Truth, and Embarrass the Powerful," October 25, 2004, at www.poynter.org/column.asp?id=34&aid=73211 (accessed November 30, 2005).
11. Mary Nesbit, "The Power to Grow Leadership: Results from the Impact Study of Readership," presentation at Institute for Journalism Excellence, June 13, 2001.
12. "The Power to Grow Readership: A Presentation of the Four Cornerstones of Readership Growth," at www.readership.org/resources/reports.htm (accessed November 30, 2005).
13. Philip Seib, *Going Live: Getting the News Right in a Real-Time, Online World* (Lanham, MD: Rowman & Littlefield, 2001), 37–40.
14. Bill Kovach and Tom Rosenstiel, *Warp Speed: America in the Age of Mixed Media* (New York: The Century Foundation, 1999), 17.

15. Av Westin, "Best Practices for Television Journalists" (Nashville: Free Press/Fair Press Project, Freedom Forum, 2000).

16. Dean Wright, interview by author, April 12, 2004.

17. Mark Seibel, "Is Including E-Mail Addresses in Reporters' Bylines a Good Idea?" *Nieman Reports* 54, no. 4 (Winter 2000): 1

18. Lori Robertson, "E-Mail Avalanche," *American Journalism Review* 23, no. 1 (Jan/Feb 2001): 16.

19. Tom Regan, interview by author, February 2004.

20. Mark Glaser, "Open Season: News Sites Add Outside Links, Free Content," October 19, 2004, at ojr.org/ojr/glaser/1098225187.php (accessed November 30, 2005).

21. Tom Heslin, interview by author, February 25, 2004.

22. Wright, interview.

23. Rosental Calmon Alves and Amy Schmitz Weiss, "Many Newspaper Sites Still Cling to Once-a-Day Publish Cycle," July 21, 2004, at ojr.org/ojr/workplace/1090395903 (accessed November 30, 2005).

24. Angela Clark, interview by author, April 12, 2004.

25. Neal Scarborough, interview by author, May 2004.

26. Heslin, interview.

27. David Underhill, interview by author, October 24, 2002.

28. Jon Schwantes, interview by author, July 5, 2003.

29. Michael Silberman, interview by author, March 23, 2004.

30. Wright, interview; Clark, interview.

31. Tom Farrey, interview by author, May 2004.

PART II

Skill Set

FOUR

Approaching the Story

GOOD STORIES come from good reporting, and good reporting comes from good sourcing, interviewing, organization, and planning. It sounds so simple and so obvious. Yet each day, turn on a television newscast, dial up a radio news brief, or open up a daily newspaper, and you can find dozens of stories with glaring problems in one or all of these areas.

Before one second of reporting is done on a story, a reporter, writer, or producer of a news piece needs to do some homework. That homework could involve finding background information to help understand the historical, political, or social context of a story. It could involve finding the people, the sources, needed to inform the story and the angle, or approach, to a story that would make the story interesting to different people.

Before a word is written, a videotape is edited, or a sound bite or quote is pulled for use, the journalist needs to know the story in order to tell the story, know the audience in order to relate to the audience, and know the outlet in order to use it effectively. Knowing the story means understanding the focus, the main point of the story. Knowing the audience means determining what others need to discern and learn from your story. Knowing your outlet means understanding how it helps people get information. Every journalist, no matter the medium or media, needs this knowledge to effectively do his or her job. Knowing the story, the audience, and the outlets affects how you go about getting the story.

KNOWING THE STORY

No matter whether you are telling your story in a newspaper, on the radio, on television, or on the Internet, you must know what you are talking or writing about before you start.

Knowing the facts of a story does not necessarily translate into knowing the story. The job of the journalist is to take facts and make them into news: a story that is timely, unusual, relevant, informative, and compelling. A police scanner can provide information about a deadly automobile accident, but a journalist must take that information to tell a story that engages people and makes them pay attention. A stenographer can record the happenings of a city council meeting, but a journalist must take that information and synthesize it to inform people about how a government action will affect them. To do that, journalists need to gather not just facts, but context and insights. They need to get information from research, from people, and from observation. These news-gathering skills are the basic work needed for any type of journalism. News-gathering involves backgrounding, interviewing, and observing.

These days, journalists have to get up to speed about a story quickly. Often, they first turn to the Internet and search engines like Google. But Google and mainstream search engines connected to portals such as Yahoo! and MSN have limitations and should be seen as only a starting point. The Web can provide a vast source of information, but its vastness can be overwhelming. Information can be scattered among thousands of sites on the Web, making useful information hard to pinpoint and hard to verify. And not everything is on the Web.

Despite those limitations, a 2003 poll by the Pew Center for Internet and Society found that some 80 percent of today's working journalists use the Web. The Web is a great source for journalists because it is accessible and searchable. But journalists need to have the skills to determine what to access on the Web and how to search through it to find usable, reliable information for stories. Journalists also need to know where to find information not available online. "Old media" resources, such as newspaper archives (formerly known as morgues),

BOX 4.1

Journalistic Disconnect

When telephone workers went on strike in the Boston area in August 1998, the local television stations dutifully reported about the work stoppage. The reporter at one station showed video of the picket lines, had sound bites from a union representative and from a phone company representative, and talked about the salary and work issues in dispute. But nowhere in the piece did the reporter explain the impact of the strike.

If you were a person expecting to get phone service turned on the next day, that story meant little to you. It was a good story for informing the phone workers, the phone company, and people with financial interests in the phone company about the strike, but it did not inform the average person. It did not answer the So What? question that news stories need to answer to fulfill their duty to their audience.

public libraries, and governmental records can provide ideas and sources for stories. Journalism involves a constant search for story ideas. Backgrounding is a way of seeking secondary sources for news stories.

But journalism is more than a term paper research project. Journalism involves people. People involved in news are primary sources. The best journalism connects to people, relating one person's story to another to inform everyone. Part of knowing the story involves knowing who to talk to about a story to get information and insights and how to talk to people to get that information and those insights. Part of knowing a story involves knowing who could be and who should be a part of a story. It requires leaving the comfort zone of the newsroom, the Internet, the circle of officials, publicists, and tipsters, and the gaggle of friends and colleagues to find different voices and different perspectives on the news. Journalism is about finding people that make stories come alive. For journalists to know the story, they must know the people who inform it.

KNOWING THE AUDIENCE

Even when journalists think they know their story, they can run into trouble by forgetting whom they are doing the story for. If you forget about the audience, you will have trouble thinking about the people you need to talk to for your story, the kinds of information you should seek from those people, and how you should organize and present that information so it is understandable.

A story about federal regulations on stem cell research for a biotechnology journal has a different audience than does a story about federal regulations on stem cell research for a television station in Cleveland. The audience for the biotech journal may be stem cell researchers with particular information needs and interests. The television audience is a broader range of people, whose interest perhaps is in how the research might bring about treatment of certain chronic conditions or diseases. The story topic may start out to be the same in each case, but the audience affects the focus and the reporting on the story.

Knowing the audience means knowing the community you are working in and reporting for. A lot of reporting for a news story never makes it into the final version, but it informs the story throughout. Knowing the community that is accessing the news story should influence every decision made about a story, from whether it should be reported to how it should be put together and how it is distributed. The people who put together the news for ESPN know that their community is sports fans. The people who work for the *Christian Science Monitor* know that their community is looking for more depth on national and international issues; it is a community who seeks "*Monitor* journalism."

The audience for news is undergoing radical change. News audiences are seeking information whenever and wherever they can get it, often in brief bits and chunks. Audiences can be organized by geography, by political, social or religious interest, and by recreational and personality types. And they are demanding more control of the news they get. Because of increased choices, they often reject outlets that do not seem to listen or care about their views and do not understand their lives and their informational needs. News outlets that know their audience tend to keep it. A 2004 State of the News Media report found that newspapers that serve small or ethnic communities are gaining audiences, while mass news outlets are struggling to maintain theirs.

KNOWING THE MEDIA

Focusing on the audience is key for anyone trying to organize stories in print, broadcast, or online. But it is even more essential in planning and organizing stories for multiple media. People turn to different media at different times to get different types of information. Understanding how people use the news media should help journalists focus on how to get stories and information for people to use.

People get news to find out the latest information about their world. Thanks to new technologies like the satellite, fiber optics, and wireless telecommunication, news can become old in minutes. The real-time capabilities of television and the Web have created a public demand for timeliness that is instantaneous. But timeliness is not the only value they expect from news. Each outlet for news provides certain value-added aspects to news (as we examine in chapter 3).

Audiences go to television to see and hear the news, so television demands a story with moving pictures and sound. Audiences expect to not only get the facts about a deadly car accident but to see the aftermath, the outcome, of the accident. They expect to see and hear someone in authority explain the impact, the relevance. Broadcast media add imagery to news.

When news of the South Asian tsunami began to develop, the impact of that disaster became real for millions of people due to the distribution of amateur video showing the tidal waves' onslaught. Still pictures could demonstrate the devastation caused by the tsunami, but only video could demonstrate the rapid rise of water and people's inability to flee to safety.

However, the Internet, with its capability for interactivity and connectivity, allowed for the firsthand experiences and images from hundreds of witnesses and victims of the tsunami to be told through Web logs. It opened up the news-gathering process on that story to not only journalists but to their audiences. The Web also linked audiences to aid organizations if they wanted to help tsunami victims and to scientific, geographic, and political information to help them better understand the context of the disaster.

In determining the stories about the tsunami, the medium or outlet for the story affected not only the information gathered but how it was gathered and how it was produced or put together for various audiences. Convergent journalists need to be thinking about how the medium and the story can dovetail to be effective in providing information to people.

Journalists can no longer think about a story as only words or only pictures. They need to think about a story as layers of information—visual, aural, textual, animated, interactive, connected—that people can mix and match in the best ways to get to what they need and want to know.

When setting out to do a story, journalists need to think of story, audience, and outlet in planning the gathering and the producing of the news. In this chapter we explore what every journalist, no matter the media or outlets, needs to do to find stories and prepare for reporting them. It looks at how to find an idea for a story, how to find the right people to talk to for a story, and how to plot out the reporting for a story. We also examine reporting techniques that help in gathering the information needed to put a story together. We look at interviewing (from the asking to the listening), observation (from gathering description to gathering images), and note taking. We outline how to develop a story idea and the sources for that story, how to determine the focus for a story, and how to gather information and images for a story.

THE JOURNALISTIC TREASURE HUNT: FINDING STORY IDEAS

"There are eight million stories in the naked city," the narrator intoned in starting the TV drama *The Naked City* each week, "and this is one of them." Journalism is about noticing those millions of stories and finding the ones that need to be told. That ability to notice stories has been called news judgment or "a nose for news." It is a skill that veteran journalists take for granted and aspiring journalists struggle to develop, but it is a skill that all journalists must have to report and produce news. It is a skill that a journalist working for a newspaper, magazine, website, television, or radio station can use, regardless of where their journalism ultimately finds an audience. All journalism starts with applying news judgment to an idea.

News judgment involves imposing news values—timeliness, proximity, impact, conflict, unusualness, relevance, and prominence—on the daily happenings of life. News judgment means knowing when something is so unusual that it will pique people's curiosity. It means knowing when seemingly disjointed things have something in common that anyone can relate to and understand. "If you can write a story about something totally, utterly unique, you probably can hook people," says Associated Press reporter Ted Anthony. "And if you write a story about something that's universal and appeals to an interest in everyone, you can hook people as well."[1] Anthony adds that the real trick to exceptional stories is to combine the unique and the universal.

Story ideas are all around us, but curiosity can help journalists notice those ideas and think about how others might be interested in them. Bob Woodward and Carl Bernstein, in their book *All the President's Men*, explain that the routine arraignment of the arrested suspects in the Watergate burglary in 1972 piqued Woodward's curiosity. That curiosity led to the duo's investigation, which ended with the downfall and resignation of a president and the conviction of several top-ranking officials of the Nixon administration.

Story ideas grow from a journalist's curiosity to find out more or to find out why. It could be something read in the paper or online, something heard in a conversation, or something seen while walking on the street. Stories can be found in public institutions and in the privacy of a home. Journalists find story ideas by taking notice of the world around them.

Story ideas come from all manner of reading. The traditional notion of reading is taking in the written or typed word through books, news articles, bulletin board notices, online discussions, government documents and public records, and even Web logs. But reading also means "to learn by observing outward expressions or signs," to make a study of a situation or activity.[2] That type of reading also generates story ideas. To find stories, journalists need to read anything and everything. First they need to determine what they need to read. Then they need to think about news values (how they know the story), the news consumers (how they know the audience), and their news outlet (how they know the medium or media) in plotting out their reporting.

The Usual Suspects

Over the years, news organizations develop lists of people and places to check to get started in the search for news on any particular day. News releases, court dockets, police scanners, and government meeting agendas are common places to start to find stories. But reporters must know how to sift through that information to find stories that will interest people.

News organizations get inundated with news releases about people and events that publicists think should be reported to a wider audience. News releases are designed to place a person or event in the best light, to garner publicity and public notice. Journalists need to decide if the person or event warrants public notice, by applying news values. News releases can serve as tip sheets, alerting journalists about new products or programs, upcoming events, or people who have done something newsworthy or are advocating an idea that is newsworthy. The best way to decide whether to pursue a story from a news release is to ask who will benefit the most from the story—the subject of the release or readers, viewers, and browsers.

Over the past two decades, companies or individuals seeking news coverage have developed video news releases, or VNRs, which can be as complete and as well-produced as news packages. In March 2004, some forty television stations aired a VNR touting the benefits of the newly enacted Medicare law that resembled a news story, but it was not put together by a journalist working for a news organization. It was created by a production company for the federal Health and Human Services Department, which runs the Medicare program. This particular VNR provoked outrage because it was funded by taxpayers' dollars. It also illuminated the way news organizations sometimes engage in the bad practice of using text or video news releases without revision, review, or source identification. In this case, the stations used the VNR not as a tip sheet for a story, or as a source of information and visuals, but as a substitute for a news story that should have been researched, reported on, and checked out by the stations. But they apparently did not have the time or personnel to do so. The VNR was thus the only source of information about the provisions of the new Medicare law, as promoted by the people favoring the law. Print and video news releases are no substitute for reporting.

Court dockets and police scanners also provide a daily dose of story ideas for the news media. Considering the number of crime and court shows on television, it is apparent that crime stories attract people's interest. But not everything going on in a courthouse or at the police station warrants a news story by every organization. A criminal trial in which a former priest is accused of rape would definitely qualify for coverage because of the unusualness of both the crime and the accused. A civil case involving a fall in a local grocer's cereal aisle might not. But a civil case in which a fast food restaurant chain was on trial for injuries to a woman who was burned by the restaurant's hot coffee warranted a lot of coverage, especially when the woman won her damages suit against the chain, McDonald's. News values were applied to decide the newsworthiness of the case in reporting it to a wider audience.

The same sifting of cases occurs in looking at crimes, car accidents, and fires. The more severe the crime, accident, or fire—the more unusual they are—the more likely those stories will warrant a news piece. A transit train accident in New York City that kills a rail worker warrants a news story, but a fender-bender at Times Square probably does not. But if that fender-bender created a huge traffic jam in the city, affecting a lot of people, it could become a news story. By monitoring police and fire scanners, news organizations can react early to a news story. They can get to the scene of the fire, accident, or crime to gather information not only from police and fire officials but from witnesses and neighbors. They also can get visuals—still pictures and video—from the scene. Sometimes newspaper and television photographers are sent to a police or fire scene before reporters to ensure that a variety of visuals is captured as the story is unfolding. Sometimes the photographer is expected to gather both visuals and information while someone back in the newsroom is "working the phones," making calls to gather information for a news story.

Because of the differences in deadlines and audiences, television and radio react more extensively to possible news events unfolding on the scanner. That's because radio and television value immediacy. Television also values visuals, so dramatic pictures of a building on fire might warrant more of story on television than in the newspaper. Newspapers and websites, because they have more space and time, include more context in their reports. Police scanner stories favor immediacy and visuals; court cases and trials favor context and explanation.

While most trials are open to the public, not all of them are open to cameras, which creates severe limitations for visual coverage. Some court and crime cases do not lend themselves to visual storytelling but the prominence of the accused or the crime demands coverage. For example, home design entrepreneur Martha Stewart's trial involving stock fraud was a dramatic story that worked far better as a text story (print and online) than a visual story because

BOX 4.2

A Story is Born

How the New York One newsroom takes a call on a police scanner to create a lead item on the six o'clock news:

July 6, 2004: Late in the afternoon, New York One, a cable news channel designed to provide hyperlocal coverage of New York City, moves into position on word that the body of a relative of actors Kirk and Michael Douglas was found dead in a Manhattan apartment.

Around 4:30 p.m.: An editor on the station's assignment desk talks to a news assistant on a walkie-talkie about what is happening at the scene. NY1 will send a news assistant with a camera to start getting information and assess the story. A NY1 truck is sent to the scene.

Around 5:15 p.m.: Another station on a newsroom monitor reports that the body has been identified as Eric Douglas, Michael Douglas's half brother. Managing editor Peter Landis confers with the assignment desk about confirming the identity before reporting it.

At about the same time, executive producer Matt Besterman has one of his writers start putting together the story, in hopes of getting video for the first minute of 6:00 p.m. news. "We knew the [satellite] truck was there but we weren't sure if we'd have the video back, so I had the story written up, thinking we could cut the video later if it was fed in time."

About 5:45 p.m.: Besterman copyedits the story but still has no video.

A few minutes before 6:00 p.m.: The video feed is in, but it is so close to the top of the hour that there is not enough time to get it cut for the first NY1 minute.

6:00 p.m.: The news show starts, and Besterman "floats" the body story, taking it out of the lineup temporarily until it has the video and planning to put it back in the lineup once the video is ready to run with the script.

About 6:05 p.m.: The story airs, with video showing exterior shots of the building where Eric Douglas's body was found.

of limited pictures (usually of people walking into and out of the courtrooms) and limited sound. Television and the Web relied on artists' drawings of activities inside the courtroom to help illustrate their stories.

Since the media frenzy during the 1995 murder trial of O.J. Simpson, where cameras were allowed in the courtroom during the nine months of testimony and arguments, such access has been greatly restricted in other cases involving prominent figures. The 2005 sexual molestation trial of pop icon Michael Jackson, like the Martha Stewart case the year before, banned courtroom cameras. Some states, like New York, prohibit cameras in the courtroom, while others allow the presiding judge to decide access. So while courts are a good place to find stories, journalists face limits as to the devices they can use within the courthouse and the courtroom in their news-gathering. The Reporters Committee for Freedom of the Press monitors legal issues relating to journalistic access to places and documents and provides background information about legal limitations being placed on reporting. Its website, rcfp.org, is a good first stop for journalists seeking to learn the ground rules, from cameras in courtrooms to open records and opening meetings laws (nicknamed Sunshine Laws).

Open meetings laws come into play in covering governmental decision-making groups, from legislatures to city and town councils and boards of education. These groups' public meetings provide fertile ground for news story ideas, as they make decisions involving thousands or millions of dollars, affecting thousands or millions of people. Most states require those decisions be made in an open or public forum. Sunshine Laws outline the requirements for those forums, such as requirements for notifying the public of the meeting time and place and items up for discussion and action. The laws also delineate topics that can be exempt from discussion in an open forum (usually personnel matters).

An agenda item might warrant a news story ahead of the meeting, informing the public on a decision that is expected to be made. This type of story is known as an "advancer," and it can generate more interest in the meeting. The discussions and decisions of the public meeting could also warrant a news story, especially if an agenda item generates a new policy or program or a change in a policy or program with wide-reaching impact. Public meetings can also provide good background information on a topic, even when the meeting itself does not result in any newsworthy action.

The News

Most news stories can be mined for other news stories, because they are usually focused snapshots of an event or a situation. A big-picture story, such as one on the new federal energy bill, can generate other stories with a smaller focus, such as how the bill will impact heating oil costs for local residents or if a local utility company might have to renovate its plants because of more stringent environmental regulations. Many national and international stories take a broad view of the news. But they can be localized so that the news and information is tailored to a specific community. When Pope John Paul II died in April 2005, many news organizations localized that story by getting reaction to the death from local Catholics.

National or international stories also provide broad information and may not take into account the impact on specific age, gender, economic, or social groups. For example, CBS News did several follow-up stories on President George W. Bush's Social Security plan, examining its impact on different age groups of workers—people in their late twenties versus those in their late forties.

This is a common storytelling technique, seen frequently on television news. Another way to think small about a big story is personalizing it. This technique is used most often to explain a complex topic, to help audiences relate to the information by having one person serve as a representative for everyone. To relate to the impact of a plan to close a state facility for severely mentally disabled adults in Waltham, Massachusetts, *Boston Globe* suburban reporter Emily Sweeney profiled six residents of the facility who had lived there for at least forty years. While Sweeney and others had done news stories over several months about the state's closure plan and public reaction to it, the profiles provided a personal side to the debate over the facility's fate.

While thinking small about a big story can generate new story ideas, thinking big and broad about a small or one-time news story can do the same. When a commuter train crash killed ten people near Los Angeles after it hit a car that police believe was deliberately left on the tracks, the *New York Times* followed up with a story on how the crash highlighted security concerns about the nation's commuter rail systems and their vulnerability to terrorism.

The *Lawrence (KS) Journal-World*, with its convergence partners in television, decided to mark the fifth anniversary of the Columbine High School shootings, with a look at safety and security at the schools in its city, rather than just recounting the events that occurred in the Colorado community. In this case, the paper, the television station, and the website decided to localize a national story. To examine the larger issue, they focused on lessons learned from the shooting in terms of safety in schools.

The old saying that when one door closes another opens applies daily to journalists' hunt for stories. Reporters can mine story ideas from news stories just by determining what questions or concerns might still need to be answered or resolved, seeking story angles that might have been missed. These stories are sometimes offered as sidebars, stories that are thematically connected to a main story but report on a different angle of the story. Sometimes those stories are run on subsequent days. Reporters can also find stories by keeping track of any further action or development that may be planned. These stories are considered follow-up stories, and reporters and assignment editors keep a futures file that includes these stories.

Weather stories, such as a lengthy heat wave or a sizable snow or rain storm, often challenge journalists—everyone experiences bad weather, so making the news unique and interesting without turning to clichés requires some creative thinking. Many a reporter has tried to fry an egg on the pavement to show how hot it really is, or has timed how long a glass of water takes to freeze up during a cold spell. More creative journalists look for other people to be the characters in stories telling their readers, listeners, viewers, or browsers how hot or how cold it really is. A story on how people (such as dry cleaners or roofing workers) who work at really hot jobs cope with a heat wave can serve as a sidebar to a main story on the severity of the hot weather.

In Boston, during the blizzard of 2005 that blanketed the area with up to three feet of snow, one sidebar explored a new city policy to collect parking space "savers." People who dig out parking spaces on the streets of the city often place a chair, garbage can, or orange traffic cones to mark the cleared space as their territory. Before the big storm, Tom Menino, mayor

BOX 4.3

Finding a Story

A bad snowstorm in Little Rock, Arkansas, tested my ingenuity as a reporter in 1979. As someone from northeastern Ohio, I was unimpressed by the storm, until I could not get out of my driveway because other cars got stuck in the snow and blocked me in. Teased by my editor for not being tough enough to get to work, I was determined to turn in a story, even if I could not get to the office.

While watching people struggle with the snow, I noticed that no one had snow shovels and decided to see if any could be had. They could not. Hardware stores either had them and ran out, or never stocked them. Although the main weather story that day was about the snowfall and how it shut down schools and businesses, I was able to produce a small sidebar on the area's snow shovel shortage.

of Boston, announced plans to collect space savers to open up street parking, angering residents. The sidebar looked at how and when that new policy would be tested. A week or so after the storm, when the policy was being carried out, newspapers and television stations in Boston did follow-up stories on its implementation.

Follow-up stories can be anniversary stories relating to what has happened in the year or years since a major news event. Mary Wiltenburg did a follow-up story for the *Christian Science Monitor* on the lives of one family who lost a loved one in the September 11 attacks. Follow-up pieces can come from sentencing hearings after the verdict of a trial, such as the December 2004 stories in which Scott Peterson, convicted of killing his wife and unborn child, was sentenced to death in California. They can also check on the implementation of a new law, such as a smoking ban in public places.

The Internet

The rise of discussion boards, Web logs, and chat rooms online has opened up another source of story ideas for journalists. New communities and new issues crop up in places on the Internet where people with similar interests can exchange viewpoints and concerns. Rebecca MacKinnon, former CNN Beijing and Tokyo bureau chief, said she started taking an interest in blogs when she found Japan-based Web log pioneer Joi Ito's Web log, with all sorts of tips and perspectives on concerns and issues being discussed in Japanese political circles, including a story idea about a power plant whistleblower. Other journalists, particularly those who cover a specific beat or topic, have turned to interactive Internet activities to find out what people are talking about and interested in. Health reporters, for example, might go to chat rooms and discussion boards for the latest buzz on a new medical study, or to pick up concerns about a side effect or reaction to a drug.

Chat rooms and message boards are often associated with a group, business, or association that promotes a special interest. Journalists need to know and understand those interests in evaluating the relevance and independence of the perspectives. For example, a discussion board on continuing the use of the painkiller Vioxx put together by a law firm might attract different responses than one put together by the Arthritis Foundation or the American Pain Foundation. The Internet does not impose filters or ratings on the validity of information on it, so rumor and innuendo can appear to have equal weight to facts and well-sourced information. Talk radio and television call-in shows have a similar problem. A tip about a story may emerge in the heat of a discussion board, chat room, blog, or call-in show dialog, but it also may end up being false or incomplete. The more you know about the people behind an Internet site, the better off you will be in judging its usefulness in getting ideas.

Jonathan Dube, who writes about online news, offers a five-point checklist for journalists for assessing Internet information:

1. Authority. Know all about who is distributing, promoting, offering the information online. Who is behind the information?
2. Objectivity. Know all about the agenda of the site where you are getting information. Is it supposed to be funny, promotional, political?
3. Timeliness. Know when the information was posted and/or updated.
4. Sourcing. Know the reliability and the credibility of the people, agencies, reports, and so forth cited on the website.
5. Verification. Know that the same information can and is found elsewhere.[3]

These five rules can be applied to any source of information gathered for a news story, from primary sources such as people and research and government studies, to secondary sources. The rule about verification is a common touchstone. The legendary rule of thumb of the former City News Bureau in Chicago was: If your mother tells you she loves you, check it out. A good story has a solid foundation of several sources of information, whose credibility, reliability, and independence are apparent.

Many Internet sites for interactivity and information have their roots in physical places and spaces. Internet bulletin boards are extensions of the old-fashioned pushpin boards found at restaurants, cafes, grocery stores, schools, church halls, sports clubs, and community activity centers. The precursors of chat rooms on the Internet are coffeehouses, libraries, and community meeting rooms and clubs. While the Internet is vast, it does not hold everything. Journalists need to go out and explore places and spaces to find stories.

Mark Douglas, a reporter for WFLA-TV and the *Tampa Tribune*, told a 2002 conference that he calls his search for story ideas "community mapping." Douglas, who produces news stories for television, newspapers, and online, relies on walking, talking, listening, and observing everyday life to find hints of stories. Topping his list: Get off the beaten trail and look for listening posts.[4] Both tips aim at getting away from the computer, out of the office and into where life is happening. Douglas's tips mirror what Jan Schaffer, formerly of the Pew Center for Civic Journalism, refers to as going to "third places," or hangout spots. She suggests listening to what people are talking about.

Finding Sources

Story ideas often come from people, and the hunt for sources goes hand in hand with the hunt for stories. A good story idea requires finding the right people to provide insight, information, and perspective in order for it to become a good story. Just as reporters and news organizations have a list of places that are "usual suspects" for getting story ideas, they also have a list of people who are usual suspects for getting comments and information for stories In many instances, it makes sense to go to the usual suspects for initial reporting: members of the city council about town policy, the prosecuting and defense attorneys in a criminal trial, the fire chief about a house fire, the chief researcher testing a new cancer drug.

But often, reaching only the same people as sources for stories provides a narrow and skewed perspective in news stories. It can promulgate stereotypes and conformity. It can lead to a disconnect between the journalist, the story, and the audience. Several studies of newspaper front pages and national and local newscasts have shown that white males predominate as sources quoted prominently in major news stories. Among the most quoted persons on the front page or in a nightly newscast is the U.S. president. And while no one will deny that when the president speaks he makes news, by quoting the usual well-known officials in many of its stories, the news media get accused of bias. Journalists also draw fire for using the usual suspects to paint the simplistic yes-no, pro-con sides of issues. For every Republican there needs to be a Democrat; for every stem cell research proponent there must be an equal and opposite stem cell opponent.

Just as there are millions of stories in the naked city, there are also millions of sources. Anyone and everyone can be a source of information. Journalists need to cultivate all types of sources at all levels in government, businesses, and communities. Good stories grow out of nurturing sources and harvesting information from a variety of them. Journalists, who work in more than one news medium can blunt the criticism about a paucity of voices in convergent news if they work at using sources that reflect and relate to the diversity of their audiences. The best reporters seek out the unique as well as the usual as sources. They create their own database of people they find are reliable, credible, and knowledgeable.

BOX 4.4

Developing Stories

As the education reporter for the *Plain Dealer* in Cleveland, I was responsible for keeping track of major federal court filings relating to the court-ordered desegregation plan for the Cleveland Public Schools. As in many courthouses, legal filings tended to get completed toward the end of the workday, so I had to rely on sources within the federal court, the school system, the court-appointed desegregation monitoring agency, and the NAACP, the lawyers for the plaintiffs, to alert me about the possibility of a legal decision or action that would warrant a news story.

The federal judge in the case did not speak with the media, so his clerks served as secondary sources of information. The legal document itself served as the initial source and a primary source for a story. Then I would contact other primary sources, lawyers representing all parties of the case, for comment and explanation. I would also contact parent and teacher representatives about a court filing, especially if it pertained to a particular class program.

Sources can usually be divided between primary sources and secondary ones. A primary source can be a person with direct knowledge of a news subject or a document, such a report or legislation. A secondary source is one or more steps removed from that direct information. *The 9/11 Commission Report* and the members of the commission would be the primary sources for a story on the commission's examination of the 2001 terrorist attack. A newspaper article summarizing the report, or a terrorism expert's comments explaining the commission's thinking, would be secondary sources. A story on reaction to the report could have primary sources that included 9/11 victims' families, intelligence officials, and security and diplomatic experts. Secondary sources best serve to provide reporters with tips and insights about a story; they inform the reporting of a story. Primary sources are crucial to a story. Secondary sources can help lead reporters to primary ones.

One of the easiest and fastest ways to find primary sources is to examine previous news stories. News stories can be mined for not only story ideas but for story sources and general knowledge or background. Most news organizations maintain archives of their work, and many of them are available online, although more are charging a fee for access to full texts. Databases that compile stories and transcripts, such as LexisNexis, can be used at libraries, which subscribe to dozens of such services.

News stories usually yield the names of public officials and experts on the story topic you are exploring. Sometimes you will find names of representatives of community or support groups with an interest in a topic. What news stories will not tell you is how to find these people and what information you can expect from them. Depending on the size of the town, business, or agency, you may be able to find a main website with phone numbers or get a main number via an Internet directory. Both online phone books and the old-fashioned print ones are good resources.

In fact, printed phone books may be faster and easier to use, because business, government, and residential numbers are compiled in separate sections. Also, printed phone books are easier to search through than an electronic database when the exact name or the exact spelling of a person or agency is not known.

Sometimes the best contact for sources may be someone sitting next to you in the newsroom who has compiled lists of the phone numbers and e-mail addresses of contact people. In television newsrooms, the assignment desk serves as a repository of such contact information. But reporters have their own lists as well. It may be in a Rolodex, PDA, beat book, or computer file, but if a story has been done before, more than likely another reporter has contact information stashed away somewhere about it. They also would be able to provide insight as to how useful the person might be on a topic or story.

Good reporters pride themselves on having contact information for hard-to-reach, prominent, and quotable people. Their contact lists often include several people who might be knowledgeable or informative on a subject. New reporters sometimes get stuck on a story by getting fixated on a handful of "must-have" sources. Veterans have a number of people they reach out to for information. They collect business cards of sources every time they go out on an assignment. Beat reporters might "work" buildings, meeting and learning about different people who work in a government or business office every time they go there. They learn the name of the security guard, office manager, secretary, executive assistant, and others who can make access to people easier or harder and who can provide tips and insights about what is happening.

You also find primary sources by going to the place where news is happening. You look for officials who can provide information and facts about the news event. You also want to find experts or witnesses who can provide insight and interpretation. And you may want to seek out people who want to give their opinion. All have value as sources for a news story, depending on the story you are trying to do.

At a legislative hearing on stem cell research, legislators and their aides—officials—can be sources about the hearing and the legislation they expect to develop from it. Scientists and ethicists—experts—may be sources for detailed explanations about the implications of the research. You may also find individuals in the audience, people with special interests, who may be affected by the legislation and may have an opinion on it. At meetings, mine the audience for sources, even though they might not serve as primary sources for a story that day; they may serve as sources for a future story.

At a fire or crime scene, you want official and eyewitness accounts for a story. Jared Stearns used a crisscross directory, which lists addresses in order and then phone numbers, to find someone who could talk to him about what was happening at the Station nightclub in West Warwick, Rhode Island, early on February 21, 2003. With a final deadline minutes away, Stearns, an intern on the late shift at the *Boston Globe*, found someone who lived on the same street as the nightclub. The nightclub neighbor got on his cell phone and described the chaotic scene, where a hundred people died in the nightclub fire, nearly seventy miles away from the *Globe* and Stearns. That description enhanced details about the fire from fire officials in the breaking news story put together by Stearns and Michael Rosenwald for the morning paper.

When talking with officials, experts, or any possible news source, always ask for a number where you can reach them after hours, should you want to follow up on the story. When talking to someone on the phone, note the number on caller ID, in case it is different from the number you used for the first contact. It also is smart to ask them for other people they know who might be good contacts, thus expanding your list of knowledgeable sources. Anytime you meet or talk to someone, you have an opportunity to make a contact and develop a source for a story.

In dealing with officials and experts, you may find that you have to go through a media relations or public information office. The people who work in these offices can bypass or create barriers to officials. They can be helpful to broadcast reporters in organizing the logistics needed to get source, reporter, and camera together. They can help find the right people to talk to within an organization or business. Often the top boss or officials may not have the best information or perspective for a story, and a public relations liaison may be able to steer you to someone who can. But their job is to put their organization or business in the best light in the media, so they will issue statements and provide information or contacts that steer you in a direction that may or may not suit your story. However, public relations people are sources that journalists need to cultivate.

Journalists also need to cultivate less obvious sources. Sometimes the best source may be someone who used to work in a job. Veteran political reporter and columnist Jack Germond says that former elected officials often have great insight into current political campaigns, although they may not speak publicly about them.[5] "Formers," as they are called in *The Investigative Reporter's Handbook*, can provide candor and supporting documents for reporters.[6]

The Pew Center for Civic Journalism also promotes cultivating nontraditional sources. Jan Schaffer, the center's former director, called this "civic mapping," a way to find new and diverse sources within a community. Journalists' usual suspects tend to be officials and quasi-official civic leaders, such as church pastors or rabbis or political activists. Schaffer has identified two types of nontraditional, nonofficial sources that can broaden perspectives in news: catalysts and connectors. These nonofficial sources often provide information and insight about the officials. Catalysts, according to Schaffer, are the people in neighborhoods and communities that others turn to. They are the "go-to" people who make things happen. Connectors are people who move between various communities and organizations and know what is going on in several places. A catalyst might be a grocery store manager who knows how to get a street light fixed or how to raise money for a girls' soccer league. A connector might be a school crossing guard who is active in a local bike trails group and works with a breast cancer support group.

Finding sources—officials, business or civic leaders, or nontraditional community activists—requires constant vigilance, curiosity, and ingenuity. Working with them for a story requires knowing the story and knowing enough about the sources to determine how they can enhance the story. A few minutes spent researching your story topic and possible sources helps inform your reporting and ultimately your producing on your news story.

BACKGROUNDING: BEFORE, DURING, AND AFTER

Research, or gathering background information and material, can make the difference between a routine news story and one that attracts an audience and keeps it reading, listening, watching, and interacting. It can mean the difference between a story that does not pass muster in terms of balance and accuracy and one that is both fair and straightforward. Gathering background helps you know the story.

Reporters who get assigned to a certain beat or area of specialty spend hours, if not days, developing background knowledge. TV correspondent Dan Harris told college students that he read several books on the Mideast before he headed out to the region for ABC News. Education reporters often subscribe to specialty newspapers and magazines, such as the *Chronicle of Higher Education*, *Education Week*, and *American School Board Journal*. Health and medicine reporters read medical journals. For many journalists, this type of backgrounding is considered "walk-around" knowledge, basic information that keeps them prepared for any unplanned news event as well as for daily reporting challenges.

Before heading out on a story, backgrounding can help you find a good angle or approach to a story. It can help you find and refine the story idea. Backgrounding can also help you seek out the best people to talk to for a story. It can help you find primary sources.

During the reporting of a story, backgrounding can help focus observations and interviewing. It can provide insights into the nuances of a story. For example, a reporter at a legislative hearing on helmet laws can do a better job sorting out key points and information presented over several hours of testimony by knowing some of the issues and some of the people at the center of previous debates. Backgrounding can also help determine what the news from the hearing is—what information is new, unusual, or relevant, as well as what areas of conflict or agreement are developing. Backgrounding a person and a topic for an interview can help break the ice in getting someone talking and can help focus an interview in order to get quotes or sound bites that speak directly to the heart of a story.

Both during the reporting of a story and in final production, backgrounding can help in finding inconsistencies or gaps in a story or in the information someone has provided for a story. If a personal injury law expert at that helmet law hearing is interpreting the state helmet law a certain way, knowing what the law says can help determine if the person really is an expert and whether the interpretation has some merit.

Everything you read, see, or hear can help provide background for a story. The more you read and take notice of people, places, and things, the better prepared you will be for tackling stories.

Using the Internet

The rise of search engines like Google and MSN Search, librarylike compilers of articles such as LexisNexis, and people-finding sites like Switchboard and PeopleSearch have proven to be a fast and easy way to get started with finding basic information about story topics and story sources. But be aware of their limitations as well as their benefits. And understand the difference between using the Internet to formulate the reporting of a story and using the Internet to put together a story. Or as technology editor Mike Wendland said in 2002, journalists should be taught "to use the Internet as a tool rather than as a news source."[7]

The Google search engine has become so popular that a verb was coined ("to google") in its honor. The Nielsen/NetRatings ranking of search engines shows that Google, Yahoo!, and MSN Search are the top three search engines, and that Google led the list in 2004. Sree Sreenivasan, who writes a technology column for the *Columbia Journalism Review*, advocates Google as the first stop on a journalist's Web hunts. A Google search of the Internet will develop a list of websites ranked in order of relevance. Relevance for Google is determined by a mathematical formula dubbed PageRank, which includes the number of links to a particular Web page. The more links, the more relevance that site is given. So instead of just listing the number of times a phrase appears, Google massages its mathematical formula to rate websites by importance or relevance.

Additionally, Google sells space to businesses, so that a Google search develops two search result lists: a main list and a commercial list in a box on the right. This boxed list is for sites that pay for first-page notice on Google searches. Surveys of Internet search engine users in 2002 and 2004 found that nearly two-thirds of them were unaware of the difference between a sponsored and an unpaid search.[8] Internet searchers also need to be aware that various businesses and individuals try to trick search engines into giving them greater rank and position in search results by creating artificial links on a site.

Search engines like Google and Yahoo! massage their search methodology and police for what are called "optimizers," people who try to increase the likelihood of getting to the top of a search result list. Search engines also revise their rankings every few days or every few weeks. So a Google, Yahoo!, or MSN search results list changes over time. Search engines search only the Web, and some of the most relevant pieces of information may not be found on a website. Internet searches can sometimes yield thousands of results that may have little relevance to the information a journalist needs to understand the background of a story, or they may contain erroneous information. Search engines do not differentiate between credible and questionable websites; they only measure popularity. As with most information, you must judge the credibility of the source.

Despite those caveats, search engines can be used to get started in finding out more about a story idea or story sources. The key to good Web searching is being specific about what you are looking for. Use quotation marks if you are looking for an exact phrase, like "Iraq War," or the engine will look for Iraq and for war, needlessly expanding the results. SearchEngineWatch.com recommends using math signs in defining searches: use a plus sign or the word "and," for example, "Iraq War" + "journalists killed." Use the minus sign to eliminate certain terms, such as "Time Warner" – "AOL merger." Use the word "or," such as "Social Security" and "privatize" or "personal" in looking for information about President Bush's proposed changes for Social Security accounts. You can use the name of your city or town to limit a search to your locality: "Smoking Bans" + "Columbus." You can also limit the dates in a search. These basics also work in searching databases, such as LexisNexis, which can provide access to articles in major newspapers, magazines and journals, and even television transcripts for paid subscribers.

Other Background Sources

One of the best Internet resources may be human: a librarian. Librarians can provide not only research tips, since they are trained researchers, but also leads and tips to useful online databases and websites. They can guide you through government websites, such as the U.S. Census Bureau website. They also can point to printed materials that may not be consolidated effectively on the Web. For example, newspaper stories that were published before 1980 may be on microfilm or microfiche files and not available on Web-accessed databases. Local libraries also may have old phone books, which are good for checking out past contact information.

THE JOURNALISTIC TREASURE HUNT: FINDING IMAGERY

If journalists need to have a nose for news in order to find story ideas and sources, they also need to develop an eye for the visual details that bring news to life. Whether it is a print reporter who uses words to paint a picture of a town's grief following the drowning of four young boys, a television reporting team that focuses its lens on an empty refrigerator to illustrate poverty and hunger, or an online producer who develops interactive charts on hidden lead poisoning dangers, all journalists need to look for and use images in their storytelling.

The images of news are in the words, the pictures, and the sound that help an audience experience and relate to your news story. Journalists need to consider these images before they go out and report a story, by planning how pictures will add to the story and the public understanding of it. They also need to consider visuals during the reporting of a story, by taking notice of details within the news setting.

Because broadcast news demands pictures and sound, more so than print, it has developed a habit of thinking about and planning for the collection of those images as part of its story development process. In convergence-oriented newspaper newsrooms, the push is to pick up a few of the cues from broadcast; reporters are being encouraged and trained to think about graphics and pictures that should accompany their stories.

For example, traditional still photographers at the *Tampa Tribune* have been given video cameras to give them the option of using both moving and still pictures. A photo essay about life on an egg farm took on new life when the photographer gathered sound as well as visual imagery for the *Lawrence Journal-World* website. MSNBC.com took a story about airport security scanning to a different level by designing interactive animation to demonstrate the difficulty of detecting illegal items. In each of these cases, visual elements were not afterthoughts but were integral parts of the story from the beginning.

Images bring a story alive for an audience. Still pictures and video can put the audience at the scene. They can also add a dimension of authenticity and support for the information and facts presented in a story. For example, reports of U.S. soldiers being charged with abuse at Abu Ghraib prison in Iraq had surfaced in March 2004, but the story did not register public outrage until CBS's *60 Minutes II* aired pictures. Graphics can make numbers understandable and relevant. A bar graph can show change from one year to the next. Animation can show how something works. A map can familiarize the audience with a location.

Just as you map out who might be a good source for a story, journalists in all media are being asked to map out what images could enhance the audience's understanding of a story. For example, an online producer of a Spanish newspaper's website developed graphics to explain the links among suspects in the March 11, 2004, bombings of a Madrid rail station. But the stories do not need to be as dramatic as a terrorist attack. A map of the streets with the most potholes, or a bar graph showing the dramatic drop in viewership of the Oscars telecast, makes for better storytelling and better audience engagement.

Before television journalists set out to cover a story, they are expected to think about "b-roll," the various visual images on video that will be needed to help an audience see a story. The common joke is that television without pictures is radio. To do TV stories, imagery has to be a part of the story beginning with the germination of the story idea. Images of someone standing at a podium, which are the basic visuals presented at a press conference, will not do on television. Images that depict the topic of the presentation, images relating to the information being presented, images of the setting of the news conference, are just some of the visuals that could comprise b-roll. Thinking about visuals, like thinking about sources, story angles, and questions, has to be an elemental part of reporting for journalists in any distribution medium.

While some images can be planned for in storytelling, others have to be experienced and observed. Journalists need to be trained observers, able to notice changes in people, communities, and situations. They must pick up on how something is phrased and the way a person says it. Good observation can lead to interesting details in a story, questions to ask about a story, and even further stories.

Magazine and newspaper writers are encouraged to observe nuance and details. Writers need to frame the story, focusing on information that is most relevant, compelling, and interesting. Photographers also need to frame the picture, focusing on what is the most relevant, compelling, and interesting. Some basics in framing visual images for a story can serve as good ground rules in developing a good eye in framing any image—visual, textual, aural. Learning how to frame a news scene through the lens of a camera can lead to more precise observation.

To shoot still pictures or video, you need to focus on the person or object. But you also need to approach the focal point from different angles. That gives you different perspectives. Shoot a subject from the left side, the right side, and straight on. Take wide, medium, and close-up shots. You can shoot down on someone, making her seem small and diminished. Or you can shoot looking up at someone, making him come across as dominating.

A close-up shot would have the person or object fill the frame, which is traditionally a ratio of four (wide) by three (high), almost a square. A close-up is aimed at scrutinizing the subject. A close-up can help an audience understand how a person looks or reacts. A close-up brings the audience and the subject of a news story close together. Use it if it is relevant to the understanding of the story. In a car accident, you may want to capture a close-up shot of a mangled seat, or a lone shoe, thrown several feet away from the wrecked car but framed with the car in the background. That close-up provides a telling detail about the severity of the accident. If you are doing a profile, you would use the close-up during the interview, when you expect the person to reveal their inner thoughts and feelings.

The close-up underscores the idea of revelation. A close-up in text often is a detailed description of how someone acts, reacts, and looks, in an effort to reveal the person. A close-up could also describe how something sounds, moves, or changes. Details provided through visual or descriptive means can bring the audience closer to the person or situation.

A medium shot aims to be less invasive and thus less revealing. But it does give an audience a sense of a subject. A medium shot provides a frame of reference for the subject but does not probe too deeply. In still photography or television, a medium shot can show someone from the waist or knees up, hinting at distance and separation while still keeping the subject as the

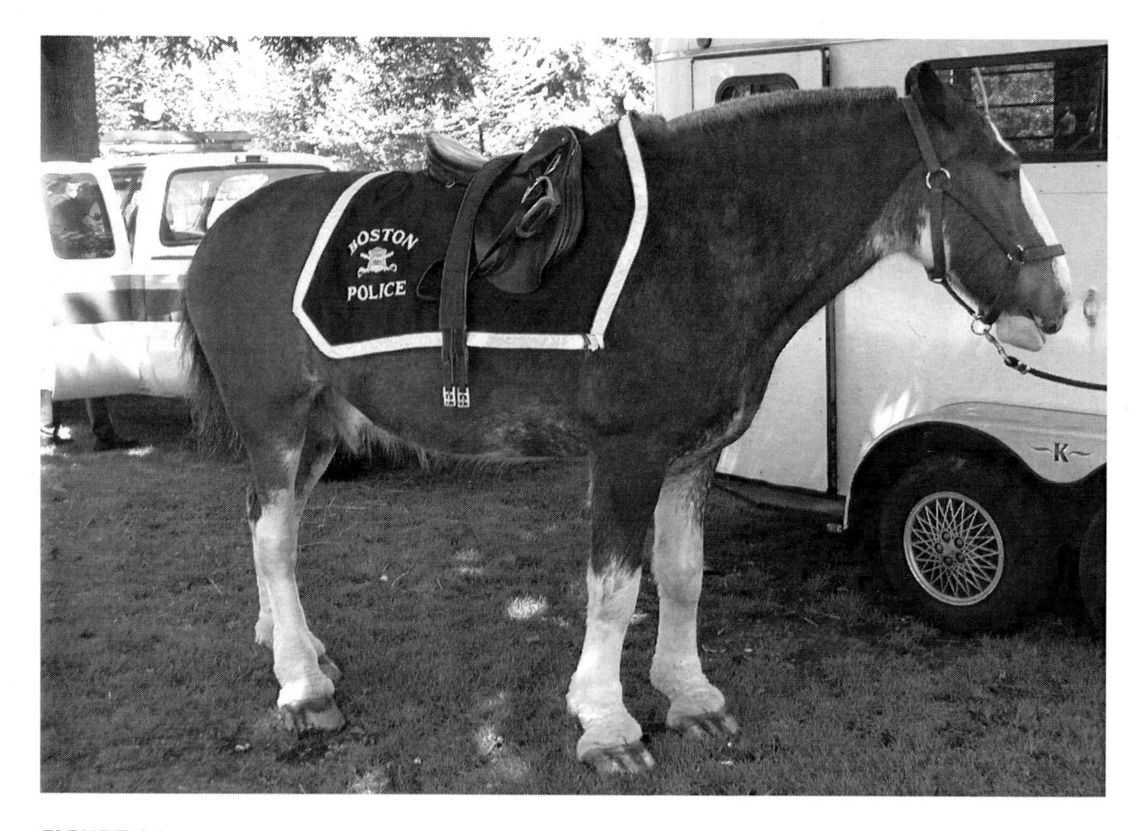

FIGURE 4.1. Wide shot. (Courtesy of David Schwab)

focus. A medium shot is neither close enough to show minute detail nor far enough to emphasize the setting more than the person in it. A lot of spot news reporting, reporting on events as they are happening, relies on the medium shot. The stories provide some detail and explanation but there is not extensive scrutiny or broad context. Basic reporting and observation is gathering that middle look at a news event.

A wide shot is often used as an establishing shot in film. It establishes the setting, the context of the subject of the story. A wide shot of a train derailment would look at the whole extent of the derailment, contrasting with a close-up detailing one area of devastating damage. Both views are needed to give the audience a better understanding of the magnitude of the derailment and its intensity. Journalists need to capture the big picture as well as the intimate portrait.

Another way of finding imagery for stories is to seek out someone to demonstrate how something happened or how they did something. Imagery is about showing, not just telling. Having someone show a crucial element of a story makes the story more human and more real. Television reporters often seek out the demonstration in an interview, as it provides

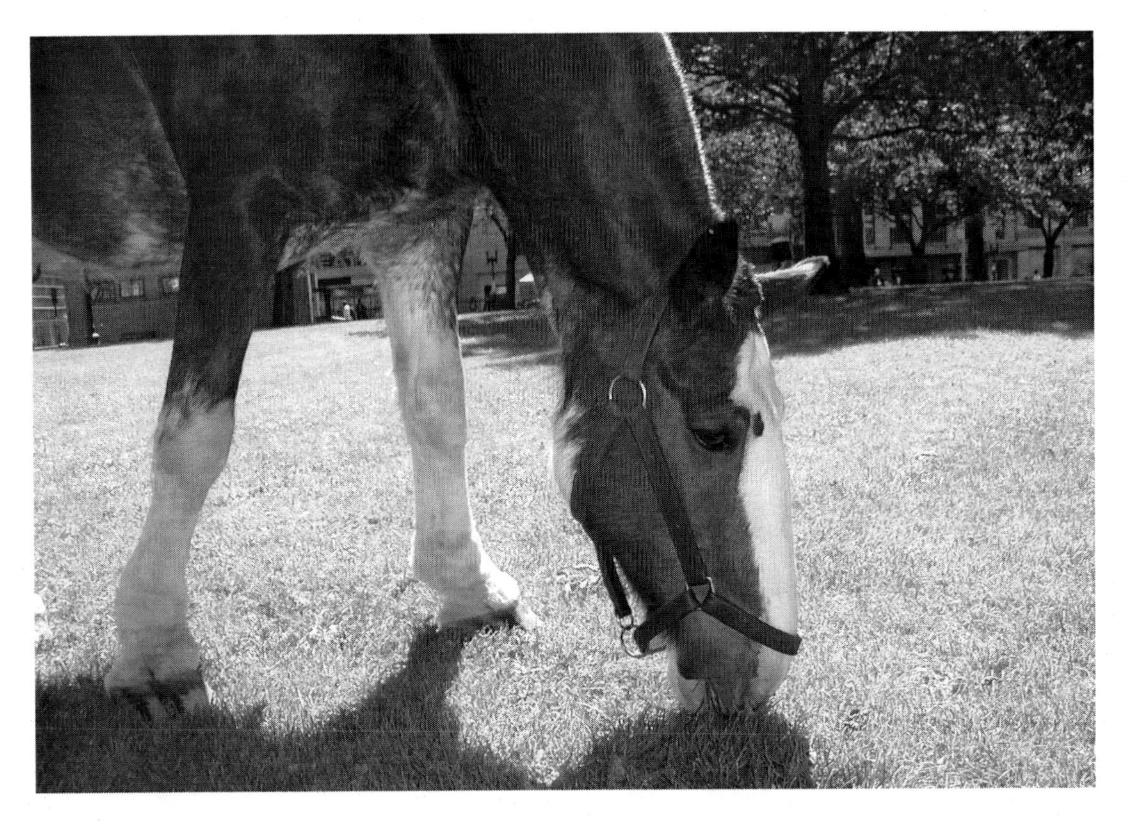

FIGURE 4.2. Close-up. (Courtesy of David Schwab)

action, something key for moving pictures. Demonstration also is a way to get people who may be uncomfortable talking to the media to relate information in a more relaxed manner. Having someone work or demonstrate their work during an interview can capture telling imagery and telling quotes.

JOURNALISTIC TREASURE HUNT: INTERVIEWING

People make a news story interesting and complete; interviews put people into stories. A good interview can yield information and insight about a person or a situation, elevating a news story from the mundane to the profound. A mediocre interview can leave a journalist scrambling to put together a story. Interviews provide quotes or sound bites to a story. Quotes or bites give a news story information, humanity, and authenticity. The best interviews get the bites that deliver all of the above. Skillful interviewing is an essential tool for all journalists, no matter if the news story appears in print, online, or on air.

Good interviewing, regardless of the medium, begins with scouting and planning. That entails knowing the story focus, knowing the interview subject, and knowing the information that might be needed from the interviewee. Barbara Walters, working on the annual pre-Oscars interview special, may have a lot of time, and lots of help, to scout and plan. Someone headed out to cover a house fire may have just a few minutes to figure out interviewing essentials.

Those essentials vary in terms of the type of interview—face-to-face or over the phone or via e-mail, in a group like at a press conference or one-on-one, confrontational or conversational—to get information and insight about a situation or information and insights about a person. Those essentials also vary in terms of the type of person being interviewed: someone accustomed to talking to reporters as opposed to someone who is not, someone who wants to talk to the media as opposed to someone who does not.

No matter the type of interview or the type of interviewee, the process is a journalistic dance, with the reporter leading the way. Few journalists get the steps down right the first few times. It takes practice and a sense of rhythm. Even seasoned reporters can make missteps by adopting the wrong tone with an interview subject, by being unfamiliar with the person or the interview topic, or by not paying attention to what the interviewee is saying. It's important to not only know the dance but to know the partner.

Preparation

Every interview is different from the one before it and the one after it because the person, the topic, the situation, and the timing all vary. Before any question is asked in an interview, answering some basic questions about the goal and focus of the interview will help in planning and shaping it.

INTERVIEW TOPIC What do you know about it? What can the interviewee tell you about it? A little knowledge can go a long way in an interview, but lack of knowledge can stop an interview in its tracks. You cannot ask good questions that elicit interesting and insightful answers if you have no idea what you need to know. If you are talking to an elementary school principal about a new reading program, know some basics of the program. If you are talking to a video game designer about trends in the industry, know something about video games. If you are talking to a firefighter at a house fire, have some idea about how fire departments respond to fires.

Having some idea about your topic sends a message to the people you are talking to that you care enough about something they care about deeply. It is a sign of respect. Starting off an interview with a line like "Tell me what you know" can seem to the person you are talking to that you are saying, "Do my job for me." Knowing something can break the ice. Often a good way to start an interview is to mention something you have read about the person or the topic.

On the television show *Inside the Actors Studio*, host James Lipton often uses tidbits of information about an actor's early career or childhood, eliciting first surprise and then a revelation.

Neal Conan of NPR has said that the best preparation for any interview is "to read all the time. We need to be information sharks. . . ."[9] Just as reading helps you find a story idea and story sources, reading can help you prepare for an interview.

INTERVIEW TYPE What do you need to get out of the interview? What does your story need from this interview? These questions help you figure out the type of interview you will be doing.

If you are at a spontaneous or breaking news event, like a house fire or car accident, you need to get details about what happened, who was involved, and what are the consequences. But if you are doing a reaction story, called a vox populi (Latin for "voice of the people") or man-on-the-street, you are looking for comments and insights about a situation, not necessarily the facts. If you are interviewing someone you are profiling, seek anecdotes and stories that reveal a person's personality and thinking. If you are at a controlled event, such as a public meeting, speech, or news conference, you may need more information about what was done or said, in addition to reaction and insight. Or you may be called upon to contact family or friends of someone whose death becomes newsworthy. This type of interview, which Gail Sedorkin and Judy McGregor call "death knocks," often involves gathering both information and insights.[10] You also may have to get a comment from someone who does not want to talk to you and has avoided you. You end up tracking them down and cornering them for a comment. These are called "ambush" interviews. Determining the desired outcome of the interview helps determine the questions that need to be asked, the tone and approach needed, and your time limitations.

INTERVIEW TIME How much time do you have? How much time does the interviewee have? The answer to the first question is easy: not enough. With only a short amount of time to get information, prepare a list of key questions that must get answered. With more time, ask more questions or more nuanced questions.

In print and radio, you can use the telephone to get comments from people in as little as five minutes. If you record an interview, most state laws require that everyone, the interviewer and the interviewee, agree to the conversation being recorded. Recorded phone interviews have limited use on television. They are most often used in breaking news settings, to get information from witnesses or officials at the scene. In television, the best interview is one that yields information and insight on camera, which takes more time than a telephone call. For television, a telephone pre-interview is used to set up a face-to-face, on-camera interview. The pre-interview determines if the interviewee can deliver tight, relevant, interesting, and quotable material for air. If a pre-interview goes well, you may decide to take a little more time to do a face-to-face interview.

You also need to think about your interviewee's time limitations. He or she may have more time to talk to you at the beginning of the day, or after a meeting wraps up, or right before lunch. He or she may be more available in the middle of the week rather than at the beginning or end. While you may have no choice but to call and interrupt someone, often someone will be more willing to talk to you when there is a break in their schedule. Reporters hate to get phone calls close to deadline; the people they need to talk to have the same concern. Knowing when to call for an interview can make interviewing easier.

On-the-spot interviews are also constrained by time: yours and the interviewees'. They may want to leave or get back to work, and your questions are keeping them from doing so. In a police story, an arresting officer may be your best source of information. At a fire, the firefighter who went in the building first might be the person you would like to talk to. But they may be busy doing their job. In large cities, police and fire departments limit media access to public information officers or to the police chief or sheriff, who may not have precise details to enliven a story.

When time is limited, learn not to waste it with long or convoluted questions. Two-part questions, questions with introductions, or those that require explanations all take time and should be avoided. At a presidential press conference, for example, long, multipart questions rarely get completely or effectively answered. At a crime or accident scene or at a disaster situation, unfocused questions can result in bland, pat answers. If time is tight, plan simple, straightforward questions that take as little time as necessary to ask, leaving as much time as possible for someone to answer them.

INTERVIEW SUBJECT AND SITUATION A few seconds spent thinking about the person you are interviewing and the situation that person is in will help establish the approach and tone. You need to determine if the person is a public figure dealing with public issues or private ones. Is the person someone who has never dealt with the news media? Is it someone who wants to talk to reporters or someone who is reluctant? Journalists may come across to uninitiated interviewees as callous, nosy, or obnoxious when they fail to see the person they are talking to as a person and not merely a quick quote or sound bite. Determining the type of person being interviewed and the situation he or she is in can make an interview easier.

In general, public figures or officials should be ready to take any and all questions about public issues; that is their job. Your tone and approach to a public figure about a public issue could be confrontational, aggressive, light-hearted, conspiratorial, respectful, or deferential, depending on the information needed and whether the person is willing and able to provide it.

If the public person, be it a celebrity, sports figure, public official, or political leader, wants to talk to the media or has an agenda or point to promote, then an interview can become a verbal tug of war between the reporter and the news subject, as each tries to pull the interview in a different direction. And public figures may be reluctant to talk about private issues.

Lawrence Grobel, in writing about interviewing famous people, notes that celebrities use their publicists to set limits and demands. He recounts how Barbra Streisand required interviewers to sign a document giving all rights to an interview to her. He also notes that actress Jodie Foster prohibited questions about John Hinkley, the man obsessed with Foster and convicted of shooting President Reagan.[11]

Publicists and consultants also provide coaching in handling the news media and interviews. George Merlis, a former television executive producer and media coach, writes about five basic "commandments" in dealing with the media. At the top of his list, he encourages his clients to be prepared for an interview by having a story or message to get across when talking to reporters. "Knowing what you will and won't say is fundamental to media success,"[12] he writes. In preparing for an interview, you need to determine how savvy you need to be in getting information by assessing how savvy your interviewee may be in controlling it.

On the other side of the spectrum are private individuals thrust into the news by an event. They may find themselves in completely unfamiliar territory and may be hesitant to deal with reporters. But an old saying, "You catch more flies with honey than with vinegar," generally applies in those situations. A little respect, empathy, and sweetness goes a long way in getting someone to talk. It sometimes can work, too, with public figures who are reluctant to talk. What works best depends on the person and the situation.

Questions

Journalists may disagree about how many questions you should prepare ahead of time, but they all prepare them. They also all agree that the questions you ask must inform the questions your story is expected to answer: the five Ws and H. All news stories need to tell their audiences who, what, when, where, why, and how. To get answers to those questions that you can use as quotes or sound bites, you need to ask the questions that get someone to talk. You want to avoid closed-ended questions that can be answered with one word or dismissed with a yes or no. You want open-ended questions, such as: How did this happen? What did you see/do? What were your first thoughts? Why did you want to try this? Questions that begin with how or why make for good open-ended questions.

You also want to avoid leading questions, which in essence put yours words in someone else's mouth, questions that are loaded with value judgments. Interviews, whether at press conferences or one-on-one sit-downs, are conversations with a purpose: to reveal interesting and pertinent information. But that revelation needs to come from the person being interviewed and for your audience, not from you or for you.

The types of questions you need to ask and the tone you take depend on how you answered the questions about the purpose and timing of your interview.

Listening

During the interview, new questions may pop up and should pop up. Listen to what is being said and how. Listen to what is not being said. Listening requires keeping quiet and paying attention.

The point is to hear someone else's voice, perspective, and information and to challenge only when that information does not ring true. That is why short, open-ended questions work best. They open the door for the interviewee's voice. They allow for the person being interviewed to fill the silence. Keeping quiet is especially important in broadcast interviews; a microphone picks up verbal encouragement (such as "Uh-huh" and "Oh really?") and can ruin a sound bite by drowning out a word or two. By keeping quiet, you can pay attention to what is being said.

When Katie Couric of *The Today Show* interviewed the brother of a victim of the 1999 Columbine High School shooting, she asked at most a half-dozen questions over almost fifteen minutes, not interrupting, letting the story unfold, leaning in to encourage the brother, but saying little. The brother filled the silence.

Sometimes a response does not provide the information you think you need. If the first way you ask a question leads to an evasive answer, rephrase it and ask again. Or if you did not understand or could not follow the answer, ask for a clarification or explanation. The person being interviewed may also want another opportunity to answer the question, as they may feel their response was wordy or inadequate.

The answer to one question, however, may reveal a topic or idea that requires further explanation or follow-up. Paying attention to what is being said allows for an interview to take another and quite possibly more interesting path. Too often an interviewer sticks to a prepared list of questions and fails to hear when a gem of a quote or idea gets uttered. Paying attention to how something is said can also lead an interview into new, more relevant, or more interesting territory. It can give you clues about inconsistencies.

Two questions should always be in a reporter's repertoire, and they should come toward the end of an interview. They are: Is there anything you would like to add that I did not ask? and Who else would you recommend that I talk to? These two questions can lead to a topic or point that you may not have thought about but that could be pertinent, and they can provide a perspective that your questions may not have focused on.

Note Taking

Note taking can complement listening in interviewing. It can help a reporter stay focused. But like listening, it is a skill that most journalists end up learning by trial and error. Note taking is an integral part of almost every type of interview. It can also help a reporter organize his or her story. And it helps speed up the writing and producing of a news story. Note taking skills develop when taking notes becomes an unconscious habit.

Reporters first must decide when to take notes. The mere sight of a note pad, a camera, or a microphone can terrify people and make them refuse to talk. Some television reporters, particularly when they have to speak to family members of someone who has been killed, first approach a front door without the accoutrements of the reporter: the note pad is in the purse or pocket, the camera and microphone is in the bag, or the camera operator is standing at a distance. Once a person starts to talk, the reporting gear comes out. Sometimes reporters who are working in print will observe a situation and talk with people only to take notes afterward, relying on what they remember was done or said.

Generally, however, note taking sends a signal to people at the center of your reporting that you are indeed a reporter and they are a part of your story. Note taking signals that what they say and what they do are on the record. Thus note taking can help reinforce the ground rules of reporting.

Ground rules for an interview need to be set at the start. You need to make it clear to the person you are talking to what those rules are. The vast majority of reporting should be on the record, for use in a story, with full name attribution, to provide audiences with a clear idea as to the sources of the information in a news story. If one of the basic tenets of good journalism is transparency in knowing where information comes from, then on-the-record sourcing provides that. Once something is said on the record, it should not and cannot become off the record. Most public officials understand this, but sometimes a person says something on the record and then asks that it not be used in any way for a news story. Here is where individual ethics come into play; the reporter must balance the need for the information against the need to keep the source of the information as a source for future stories. A reporter should aim for every piece of information to be on the record and should work to encourage that, but that resolve is often tested and abandoned in doing daily journalism.

Off the record means just that; the information does not get used. Many government officials allow information they provide reporters to be used in stories provided the attribution of that information does not include their name but may include a general identification, such as "a White House official" or "a Senate aide." They may refer to this as being "on background" or "not for attribution." This is sourcing the information while allowing the source to remain anonymous, and it raises ethical and credibility issues when used.

Once you decide you need to take notes, how you take them depends on the individual. Most journalists develop their own shorthand for common words. They may drop articles such as "a," "an," or "the." They may refer to persons by their initials and use abbreviations for often-used words. The last thing you want to do is spend time searching through a recording or relistening to an entire interview. Note taking, along with good listening in interviews,

BOX 4.5

Note Taking Tips

As an education reporter, I would abbreviate curriculum to "curr," superintendent to "supt," junior high school to "jhi," and so on. I also developed little notations along the way to highlight certain points in my notes. I would always mark a star next to a sentence or quote that I sensed was a point well-stated, dramatic, or interesting. When I was recording an interview, I would also try to note the time I asked a question. With that star, when I heard something good, I had a general idea where that quote or comment could be found.

can help you process the information you have in order to determine what information you need for your story.

JOURNALISTIC TREASURE HUNT: FINDING THE FOCUS

The search for the focus of a story begins with the hunt for the story idea and continues through the news-gathering process. By the time the story is ready to be produced, the focus of the story may have emerged. But often the focus can still seem a bit fuzzy. The next and perhaps most crucial step of reporting and producing a news story may be among the hardest to learn: thinking. While there are techniques to help find a story focus, the key is to stop and think about the story before you start putting it together.

One way to think about the focus of a story is to think about how you find the focus when aiming a camera. One of the first lessons in handling a video camera is setting the focus. It requires the shooter to zoom in as close as possible on a person's eye. If that eye is so clear, so well-defined, that the iris shows many colors, and if the eyelashes are so distinct they can be counted, then the eye is in focus, and the shooter can zoom out and be confident the subject of the video is in focus.

The same holds true in a news story. If the reporter finds the focus, the rest of the story will fall into place. But finding the focus of a story, just as in video, is not a one-time event. The focus of the story needs to be set during the idea stage, rechecked at the reporting stage, and checked again at the production stage. Sometimes the focus of a news story never changes from the idea stage to the writing and editing stage. Sometimes it needs slight adjustments. But developing a good news story always involves finding the focus of the story and consistently and periodically checking it out to ensure that the center, the subject of the story, remains clear and in sight.

The first time you should begin seeking the focus of the story is in the idea stage. A story idea can come from observation, reading previous stories, a source tip, a news release, a police scanner, a court docket, a budget, or a report, to name just a few. But to find the focus of a story, you need to determine not just the topic of your story, your story idea, but the point or purpose of it. For example, you might have an idea for a story about the one-year anniversary of the citywide smoking ban in all public places, including bars and restaurants. This would be a follow-up story. But what exactly are you following up on? What is the purpose of the story?

The purpose could be to see how bars and restaurants, and their workers, have adjusted to a smoke-free environment. Or the story could be aimed at finding out what smokers are doing, and where they are going, now that they cannot light up in bars and restaurants. Or the story could focus on the rise of private smoking clubs and bars designed to accommodate smokers.

Just like the videographer zooming in to find the focus of a picture, the reporter can zoom in on several themes or topics in trying to get to the focus of a story. In seeking out a focus, follow the example of the videographer by looking for something that has nuance and detail. To find the focus of a story, look for a person, or several people, or an activity, or a discussion that allows you to zoom in from the large and fuzzy idea to see an angle or aspect that helps clarify the larger idea. To find the focus, think about your audience and the outlets for your story. If your audience for the smoking ban follow-up story is readers of a magazine for cigar smokers, then the rise of smoking clubs might make a better story focus.

The first step to finding a story's focus is to think about several different themes, to brainstorm. You can brainstorm by yourself, or you can bounce your ideas off other people. But brainstorming allows you to take your topic and examine different themes or points to explore in your story. The best brainstorming ends up with several possible areas of focus. Brainstorming can involve just writing down ideas, the more ideas the better. Do not worry if the ideas might seem silly or implausible; you are seeking multiple themes or ideas so you can choose the best. That list of angles on the smoking ban anniversary, for example, was brainstorming.

A more graphic, visual form of brainstorming involves story mapping. You start out with your main idea or topic at the center of the page and then put down around it all the various aspects and angles you think might be interesting and worthwhile for your audience. Just like a jigsaw puzzle, some pieces of news-gathering will fit together with others, and a pattern of prominent or tangential themes may emerge.

For most journalists, the hard part is determining what needs to get left out because of time and space limitations. Most stories cannot include all the anecdotes, every clever quote, all the descriptive detail, or even all the sources interviewed or researched. Here is where news judgment comes into play and where notes help in sorting through the important and the memorable. Through story mapping, you can also see what news-gathering pieces fit together, as well as the central theme or focus of those pieces.

BOX 4.6

Story Mapping: An Example

As the education reporter for the *Plain Dealer* in Cleveland, I was faced with a "first day of school" story every year. In mapping out some ideas, I thought about stories about the first day for a new teacher, a new principal, or a new student, the cost of school supplies for teachers and for students, school dress codes, repairs on the schools, training of new bus drivers and new routes, new curriculum changes beginning that year, the first day of school for high school freshmen, and returning teachers. I ended up one year with a story of a school administrator who returned to the classroom after more than a decade away and her first-day jitters.

Sometimes a story requires very little brainstorming to find its focus, although it requires some thought or reflection. In breaking news or events stories, that thought and reflection might last only a few seconds or minutes. For a story about the crash of a bus carrying disabled students, the focus is on what happened to the students. If they all escaped injury, the focus is on how that happened. When confronted with this story, Boston Fox 25 reporter Glenn Jones found that the focus of his story was how the bus's hitting a tree actually saved the lives of a group of students in the accident. The tree prevented the bus from falling into water, where some of the students with severe disabilities would have likely drowned.

Finding the focus helps shape the reporting of the story, although sometimes the focus changes during the reporting, The focus of Jones's bus accident story did not start out to be on the tree, but it was something that he learned through observation, listening, and interviewing. The tree was a detail that Jones could not forget. Often during reporting, a detail that stands out helps you center or pinpoint your story. It also helps you in producing your story.

A focus statement can help you think how you should organize your story. A focus statement should be no more than one or two sentences. It should succinctly tell what your story is about. Often it can help you formulate your lead or opening. For the smoking ban story, a focus statement could be: New private clubs are cropping up to cater to smokers left out in the cold by the city's year-old public smoking ban. For the bus accident, the focus statement could be: Police and parents say a tree may have saved the lives of a bus full of disabled students. A focus statement aims to answer the five Ws and H as well as "So what?" It outlines a story's theme and approach. In each of the examples, the focus statement states an action but also a cause, effect, or reason.

Focus statements can be a part of a larger explanation of a story: a story memo. For a daily news story, a story memo can be short, just a few sentences, so it can be included in the day's budget for the newscast, newspaper, or website. For more extensive stories, it could be a page or two. A story memo is designed to "sell" your story to an editor or producer. But it really is a sales pitch to your audience, with the editor or producer representing the thinking of the people you want to reach with your story. A story memo includes information about what the story is about, what you already know, what you need to know, who you have talked to and still need to talk to, what images can and should be gathered, and ways you can engage the audience in the story, such as interactive forums, demonstrations, and games. A story memo helps put down on paper your thinking about the various elements of storytelling and helps organize them.

Chip Scanlan, a writing coach at the Poynter Institute, a program aimed to enhance the journalism profession, uses five questions to help practicing reporters find the focus of their stories. Scanlan attributes the first four questions to *Washington Post* reporter David von Drehle; Scanlan added a fifth:

1. Why does this story matter?
2. What is the point?
3. Why are we telling this story?
4. What does this story say about us and our world?
5. What is the story really about, in one word?[13]

By answering those questions, a universal theme can emerge, making the telling of the story easier to do.

Once you have found your story idea, your sources, your information, and your focus, you just might be ready to start thinking about putting together all the images of news to produce a story for your audience.

BOX 4.7

Approaching a Story: Convergence Thinking

Tom Farrey began his journalism career in newspapers, spending nearly eight years at the *Seattle Times* before heading east. These days, he does his journalism on all platforms—online, on television, and in print—for ESPN. He sees convergence as a plus, not just for his audience—sports fans—but for himself as a reporter. When Farrey works on a story for *ESPN the Magazine*, he is also working on a story for ESPN the sports network and ESPN

continued

FIGURE 4.3. Tom Farrey, ESPN. (Courtesy of ESPN)

the website, gaining reporting insight and perspective from producers and designers along the way.

By working in a team and for different media, Farrey says he has developed nuances in the way he approaches reporting for a story, interviewing for a story, and ultimately producing and writing a story. "I'm thinking as a multimedia reporter," Farrey says, adding, "It's a lot of coordination and strategy."

On approaching a story, Farrey keeps in mind the storytelling goals of each medium. "The thinking in magazines is of scene setting, anecdotal material," so he works on looking and getting that kind of material. But when he is thinking about online, he thinks about getting notes for "chat sessions" for example. "I'm always thinking about all three [platforms] in terms of content as well as when to do certain interviews and to gather certain information," he says. Reporting in multiple media means doing the reporting work concurrently as opposed to consecutively. "It's not like you can get the online series done and then focus on TV."

Farrey has given a lot of thought to the pacing and the timing of interviews for his stories in terms of making them work for all media. He notes that if he needs to ask someone a tough question, and is only doing a print story, he could do it in a telephone interview. But if he tries to get the person to answer that tough question again on camera, he might be out of luck. "When TV is in the picture, I often save the tough questions for in front of the camera, and that changes the arc of my reporting," Farrey says. Because of that, sometimes key interviews for a story might not get done until very late in the reporting process, and he has found that he has had to scramble a bit to add the information.

Still, Farrey notes that while the content of his stories on the different ESPN platforms is similar, each medium affords him a different way of reaching sports audiences. "The writing in my magazine piece is authoritative, scene setting," he says, while online gives him space to put information he could not squeeze into his television report or magazine story. Plus, the cross-promotion of the different ESPN outlets opens up his story to wider audiences. "You have to step away from that selfish competitive impulse," of worrying about which medium breaks the story, he says, and realize a story can work in all media. "It's got to be a real cooperative venture from the get-go."

Source: Tom Farrey, interview by author, May 2005.

BOX 4.8

Approaching the Story: Convergence of One

Kevin Sites might be considered the poster boy for what he calls "SoJos," solo journalists. Since 2001, when he was handed the digital technology (camera, computer, satellite videophone) to go out and report in places like Afghanistan, Indonesia, and Iraq, Sites has been putting together stories for television, mostly for NBC News, and for the Web, for his blog, www.kevinsites.net.

SoJos may be the ultimate embodiment of the convergence strategy: one person reporting and distributing news to diverse audiences along various formats or platforms. But Sites cautions that SoJos are just one way of doing convergence, and not necessarily the only way. "I think this is one aspect of the tool chest that we really need to delve into as we progress with electronic journalism." Every journalist, Sites argues, needs to have a basic understanding of all the skills to work in various media—print, broadcast, or

continued

online—whether the journalist will be reporting in multiple media on every story or not. Sites says that understanding the different news-gathering needs of print, online, and television makes for better journalism.

"You basically enlarge the reporting net a bit more," he says. Because Sites worked in television as a field producer before going solo, he had to enlarge his net to capture the details and additional information needed for text. He still starts out his reporting thinking about getting the visuals, "making sure you've got several interviews on camera and that you've got all the visual elements you need to do a [television] package." But the difference Sites finds in the reporting is in having to gather information that often gets passed over for a ninety-second or two-minute television piece. "Yes, I need all these visual elements for a TV story, but additionally I need to get details, and the spelling has to be precise. All those things that a print reporter has to get I have to get as well." On the other hand, he adds, a print reporter who starts recording video and audio images has the advantage of being able to be precise in interviews and descriptions because he does not have to rely on what he remembers or jots down. But being a SoJo has its limitations, Sites notes, because you often do not have the time to get all the information or visuals you want or the freedom to talk with a source while a videographer is gathering the visual elements

Sometimes Sites worked on stories that did not come together for a television report but that he felt still could and should be told. The Web liberated some of that storytelling, as Sites found still pictures to be a very powerful storytelling tool. A story he did that appeared as a May 3, 2003, blog started out as a television story, and he transmitted it via videophone but it did not air, as other events were happening in Iraq. He ended up blogging the story about how a group of Marines reacted to a roadside bomb that barely missed their patrol, using the captured stills from the video that did not air and making a powerful sequence of images intermixed with the text of the story.

Working as a solo journalist has also liberated some of his reporting, Sites has found, as people see SoJos as less intrusive and less elite. With a big TV camera, story subjects would act "like deer in the headlights or PR pros." But with a smaller camera at his side, Sites says he is able to make eye contact and get people to talk with him. And in covering the war, soldiers respected the fact that he was toting his own gear and getting dirty and sweaty, just like them. One result of that was access.

Sites's access to the 101st Airborne division during an offensive in Fallujah in November 2004 earned him both controversy and kudos. While reporting as an embedded reporter with that division, a group of soldiers encountered a handful of wounded insurgents inside a mosque. During the encounter, one soldier saw one insurgent move and opened fire on the injured man, killing him. Sites captured the encounter on videotape.

FIGURE 4.4. Solo journalist Kevin Sites. (Courtesy of Kevin Sites)

"I'm pretty aggressive when I'm out there and I'm a one-man band, and I get into places other people won't be able to get into," Sites says, especially places that would be difficult for a television correspondent with a crew. His report on the encounter aired two days later on NBC as a packaged report, but the video was part of a pool sent out and available to other news agencies to air. The video created a firestorm about U.S. actions in Iraq and led to Sites losing his SoJo reporting privileges as an embedded reporter. He used his blog to explain how he came to tell the story of the encounter, for which he won the 2005 Payne Awards for Ethics in Journalism.

While Sites is a convert to solo journalism, or what Jane Stevens has called backpack journalism, others are not. Sites says that traditional journalists worry that SoJos lessen the production value of TV news stories and result in job losses. The best use of SoJos so far has been in covering war or natural disasters, Sites says. "The more chaotic the story and more hostile the environment, the more likely viewers and television people are to accept lower production values," as just having a story at all becomes essential.

The key Sites has found to being a journalist in any outlet is to focus on the story, the narrative, "otherwise you're gathering strings on a number of different incidents." Journalists need to not only say what is happening but give their audiences information as to where it goes from there, Sites says—the action, reaction, and result. "Once I understood the narrative, everything became so much easier" like the visual information gathering and the writing of the story. The narrative is "the big picture to have all the other things makes sense."

Source: Kevin Sites, interview by author, May 2005.

SUMMARY

Journalists need to know the story, the audience, and the media they are using to be effective storytellers. To do that, journalists use simple research techniques to background story ideas and the sources for those stories. Journalists use every means available, not just the Internet, to find necessary information to help them understand the topics and the people at the focus of their reporting.

Story ideas can come from observing everyday life, reading the news and finding questions left unanswered, checking out the comings and goings of government agencies, and getting tips from people in any and every walk of life. Most news stories are developed from primary sources, although secondary sources can be helpful in providing background information.

Interviewing, observation, and note taking are primary tools of news-gathering. Observation aims at providing imagery of a situation or a person. Imagery can come in words, pictures, or sound. Interviews can provide not only information for a story but insight into the reason for a story. Interviews put people at the center of the storytelling. Note taking helps journalists listen in interviews and keep track of key points in gathering imagery. Note taking helps keep reporting organized and on target.

The final critical step in story reporting is thinking. Before a story can be produced in any medium, journalists need to stop and think about the universal theme or focus of their story. Writing a focus statement or story mapping can help organize material to determine a story's focus.

LEARNING THE LINGO

Beat book
Civic mapping
Close-up shot
Off the record
On background
PageRank
Primary source
Secondary source
Story mapping
VNRs
Wide shot

NOTES

1. Jerry Schwartz, *Associated Press Reporting Handbook* (New York: Associated Press, 2002), 32.

2. *Webster's Ninth Collegiate Dictionary*, s.v. "read."

3. "Internet IQ Checklist for Journalists," May 31, 2002, at www.poynter.org (accessed November 30, 2005).

4. Mark Douglas, presentation at Tapping New Data Territories workshop, Tampa, Florida, Feb. 23, 2004.

5. "Broaden Your Source Base," February 7, 2004, at www.journalism.org/resources/tools/reporting/politics/sourcebase.asp (accessed November 30, 2005).

6. Brant Houston, Len Bruzzese, and Steve Weinberg, *The Investigative Reporter' Handbook: A Guide to Documents, Databases and Techniques*, 4th ed. (New York: Bedford/St. Martin's, 2004), 6.

7. www.poynter.org/column.asp?id=34&aid=2663 (May 31, 2002, accessed November 30, 2005).

8. Deborah Fallows, "Search Engine Users: Internet search engine searchers are confident, satisfied and trusting—but they are also unaware and naïve," January 23, 2005, at www.pewinternet.org/PPF/r/146/report_display.asp (accessed December 8, 2005).

9. "The Art of the Interview," July 11, 2002, at poynteronline.org/content/content_view.asp?id=9572 (accessed November 30, 2005).

10. Gail Sedorkin and Judy McGregor, *Interviewing: A Guide for Journalists and Writers* (New York: Allen & Unwin, 2002), 5.

11. Lawrence Grobel, *The Art of the Interview* (New York: Three Rivers Press, 2004), 73–74.

12. George Merlis, *How to Make the Most of Every Media Appearance* (New York: McGraw-Hill, 2004), 26.

13. Chip Scanlon, "Selling the Power of Focus," November 24, 2003, at www.poynter.org/column.asp?id=52&aid=55118 (accessed November 30, 2005).

FIVE

Broadcast Basics: Write Simply, Think Visually

BROADCAST NEWS is not as simple or as easy as it looks. While the writing requires fewer sentences and words, it also requires those sentences and words to be focused and precise. While its stories are enhanced with pictures and sound, those pictures and that sound must provide meaning and description.

A good broadcast news story uses sound and pictures to put the audience at the scene. It uses words for narration to explain the meaning of the event. Good pictures provide the foundation of a good television story, and good sound provides the basis of a good radio story. But good writing provides the mortar that holds them together. A broadcast story organizes and layers the best materials, such as narration, sound bites, ambient or natural sound, pictures, animation, and graphics, to build a strong, cohesive report.

Broadcast news places technical as well as informational demands in gathering the best materials. The key tools of the trade, the microphone and the camera, are much more intrusive, cumbersome, and distracting than the pad and pencil. But they are essential to providing the emotion and the immediacy audiences expect. Audiences expect broadcast stories to sound good and look good. If a broadcast story has the information but not the sound or the visuals, it lacks the materials necessary to best capitalize on its unique way of storytelling.

That is why broadcast news stories are more complicated to report and put together than stories relying on text alone. For example, a simple story about a house fire for television requires pictures of flames, rubble, firefighters, and fire trucks. It should have sound bites or quotes from the fire chief, residents of the house, and the neighbors. Of course, it also needs basic factual information about people killed, hurt, and homeless, how the fire started, when

BOX 5.1

Print versus Broadcast

When I was a print education reporter working alongside radio and television reporters, I would never have thought they could teach me anything about journalism. I spent a lot of time being annoyed with them, having to squeeze past TV and radio microphones and cameras so I could get close enough to hear what someone was saying. I did not think many of them thoroughly backgrounded the story or the key people they were interviewing, so they asked simplistic questions. I thought they relied on me, the beat reporter, to fill them in on what they needed to know. I hated the way sources would either clam up or gush for the microphone or camera, so I would wait until they were alone to get the "real" story or reaction.

When I heard or watched the broadcast story, I thought about how little they had to write and do to put it on air (maybe 200 words?), while I had to write so much more. Broadcast journalists were my enemy and my inferiors. Or so I thought.

Then I became a television news writer and a producer, and the limitations of time, sound, and visuals brought a new appreciation of the difficulty of good broadcast storytelling. I saw how I got away with some flabby writing in print: stories that lacked focus or were bogged down by lack of clarity. I realized the impact of images and the challenges in getting them.

it started, damages, and how long it took to get it out. A good broadcast story relies on every element, on several pieces of news material gathered, to relay information to audiences.

A bad broadcast story throws out bits of information, using pictures and sound to entice audiences but never tying them together. It leaves audiences asking more questions than when the story began. Worse, it leaves them not caring or remembering anything. Broadcast stories, because of their inherent need for simplicity, cannot disguise their lack of organization or lack of focus. Those flaws are apparent to anyone who hears or sees them.

The lack of connection between the elements of a broadcast story also is apparent when news is delivered on air for everyone to see and hear. When a broadcast story relies on great pictures but lacks the information to explain what they mean, the pictures lose relevance. For example, the initial pictures of the devastating December 26, 2004, tidal wave that engulfed the coastlines of nearly a dozen South Asian and African countries, showed buildings, trees, and people being swept away by the force of the water. But as dramatic as those pictures were, audiences needed to hear about the number of countries hit by the disaster and the number of people killed and missing to fully grasp the enormity of the disaster. The pictures gained greater meaning to news audiences because of the additional information provided by the words. The pictures also gained greater meaning to audiences when people heard the rush of the water and the eerie silence that followed the devastation. With the elements of a broadcast story, audiences can experience the news as well as understand it.

This chapter begins a discussion of the basic skills needed to produce news in different media. Broadcast storytelling leads off because its writing format is simple and focused. But do not be fooled. Its presentation format is complex, requiring multiple elements—words plus sound for radio, words plus sound plus pictures for television. Learning the basics of broadcast news can make all writing more straightforward and succinct. It also helps in using images and visuals in storytelling.

Writing for broadcast requires a lot of discipline to see good results; it is sort of like putting writing on a diet. Years of writing essays, e-mails, and term papers may have led to some unhealthy writing habits: binges of adverbs and adjectives, flabby verbs that need toning, addiction to complex sentences. The broadcast writing "diet" aims to cleanse your system of all the bad writing habits you have adopted over the years. By abstaining from them in broadcast, you may discover that all your writing can be healthier.

Broadcast writing has to be simple and focused because it is heard, not read. One of the tricks writing teachers suggest to students is to read their writing aloud. Words sound different when heard rather than read, because they often are heard just once. If they are not heard clearly, they will not be understood. Disorganization and a lack of information cannot be disguised in a broadcast story. If you cannot follow the story when you hear it, it is disorganized and unfocused.

As any actor knows, the meaning of a sentence can be radically changed by placing the emphasis on different words within that sentence. The meaning can be lost if a word is left out or mispronounced. In broadcast news, the audience needs to hear the words, not just see them. Broadcast news writing entails giving words a voice, one that is clear, concise, and conversational.

In addition to the voice of the storyteller, broadcast journalism can give voice to the people and places in the news. In this chapter we discuss the basics of using the sound of people and the sound of places. Then we work with how a moving picture adds not just a voice but an image to the understanding of news.

BROADCAST WRITING

If print news writing can be compared to prose, broadcast writing can be thought of as the poetry of news writing. Good broadcast writing is nonfiction storytelling with rhythm. Good broadcast writing needs to be short so the information can be grasped in quick chunks. It needs to be simple so it can be understood when first heard. And it needs to be strong to catch the audience's attention.

FIGURE 5.1. Inside the Northwest Cable News newsroom. (Photo by the author)

Broadcast writing might seem like the Rodney Dangerfield of news writing in that it gets no respect. Bad broadcast writing tends to draw more attention than the good, and obviously it draws more ridicule. Like bad poetry, bad broadcast writing can be easily found and painful to hear. Bad writing for broadcast, in an attempt to be short and simple, lacks creativity and relies on hackneyed, overworked words and phrases: The latest information is a new development, the latest deadly car accident is a tragedy, and the latest political dispute or conflict is a controversy. In an attempt to be strong, bad broadcast writing uses hype and alarm to gain attention: The newest medical finding may be the long-awaited cure, and the latest violence is a blood-letting. In an attempt to be clever, bad broadcast writing relies on forced puns and humor.

Good broadcast writing often does not call attention to itself because it enhances the storytelling without distracting from it. It lets the pictures and the sound of a story stand out.

"The purpose of television writing is to tell a story, not to call attention to the writing," writes Bob Schieffer, anchor for the *CBS Evening News* and *Face the Nation*, in his 2003 memoir of the news business. "To me the test of good television writing is when we combine pictures with clear declarative sentences to tell the story in such a way that the story, not the writing is remembered."[1]

Unlike poetry, in which audiences can ponder the meaning of the words and why the author chose them, the poetry of broadcast writing requires clarity, because a news audience does not have the time or the inclination to ponder what the writer is trying to say. The broadcast writer generally has one chance to get the story across to listeners and viewers. The good broadcast news writer always thinks about how the story will sound to someone else, aiming to make it sound natural and conversational.

Keeping It Simple

Making a broadcast story sound effortless takes a lot of work. The story must contain all the key information, but not so much information as to lose the listener. It must sound like a conversation, but each thought must be tied to the next and not ramble the way informal conversations tend to do. It must rely on familiar phrases but not get caught up in clichés. It cannot talk down to listeners or confuse them by its complexity.

Beginning broadcast writers tend to complain that the format allows for little creativity: no flourishes of phrases, cleverness of clauses, or details of description. The true creativity in broadcast writing is to work within its limits to provide nuance and context to a news story. That creativity involves finding a detail that represents a larger trend, seeking out the strongest, most accurate verbs to represent the best tone and emotion, and weeding out all but the most relevant information to help audiences understand a story. That creativity involves tying together information so that a listener can follow what is happening, even when they know nothing about a situation. Broadcast news requires simple sentence structure and simple story organization.

STARTING STRONG The lead, or opening sentence, of a news story provides key information, attracts someone to listen, and sets the tone for the entire report. In broadcast news, the lead is one sentence long. It contains many of the five Ws (who, what, when, where, why) but may not have all of them. The lead follows a simple sentence structure. It uses the active voice, and it is generally in present tense. Questions and quotations make for weak leads, as does any variation of the phrase "there is."

A broadcast story begins with a simple, declarative sentence. In that sentence, the listener gets basic information and an indication of what is to come. The lead of a news story must entice the listener to keep listening. Lead writers need to avoid the "So what?" factor, when a listener reacts to an opening sentence to a news story with a shrug. They want their audiences to want to hear more.

For example: "NASA grounds future shuttle missions until it can address debris problems during liftoffs." (What debris problems? How long will this last? Tell me more.) "Hundreds of Boy Scouts fall ill at their Jamboree in Virginia." (What made them sick? Are they OK now? Will this force the Jamboree to be shut down? Tell me more.)

SO WHAT? New writers can fall into the so-what trap in writing about speeches, meetings, or other planned events. It happens when news writers have not found the focus or point of their story. They state the obvious rather than the meaningful.

Consider the following leads: "President Bush will present the State of the Union address tonight." "The city council is meeting to discuss new legislation." "A new monument to war veterans was unveiled." "The Scott Peterson murder trial continues for a fourth day." In none of these leads does the listener get any new, insightful, or relevant information. The president annually delivers the State of the Union, the city council routinely discusses legislation, a monument is usually erected or unveiled, and a trial, unless there is a verdict, goes on from one day to the next. The lead should have listeners thinking, "Tell me more," not "Why should I care?"

To eliminate the so-what, the lead needs to provide some specific new information: The president is expected to address concerns about the Iraq war, the city council is scheduled to debate rent control measures, the prosecution is planning to outline forensic evidence. The lead needs to find a topic that will make people want to hear more.

In each of the so-what leads, the sentences use flabby or imprecise verbs. It is more important to know what is happening at a trial rather than that it is still going on. It is more important to know what the president will discuss than that he will be speaking. It is more important to know what the city council will meet about than the fact of it meeting. If a writer does not know the most important topic to be discussed or addressed, that confusion gets passed on to audiences in so-what leads. If a writer does not take the time to discern what is important, that lack of clarity gets passed along to listeners. Writers need to know the story to tell the story. Trying to disguise ignorance with weak words or complicated sentences turns off listeners and viewers. In broadcast, the audience does not go back, it just goes away.

S-V-O OR SUBJECT-VERB-OBJECT Broadcast leads use simple sentence structure or what grammarians refer to as a sentence with one dependent clause. The subject-verb-object construction is the most common form of simple sentence. Simple sentences are easy to follow because listeners are not trying to figure out how additional clauses and phrases relate to the main point.

Here is a simple sentence: "Americans are pledging millions of dollars of aid for tsunami victims." "Americans" is the subject; "are pledging" is the verb; "dollars" is the object. The rest of the words are modifiers.

Here is a more complex sentence, with more clauses: "In an effort to respond to what aid officials are calling the worst natural disaster in modern times, Americans are going online and pledging millions of dollars to charities in hopes of helping the thousands of victims of the December 26th tsunami in Asia and Africa."

While a reader could keep track of the twists and turns of that one sentence, a listener would not and would probably turn off the radio or television. To make that long sentence work in broadcast, those subordinate clauses, such as "in an effort to respond to what aid officials are calling the worst natural disaster in modern times," would become separate sentences.

Simple: "The Boston Red Sox win their first World Series in 86 years." "The Boston Red Sox" is the subject; "win" is the verb; "World Series" is the object.

More complex: "Relying on dominating pitching and timely power hitting, the Boston Red Sox sweep the Saint Louis Cardinals in four games to claim their first World Series in 86 years, elating generations of fans in Boston and New England."

A lot of the clauses in this second example could be separate sentences, as they represent individual pieces of pertinent information. For example, celebrating fans could be the lead piece of information: "Generations of Boston Red Sox fans are celebrating the team's first World Series' victory in 86 years." Information about how the team won could be the lead of a baseball analysis piece: "The Boston Red Sox relied on timely power hitting and dominating pitching to win their first World Series in 86 years."

Jamming all the information into one sentence lessens the impact of each element. The broadcast story could read: "The Boston Red Sox win their first World Series in 86 years. Fans across New England are celebrating as the team swept the Saint Louis Cardinals in four games. The Red Sox relied on timely power hitting and dominant pitching in their historic victory."

ACTIVE VERSUS PASSIVE VOICE Notice that each sentence in the Red Sox story uses the active voice. One of the easiest ways to keep sentences tight is to write them in the active voice. But many beginning news writers are confused about what the active voice is. In most cases, the active voice means that the subject of a sentence is taking action rather than being acted upon. Rather than writing, "The World Series was won by the Boston Red Sox," you would write, "The Red Sox win the World Series."

The passive voice often shows up in routine crime or disaster stories. Rather than writing, "Four men were arrested by Israeli authorities on fraud charges," (passive voice), write, "Israeli authorities arrest four men on fraud charges" (active voice). Rather than writing, "Eleven countries were hit by the tsunami triggered by an earthquake off Indonesia," write, "An earthquake off Indonesia triggered the tsunami that hit 11 countries" or "The tsunami hit 11 countries. An earthquake off Indonesia triggered the tidal waves." Notice that active voice sentences are generally S-V-O sentences.

WRITING IN THE PRESENT The passive voice often gets confused with past tense, which is also avoided in leads in broadcast stories. Past tense is used when something happened in the past. Broadcast news aims to emphasize the immediate, so the present tense or the present perfect tense, such as "fans are celebrating," is used. This indicates action that could still be going on. Rather than writing, "The search for victims of the plane crash continued," it is stronger to write, "Crews search for more victims," using both active voice and present tense.

Because of this emphasis on the immediate, terms like "yesterday" and "last night" are avoided in broadcast leads. Those terms emphasize the "oldness" of the information. In fact, broadcast lead writers are encouraged to find the latest angle to a story. So rather than writing, "A plane crashed last night in a remote area of New Hampshire's White Mountains. Crews have been dispatched to see if anyone survived the crash," a broadcast lead would talk about the search for survivors following the crash. References to "today" can be avoided in broadcast stories as well, because it is assumed that you are talking about an event of that day.

ATTRIBUTION AND QUOTES When you listen to or watch a broadcast story, the first voice you hear is the narrator, usually the anchor or reporter. So when a broadcast story starts by providing information or comments from someone else, it needs to alert audiences to that fact. It needs to tell the audience that the voice of authority in the story is changing; it needs to first attribute that information. If the attribution does not come first, it will confuse the listener as to who is providing the information. In text, the attribution can go in the front, in the middle, or at the end, as long as it is associated with the information being provided. Doing that in broadcast creates confusion.

Broadcast: "Secretary of State Colin Powell says the United States responded appropriately to the tsunami disaster. He denied that the U.S. was too slow in providing aid."

Text: "The United States responded appropriately to the tsunami disaster, said the secretary of state. Colin Powell denied accusations that the U.S. moved too slowly in providing aid."

If listeners do not get told right away who is saying that the response was appropriate, they can assume that the narrator, anchor, or reporter is making that point. By failing to attribute comments and information early and often in broadcast story, a news writer undercuts the story's believability.

Quote leads also do not work well in broadcast, because they lack beginning attribution. Consider this lead: "I'm not going to lick my wounds or hide under a rock." For broadcast, you would have no idea who is speaking those words because you would hear the reporter or anchor actually voice them. They could belong to a losing football coach, a failed business executive, or someone convicted of a crime. But John Kerry, the former 2004 presidential candidate, delivered those words in an interview in *Newsweek* magazine.[2]

Broadcast writers sometimes try to make their news scripts function like print stories by using direct quotes, if they lack the actual sound of the person speaking. But broadcast audiences cannot hear quote marks. That John Kerry story might look like this in broadcast: "In a newly published interview, former presidential candidate John Kerry says he has no plans to, quote, hide under a rock, following his November election loss. Kerry told *Newsweek* magazine his election defeat may be due his failure to connect to voters."

Even though it is a partial quote, the format does not work well. The writer has to make the audience hear the quotation marks, something that is not done in normal conversation. Because you want the listeners to understand exactly who is saying the words, you have to use some awkward phrasing. It would be better to paraphrase than to use a partial quote that does not say much. A better story lead might be: "Former presidential candidate John Kerry is promising to remain visible and active in politics despite the November election loss."

Quotes can be used in broadcast leads if the exact words are so powerful or unique that they demand attention in the news story. For example: "Entertainer Justin Timberlake says a quote wardrobe malfunction caused the baring of Janet Jackson's breast during the Super Bowl half-time show." Those two words were issued in the text of a statement and were so unique in describing the incident that a quote had to be used.

More common than the quote lead but equally problematic is the question lead, because the anchor or reporter is asking a question to the audience. Most broadcast listeners expect the news to answer questions, not ask them. Question leads signal a lack of creativity and a dose of laziness to audiences. Questions are more likely to appear in broadcast scripts to tease an upcoming story rather than actually start a report.

HARD VERSUS SOFT LEADS The lead establishes the tone of the story. If the story requires a serious, straightforward approach to the information, the story requires a hard lead, addressing the latest, most pertinent information. If the story requires a lighter or more emotional tone, the lead can be softer, less of the "just the facts, ma'am" approach. A story about a summit on the tsunami relief efforts would demand a hard lead, while a story on how a family or a village is finally getting relief could warrant a softer lead. But what if a riot broke out among the people in the village trying to get aid? Could that warrant a hard news lead? Again, the tone of the story and the information in it determine whether you should take a hard-edged approach or a softer or lighter approach.

Often broadcast leads use a play on words to set a less somber tone. But a lead you might consider clever might fall flat for others, eliciting "the groan factor." Consider these leads: "The Templeton city council put Jack Frost's plan for a new mall on ice." Or "Donut maker Krispy Kreme lost a lot of dough in the last quarter of 2004." They both lend a lighter tone to what could be serious stories. The first makes a play on someone's name, always a risky proposition, as few people like having their name be the butt of humor.

Sometimes cultural references may not click with an audience. A story about Cuban refugees using an old Chevrolet truck to sail across the Florida Straits prompted this lead:

BOX 5.2

Common Phrases, Common Problems

Colloquialisms or phrases common in certain regions may not be well known in others. For example, in my hometown of Akron, Ohio, the area of grass between the curb and the sidewalk is called "the devil strip." But if I wrote a story about a car accident, saying a passenger was thrown out of the car onto the devil strip, most people outside of northeast Ohio would not know what I was talking about. But in and around Akron, if you called the devil strip the shoulder of the road, you would confuse people. When writing for an international audience, I would be tempted to use a colloquialism (like "on the stump,' meaning campaigning) or a baseball reference (like "pinch hit," meaning to replace) to make a story more conversational. But then I would read the script to a colleague from Bulgaria or Great Britain, and they would give me a puzzled look. That meant it was time to make a change.

"A dozen Cubans try to see the U-S-A in a Chevrolet." Anyone over forty years old probably remembers that 1960s slogan for the U.S. car brand, and they understood the reference. But it did not register with a younger audience. Reading a lead and a story aloud to someone else is one way to see if the script maintains the intended tone. Check to see how an audience reacts to the story.

BROADCAST STYLE All the stylistic rules of broadcast writing relate to the central fact that every broadcast story is heard, not read. The audience hears someone's voice tell the story, so it has to be written to give the audience aural cues about the story and the information in it. Making these rules part of a broadcast writing habit will enable greater creativity in story organization later on.

Avoid abbreviations and acronyms. Unless everyone agrees on every abbreviation, using them in broadcast copy opens up the possibility of misinterpretation, misreading, and mispronunciation. Does "St." mean street or saint? Does "comm." mean commissioner, communications, community, committee, or commonwealth? While abbreviations save space on the printed page, they can create confusion and mistakes on air. Abbreviations for states, days of the week, and months of the year are unacceptable. Every word needs to be spelled out in broadcast copy.

Acronyms, or letters that represent the full title of an agency or organization, can also cause problems in broadcast news, especially if the acronyms are not commonly known. Some acronyms, like UN for the United Nations or NASA for the National Aeronautics and Space Administration, can be used without any concern. But others cannot. DHS could mean the federal Department of Homeland Security or a local or state Department of Health Services or Department of Human Services. MP stands for "member of parliament" in Great Britain and "military police" in the United States.

Many news organizations provide a stylebook of common acronyms that can be used on first reference in a story or they follow the *Associated Press Stylebook*. NASA, CIA, and FBI are a few acronyms listed as commonly known in the *AP Stylebook*. The easiest rule for broadcast writers to follow is: Avoid acronyms that require your audience to have to stop and figure out what the story is referring to. Just because you know its meaning does not mean your audience does, so think about what a general audience might understand when using acronyms.

When naming names, use titles first, initials rarely. Peter Jackson, George Pataki, Orrin Hatch, Russell Jones, and Kathleen O'Toole are prominent public figures and might be mentioned often in news stories. But not everyone knows them or why they would be prominent. Identifying titles or phrases are used to help audiences. In print, those titles or phrases can follow a name. But in broadcast, it is clearer and shorter to put the title ahead of the name rather than behind it.

For example: "*Lord of the Rings* director Peter Jackson" or "Canadian newspaper columnist Peter Jackson," rather than "Peter Jackson, director of *Lord of the Rings*," or "Peter Jackson, columnist for the *Newfoundland Telegraph*." "New York governor George Pataki," rather than "George Pataki, governor of New York." "Utah senator Orrin Hatch," "rap artist Russell Jones also known as ODB," "Boston police commissioner Kathleen O'Toole."

By putting the title first, the broadcast audience grasps the importance and relevance of the person right away. The name and the title also need to go together for quick and easy comprehension for a listening audience.

Consider this sports story rewritten from the wire services on December 29, 2004: "The all-pro safety of the Dallas Cowboys says he is planning to retire from pro football after the last game of this season. Darren Woodson told the *Dallas Morning News* that it is time for him to leave the game he has played for twelve years."

Reading those two sentences, it is easy to associate Woodson as the all-pro safety, but that is not necessarily the case when hearing it. So for broadcast, it is better to write: "Dallas Cowboys' all-pro safety Darren Woodson says he's ready to retire after the season's last game. Woodson is leaving after twelve years in the NFL."

However, broadcast writers need to keep titles short and often must reduce or summarize a long official title into a shorter, more easily digested phrase. When Jami A. Miscik, deputy director of intelligence for the CIA, resigned in December 2004, broadcast stories would tighten her official title to "CIA analysis chief" or "CIA intelligence deputy."

Also, notice that while print stories often use initials to provide more specificity in names, such as Jami A. Miscik, broadcast stories leave out the initials. Broadcast stories aim to conform with how we normally hear and speak. Generally, middle initials are not mentioned in conversation; people normally use just first and last names for an introduction. But for every rule, there is the exception. The forty-third president of the United States, George W. Bush, is often referred to on air with his middle initial, to differentiate him from the forty-first president, his father, George (H. W.) Bush.

Sometimes in broadcast stories, names are not even used if the person's job or position is more relevant to the story's understanding than the name. For example, the newspaper and online stories about the rejected appeal for a recount in the December 26, 2004, Ukrainian presidential election quote a spokeswoman for the country's supreme court, Liana Shlyaposhnikova. A story for air would refer to a Ukrainian supreme court spokeswoman and not include the name. The name would also be excluded because it is long and multisyllabic, opening up the possibility of mispronunciation. Few things sound as bad in broadcast as someone stumbling over a name.

A broadcast story would also avoid reciting a list of names, such as a group of arrested criminal suspects. When four antiquities dealers were charged with fraud relating to a hoax claiming a burial box held the bones of Jesus' brother James, few broadcast stories included all four names. Many broadcast stories about the resignation of four cabinet secretaries on November 15, 2004, did not include all the names. Often the most prominent person, such as Secretary of State Colin Powell, would be named, and the others would be wrapped up in one sentence such as: "The heads of agriculture, energy, and education also tendered their resignations."

Few people can listen to several numbers being rattled off and then understand and compute them. For most of us, numbers are more easily comprehended when seen, not heard. But numbers are a part of news stories all the time; stories about government spending, business investment, even social and political trends. Using numbers in broadcast stories requires simplicity and clarity.

Numbers under ten are spelled out. Large numbers are often rounded out as well as spelled out, so 518 might be "more than five hundred," and 48,663 might be "slightly less than fifty thousand." More precise numbers are used in broadcast stories if necessary to delineate small differences. For example, the third recount of the Washington State governor's vote showed a margin of victory of just 129 votes out of 2.8 million cast. The exact number, 129, was critical information to every story about the election's vote tally, although the number of votes cast could have been and was rounded out to "nearly three million."

One use of numbers, in dates, does not require spelling them out. November twenty-second, nineteen sixty-three is not needed when November 22nd, 1963, will do.

Money amounts also can be spelled out and rounded out, but the dollar sign needs to be eliminated and replaced with the word, "dollar." A $257,000 increase in donations to the local food bank would read "more than a quarter-million-dollar increase" or "a 257-thousand-dollar increase" in a broadcast script. The word, "percent," and not the symbol (%) is used in broadcast scripts, such as "President Bush wins with 52 percent of the popular vote, compared to John Kerry's 48 percent." Broadcast audiences cannot hear symbols, so do not use them.

Pay attention to spelling. This might not seem necessary because the audience never sees the words, they only hear them. But the people reading the words aloud do see them, and a misspelling can create problems of inaccuracy, and can harm credibility in broadcast. The misspelling of the word "public" can be disastrous on air. Relying on computer spell checking software can also be dangerous, as it may provide a correctly spelled word but it may be the wrong one.

Spelling software got writers in trouble when it wrote "assignation" (an affair) instead of "assassination" (the murder of an official), "copulation" (sex) instead of "compilation" (an anthology of work), and "vinaigrettes" (salad dressings) instead of "vignettes" (short tales).

Good writers, no matter for which medium, need to pay attention to spelling.

Broadcast writing also must pay attention to pronunciation. A word mispronounced on air may be just a slip of the tongue, like a typographical error may be a slip of the fingers. But mispronunciations of names, like their misspelling in print, raises questions of accuracy and credibility. Geographical dictionaries are one source for pronunciations of towns and cities. For example, Quincy, Illinois, is pronounced slightly differently than Quincy, Massachusetts. News organizations also keep pronunciation lists of prominent names in the news, such as Palestinian president Mahmoud Abbas or Chinese president Hu Jintao.

All of these tips and rules relating to broadcast writing boil down to making your news writing clear, concise, conversational, and complete. These writing goals, which are utterly essential for writing for the ear, can apply to all forms of news writing. They can be habit-forming.

Keeping It Organized

Because broadcast writing allows for the addition of sound and images, its organization requires discipline. Writers have to not only be disciplined in the words and facts chosen, but they have to pay attention to the impact of the different elements chosen for the story and the

BOX 5.3

Rookie Mistakes

- Forget to read the story aloud.
- Use too many clauses.
- Fail to tie the story pieces together.
- Fail to know the story before writing.
- Fail to provide adequate attribution.
- Forget to rewrite a script.

time devoted to it. Timing and organization play key roles in the understanding and presentation of broadcast news.

TIMING IS EVERYTHING Broadcast news lives and dies by the second. The number of words matter for text journalism, but the amount of time it takes to read those words aloud matters more in broadcast. The amount of time devoted to a news item signals its importance to an audience. The amount of time for a news story depends on the elements used in a story.

A newscast consists of a variety of stories, such as "readers," which are usually less than thirty seconds long, to "packages," prerecorded reporter's stories, which average about ninety seconds. Newscasts generally run in thirty-minute intervals, and that thirty minutes is interrupted by commercial breaks. The news "hole," the amount of time in the thirty minutes devoted to news, runs twenty-two minutes. Within those twenty-two minutes, the elements and the importance of the story determine the length of that story.

Readers are usually the shortest stories in a broadcast lineup, because they have the fewest elements. Readers are word stories, read aloud by an anchor. They can range from fifteen to thirty seconds in length, but they rarely go beyond thirty-five seconds. The shorter the length of each sentence, the more sentences a news writer has to tell a story. A sentence that exceeds eight seconds in broadcast is probably too long.

Look back at the Darren Woodson retirement story above. The first version, two sentences and forty-six words long, takes about twelve or thirteen seconds to read aloud. The second version, two sentences and twenty-five words long, takes about seven seconds, allowing the writer at least two to three more sentences to include information about Woodson and the Cowboys to complete a twenty- or twenty-five-second story.

Readers or "tells" are the most basic of broadcast stories and these days, even a twenty-five-second story can be considered lengthy. As many television and radio stations push to do more news stories in the same limited amount of time, they may produce a "headlines" segment, thirty seconds or one minute devoted to several stories consisting of one sentence each. Each sentence would be similar to a newspaper headline, giving just the bare minimum of information about a story. A headlines segment could look something like this:

"Here's a look at our top stories: The tsunami death toll rises to 160 thousand. The Ukrainian Supreme Court rejects challenges to Sunday's presidential election. A workers' sick-out creates major delays and cancellations for U.S. Airways. And in weather, the Boston area digs out from up to a foot of snow, while heavy rains set off mudslides in southern California."

A headlines segment represents a quick review. Readers or tells aim to provide a complete story to audiences when neither time nor sound is available. A producer might choose to do a reader on a story that warrants telling but is not as important as other stories that day.

ADDING SOUND While readers are essential building blocks in every radio and television newscast, they fail to take advantage of broadcast's greatest strength: the ability to allow audiences to experience news through sound. Broadcast news uses three types of sound: narration or track, sound bites or actualities, and natural or ambient sound. Good broadcast stories rely on good sound to help the audience understand a story.

Sound bites are used in broadcast to provide another voice to a story. That voice can provide information, authenticity, and humanity to a story. A story about a female high school place kicker could include a sound bite from her coach about her ability to play the game (authenticity) and from her about whether she fits in with the guys on the team (humanity). A story about a deadly warehouse fire could have a sound bite from the fire chief, talking about how long it took firefighters to contain the blaze (authenticity and information). Put another way, sound bites can "provide factual information . . . add a dimension of realism and reveal a person's inner self."[3] A sound bite can help people understand a story by putting the audience at the scene of the news, by underscoring and illustrating the narrative or track, and by giving the story the voice of an expert or an official to provide credibility.

Picking sound bites is a lot like picking a wine for a meal: You need to know enough about the story (the meal) to determine the best sound (the wine) to enhance overall enjoyment. Just as different wines have different functions in a meal, so too different sound bites serve a story differently. For a story about a traffic accident that just happened, look for bites that

BOX 5.4

Vocabulary of Sound

- Track: the narration of a news story read by an anchor or reporter.
- Sound bite or actuality: the audio sound of a quote from a person. Its common abbreviation in broadcast is SOT (sound on tape).
- Natural or ambient sound: the sound heard at the scene of a news event that helps distinguish the atmosphere and the environment, such as the whine of an ambulance siren, the cries of babies in a nursery, the whoosh of a space shuttle blastoff. Its common abbreviation is NATSOT (natural sound on tape).
- Wraparound: a radio story using a sound bite.
- Tag: the track or story following an SOT that completes the story.
- Sig-out or sign-off: the final identifiers of a story that include the reporter's name, station, and location.

inform and lend credibility. For a story about a pumpkin-carving contest, seek out a sound bite from a carver to put the audience at the scene, or to explain the action.

To find a good bite, look for something said in an interesting way. Look for variety—in words, pacing, and context. Avoid a bite that recites a long list of facts or statistics; you could probably write something shorter and more to the point. Avoid a bite full of jargon; you will waste words having to explain what was said. Avoid a bite that draws conclusions not apparent or relevant in the story; you will be taking your story in a direction you cannot support. Look for something that is short and gets to the heart of the matter.

Sound bites should run on average between six and fifteen seconds. They are not sound chomps, which run about a minute, or sound nibbles, which run for three seconds or less. If a bite runs too long, the audience will stop listening; if it runs too short, they cannot grasp what is being said. Good sound bites can be found in eyewitness accounts, expert evaluations, and comments or responses to a situation or claim. The general rules in choosing sound bites can easily apply to choosing quotes in text stories. But broadcast does not allow ellipses to indicate part of the comment left out or to link similar comments. Print allows for ellipses. Linking two unconnected sound bites results in a jump cut that actually sounds jumpy. While technology now allow for a clean and smooth edit connecting two things said separately, such editing is considered ethically unsound if it changes the meaning and context of the words spoken.

Many broadcast writers and reporters pick their sound bites first for their story. In radio, a story in which a sound bite serves as the center or core of the story is called a wraparound, as the track or narration leads into the bite and follows after it. In both radio and television, a story tracked and prerecorded by a reporter, often using one or more bites, which can stand alone with a beginning, middle, and end is called a package. Wraparounds and packages are built around the sound bites, because the sound should represent the most interesting, unique, and key points of the story. Sound bites reflect and underscore the story's focus. If you cannot find the right bites, it may mean you are still searching for the story's focus. Good bites will jump out, or as veteran NBC News correspondent Bob Dotson puts it, "They should stick in memory."[4]

Natural or ambient sound also should stick in the memory of listeners or viewers. Natural sound can put the audience in the middle of the action, lending credibility and emotion to a story. Rather than relying on description to get an audience to relate to what is happening, natural sound envelops the audience with a sense of place and a sense of people. Want to demonstrate the frustration of drivers in a traffic jam? A few seconds of honking horns will do. What could make an audience relate to the joy of school children finishing up the last day of classes? Try the sound of shouts and laughter on a playground after the last school bell rings. The sound of "Taps" at a military funeral, the rat-a-tat of gunfire in battle, the chants of protesters during a march, all help define a story and provide depth to the reporting.

WRITING TO SOUND Using sound effectively requires some deftness in writing into it and out of it. Sound bites need to be set up so the audience understands who is talking and what is being talked about. That means that you as the writer need to know this information.

To write to a bite, you need to know:

1. How long it is in seconds. This is known as the TRT, or total running time.
2. How it begins. This is known as the in queue, or IC, and it is usually the first two or three words of the sound on tape (SOT).
3. How it ends. This is known as the out queue, or OC, and it is usually the last two or three words.

Also, plan on using a sound bite high, or early, in a story. If it truly highlights the heart of the story, it deserves a prominent place. With stories that focus on attributed information, the audience expects a sound bite from your person of authority, and they expect it early.

To lead into a bite, tell the audience who is talking and provide some context for the sound bite. Avoid using words similar to what is in the bite to lead into it. Instead, write the sentence into the sound bite that makes your listener and viewer want and expect more. Think of a conversation where someone sets up a key revelation and you lean in for it; you want your audience to lean in for the sound bite.

For example, a story about the firing of four CBS News executives over the journalistic lapses in an investigative report on President George W. Bush's Texas National Guard service might include a sound bite from CBS president Leslie Moonves. The lead could be a sentence on the outcome of the three-month investigation, followed by some detailed information on the investigation's conclusions, then the setup to a bite. The sound bite is: "As far as the question of the reporting was concerned, the bottom line is that much of the September 8th broadcast was wrong, incomplete, or unfair."

Here's an example of how it might be written:

> Four CBS News employees have lost their jobs following a three-month independent investigation of journalistic lapses in a "60 Minutes Wednesday" report on the president's National Guard service that aired last fall.
>
> The investigation concluded that competitive pressures and not political bias led to a breakdown in the basic process of checking sources and authenticating documents.
>
> But CBS president Leslie Moonves admits the investigation showed problems with the story from beginning to end.
>
> ——(SOT)——
>
> IQ: as far as . . .

OQ: . . . wrong, incomplete or unfair."

Moonves promises new safeguards in the wake of the scandal and has created a news standards executive position to ensure those safeguards are enforced.

Notice that the line into the SOT hints at what Moonves would say, but does not parrot the bite. A lead-in such as "CBS president Leslie Moonves called the story wrong and unfair" would annoy listeners because of the repetition. A lead-in that merely announces a sound bite, such as "CBS president Leslie Moonves had this to say about the investigation," is annoying as well because it breaks up the conversational flow and adds no information.

After the bite, this story can go further with information about the investigation's conclusions and about the actions being taken by CBS. This story needs to go further; it should not end on the sound bite, as that leaves the audience hanging. Sound bites need a tag, a wrap-up sentence or two to complete the story and alert the audience that this report on this topic is ending. The story is incomplete without a tag. The tag should include some worthwhile information, not a repetition of information already presented. A tag that is often heard but should be avoided is one such as "That was CBS president Leslie Moonves on the '60 Minutes Wednesday' scandal." With so few seconds available to tell stories in broadcast, each second should convey useful information to an audience.

Natural sound, as with sound bites, conveys authenticity, because it gives the audience a sense of what it is like to be at a news event. But while you do not want to start or end a story on a sound bite, you can start or end a story on natural sound. Natural sound at the top of a story is a scene-setter, establishing the tone or feel of the story. A story about Chinese New Year celebrations could feature the sound of the gongs and cymbals of the dragon dance, immediately connecting the audience to the street. A story about a pianist might open and close with him playing piano. Natural sound at the end of a story leaves the audience with a souvenir. In the middle, natural sound can act like a sound bite, adding a voice of authenticity. Natural sound can be played full, at full volume and without a track. Or it can be played under, at partial volume underneath the narration.

ADDING VISUALS The addition of images—graphics, animation, and video—takes storytelling in the news to a more complex but also a more creative level. You have a wider selection of tools to choose for getting information across to the audience. Just as sound can transport your audience to the scene of the action, video images can do that and more, literally adding another dimension to the story. The pictures provide the description, which should allow time in the script to explain the context of those pictures. Graphics can help an audience follow key points of the story. Animation can help an audience visualize something that has yet to happen or has happened long ago.

Learning how to think visually in storytelling, essential in television news, improves the use of visuals in any type of storytelling in any media. Understanding the best way to put together a graphic of key points on a government report to be seen on television can translate into understanding how that type of graphic could be used to accompany a print or online story. Using a map to show the location of a story for television can help to develop the habit of thinking about maps to illustrate stories in other media. Looking for pictures for television storytelling will help develop an eye for visuals that can add description, detail, and illustration to all other types of storytelling.

Graphics and maps are the easiest visuals to use in television news because they usually are static, unchanging. The key to the effective use of maps or graphic lists in a television story is to refer to what is on the screen, or to write to the visual. That does not mean describing the graphic, but it does mean giving information to the audience that explains it.

A full-screen graphic can be useful in helping audiences understand numbers and statistics, such as a pie chart that shows how a city budget is allocated, or a bar graph that shows the decrease in teenage pregnancy over several years. Avoid writing sentences like "As this map shows, the train derailment occurred near Selma, North Carolina, which is near Charlotte," when looking at a full-screen map locating the derailment. Instead, add some pertinent information: "Some five thousand residents of Selma, North Carolina, were forced from their

BOX 5.5

Vocabulary of Visuals

- OTS or BOX graphic: a graphic or picture that appears "over the shoulder" or in a box next to an anchor.
- FS graphic/FSG: a full-screen graphic that fills up the entire TV screen, usually a map or a list of bullet points.
- VO: The abbreviation for voice-over, the name for video that airs during track or narration.
- VOSOT: a story that has a piece of video (VO) and a sound bite.
- OC: on camera.
- Beeper or phoner: a live report from a telephone put on air.
- Live shot: a real-time report from a news scene, often including a package or video and sound clips.
- PKG: a self-contained, preedited report.
- Donut: a package without a sig-out, usually played in a live shot to allow the reporter to tag it live and on air.

homes because of the toxic fumes from the derailment." The key is to refer to what people are seeing and put it into context.

When putting together a bullet or list graphic as a full-screen graphic (FSG), the key is to use at most three or four points, with each point only being three or four words. An FSG could also be a quote from a statement, when no audio or video is available, or from a report or document. Both the visual design and the copy accompanying the graphic should be sparse and simple. Above all, the copy, the words being said, must resemble the words that the audience is seeing on the screen.

That is even more important in writing for video; the words must refer to what is being seen. When they do not match, you get what former television news director and reporter Catherine Harwood calls "cognitive dissonance . . . people generally can't digest and retain a story if you show pictures of one thing while describing something else."[5] To avoid such a disconnect, Larry Rickel and Ed Sardella recommend that their clients in the Broadcast Image Talent Group think of the acronym SWAP, or synchronize words and pictures, "so that you show what you tell and tell what you show."[6]

One way to ensure that words and pictures match is to jot down a list of the shots in a piece of video. A piece of raw or unedited video from a house fire might include the following: the house on fire, flames at window, fire trucks, hoses on the ground, a fire hydrant, a firefighter on a ladder, a firefighter on a cherry picker, neighbors watching, smoldering rubble, firefighters shooting water, a resident wrapped in a blanket, a family hugging. As the words of the story unfold, so do the images of the story, in coordination. For example, you

BOX 5.6

Disconnected

One morning in early July 2002, while watching the morning news, a story about actress Julia Roberts's marriage came on the air. I was expecting to see pictures of Roberts and her new husband, Daniel Moder, since that was what the story was all about. Instead, the station showed video of her with a previous boyfriend, Benjamin Bratt. The station aired file video and used it as "wallpaper," a derogatory term in which video is more or less plastered on air without much thought given to connecting words and pictures. So when I heard the words "Julia Roberts and her new husband" but saw generic Roberts pictures, I added my own script, "not seen here."

Every time a story's words, such as "fighting in Fallujah," do not connect with pictures (U.S. soldiers in trucks on a highway), you have a "not seen here" moment, and it registers with audiences that this station does not know how to get its story straight.

would want information in the script about who might be homeless from the fire to be heard when the audience sees the images of the family hugging and/or the person huddled in the blanket. You would provide information about how long it took firefighters to put out the fire with shots of firefighters battling the blaze. You would create dissonance or disconnect if you talked about the firefighters while showing pictures of the family.

PUTTING IT TOGETHER A television newscast has a mix of stories and a mix of elements. Some stories have video, others have video and sound bites, and still others have video, sound bites, and graphics. A package pools all the broadcast elements together: words, pictures, and sound. Much reporting for television is turned into packages for air. With a package, choose the best elements to tell a story and organize them in ways that makes the news an informative experience.

Pictures and sound, the hallmarks of broadcast news, should be used early and often in a television package. A package should open with the pictures and the sounds that set the tone of the story, that establish the scene. Most veteran broadcast storytellers advise writers to lead

FIGURE 5.2. NY 1 reporter Roger Clark edited using natural sound to enhance a Chinese street celebration package. (Photo by the author)

packages with the best video, and the best video generally has the best sound to go along with it. When NY 1 reporter Roger Clark put together his report on Chinese New Year, he opened with his best piece of video of the dragon dance. When former CNN reporter Brian Cabell and field producer Wade Ricks put together a profile of a female high school place kicker, they opened with the sight and sound of the football team ripping through a sign at the start of a state championship football game.

A package not only should start strong, it needs to end strong. Television feature reporter Wayne Freedman refers to package openers and closers as entrance and exit routes, adding that if you plan for those, the middle part of a package will write itself.[7]

Sometimes that means bringing the audience back to the beginning. This might be called the diamond approach, with a beginning or top tip that introduces a problem by finding a person who has it and who serves as the story's "main character." The middle or center of the diamond explores and explains the problem and offers expert comments and information on it. Then the bottom tip of the diamond or end refers back to the main character, the person and the problem at the heart of this story, and concludes with some information and picture you want the audience to carry away from the piece. TV newsman Bob Dotson advises package writers to end with "something the audience won't forget. Then, like a good poet, help the viewer understand the story's meaning. Summarize the point of the piece . . ."[8]

Good packages also demonstrate the writer's attention to detail about content and the audience. Weak leads not only use imprecise verbs, they lack precise information and detail to make them appealing to listeners. Good broadcast lead writers seek a piece of information that a listener can relate to. Bob Dotson suggests looking for a detail that will make a broadcast story unique or stand out. Dotson and others suggest sprinkling such bits of detail throughout a story, to coax the audience to continue to follow along and pull them through to the end.

The challenge is finding the best details to include and then tying them together. The more sources providing you key information, the easier it is to find the details needed for the story. Finding the common points from a variety of sources underscores the necessary information.

Consider having to write a broadcast package about the new federal food and exercise guidelines to stay healthy. This story was widely reported by various wire services and newspapers after first appearing in a medical journal. All of those outlets can provide information for the basis of a broadcast story. The key details are mentioned in all of those reports. Once you have taken in the key points of the story, you can begin to tell the story in your words, in your voice. You can start putting your story together.

Now that you understand the story, you need to find people who can comment on it and who can provide visuals to explain it. You need someone to serve as the touchstone character of your report. One of the most common ways to approach this story is to look for someone who is struggling with their diet. The package might start with someone scanning labels at a grocery store, or a family preparing a meal for dinner, or people eating at a restaurant. From there you might want a sound bite from your "Everywoman dieter" and then from food experts about the new guidelines, ending with your Everywoman still struggling with trying to follow a healthy lifestyle.

Television packages almost always contain a reporter stand-up, in which the reporter is on camera talking directly to the audience, providing some pertinent information. A stand-up is the broadcast equivalent of a dateline and byline in print, putting a name and a place to a news story. Many reporter stand-ups are bridges, a bit of narration that connects one point of the story to another point. Some stand-ups are at the end of the package and include the sig-out, or sign-off. Stand-ups allow reporters to describe information they may not be able to show, or to demonstrate or indicate a part of the story. Stand-ups establish a connection between the reporter, the audience, and the people and places in the news.

Because stand-ups are recorded at the news site, think about how to organize the writing of the story and the points that could best be made or demonstrated in a stand-up. A demonstration stand-up for the new food guidelines might involve taking a box of cereal off a grocery shelf and demonstrating how to look for nutritional information. Or it could be unloading a grocery cart of items onto the checkout line. The stand-up bridge could be used to demonstrate the additional effort that following the guidelines might take.

Sometimes a story should not have a stand-up. A stand-up in the middle or at the end of a profile, such as a story about a local athletic hero killed in Iraq, might seem intrusive and

BOX 5.7

Stand-Up Tips

- Avoid standing in direct sunlight to avoid squinting into the camera.
- Stand comfortably at ease, without slouching or being too stiff.
- Face the camera at a slight but natural angle, not directly head-on.
- Position yourself with a background setting that shows something about the story without distracting too much from the informational points you are making.
- Use your space and place to demonstrate a point.
- Make sure the stand-up action fits the pace and mood of the story.
- Wear clothes that do not draw attention from the face or blend in with the background.
- Allow for some natural sound before and after a stand-up to deal with noticeable audio shift from the recorded track to the stand-up at the scene.
- Hold your position a few seconds after you finish talking to allow for some "padding," just in case.

egotistical. The main purpose of a stand-up should be informing the audience about aspects of the story and not merely providing "face time."

GETTING THE SHOTS In order to put all the elements of a package together, you need to have gathered enough elements, and here is where problems arise in broadcast stories. Information provided in an interview might be great to use in the story, but if all you shot was the person talking to you for the interview, you have little b-roll, or additional visual elements, to explain your story. Getting someone to talk to you while they are doing something, a technique mentioned in chapter 4, can help. You can take pictures of the person working or demonstrating something. You can also shoot the surroundings as a means of providing description and scene-setting.

When shooting video, you can pan or swivel from left to right, or tilt from top to bottom, and vice versa. But too often beginning shooters hurry the pan or tilt and make it jerky. The purpose of the pan or tilt is to show the entire scene by gathering up the various perspectives on the setting. A good pan follows a central subject, moving from one object to another. Another way to gather up the scene or setting is to shoot various types of shots: close, medium, and wide.

Two other camera movements to think about are a zoom-in or a pullout. With a zoom-in, the camera starts wide and slowly moves in to a very close shot. A pullout is the opposite, starting very tight and pulling out wide. A zoom-in shot aims to take the viewer from the broader scene or context to the specific and detailed. A pullout shot takes the viewer from a key specific to the wider setting.

But no matter the shot or the movement, the key is to hold the shot for the several seconds needed to capture all the action or portray the subject adequately, so you can eliminate excess rather than regret not having enough. In gathering pictures, just like information, it is better to have more than less.

Also with news, as opposed to filmmaking, the shooting aims at capturing reality, not creating or enhancing it. Some news organizations have policies that severely restrict if not outright forbid any staging or manipulating of the images for a news story. Adding sound effects or asking protestors to shout on cue for a live shot are just two examples of ways broadcast storytellers can be tempted to stray from truth and accuracy in hopes of making news more interesting. But the drama of recording news as it happens often proves exciting enough in broadcast storytelling.

SUMMARY

Broadcast storytelling is both simple and complex. Its writing has to be simple to get the main points of the story across to an audience that usually has only one opportunity to hear and grasp them. But it also involves the complex layering of sound and moving pictures to provide emotion and immediacy.

Broadcast writing requires simple subject-verb-object sentences, no abbreviations, active voice, present tense, and attribution first. Sound bites are the core elements of stories, and scripts are often built around them. They can provide information, authenticity, and humanity to a story. They can reflect and underscore the story's focus. In choosing a sound bite, look for something that was said in an interesting or unique way.

Visuals add yet another dimension to broadcast storytelling. The visuals need to connect to the words and information being presented, or else audiences will become confused and disconnected from the story. To gather good video visuals, journalists use a variety of shots to help depict the scene, the setting, and the people in a story.

LEARNING THE LINGO

Active voice
Donut
Hard lead
In cue/out cue
Package
Pan
Reader
Soft lead
SOT (sound on tape)
Tilt
TRT (total running time)
Voice-over
Zoom

NOTES

1. Bob Schieffer, *This Just In: What I Couldn't Tell You on TV* (New York: Berkley, 2003), 146.
2. Evan Thomas, "I'm Going to Learn," *Newsweek*, January 10, 2005, 46–48.
3. James Redmond, Frederick Shook, and Dan Lattimore, *The Broadcast News Process*, 6th ed. (New York: Morton, 2001), 176.
4. Bob Dotson, *Make It Memorable* (New York: Bonus Books, 2000), 57.
5. Sharyl Attkisson and Don R.Vaughan, *Writing Right for Broadcast and Internet News* (New York: Allyn and Bacon, 2003), 144.
6. Larry M. Rickel and Ed Sardella, with Carol Owen, *The Producing Strategy* (1995), 112.
7. Wayne Freedman, *It Takes More Than Good Looks to Succeed at Television News Reporting* (New York: Bonus Books, 2003), 74.
8. Dotson, *Make It Memorable*, 66.

SIX

Print Basics: Value Plus

DURING THE low-carbohydrate fad of a few years back, thousands of Americans religiously followed the South Beach diet, which requires dieters to purge almost all carbohydrates from their system for two weeks. After two weeks, they can start phase two, when they gradually start adding carbs again, in moderation and with some guidelines as to good and bad carbohydrates. Consider producing news for print as phase two of learning how to add detail, description, and nuance to news stories, in moderation and with some guidelines.

Many of the guidelines for writing broadcast news copy apply to stories written to be read, not heard or seen. Print news stories still need to be in active voice. They need to be clear and concise. They need to have the basic who, what, when, where, why, and how. Sentences should not be complex. Attribution and sourcing provide credibility. Stories need to have a focus and a purpose. Quotes, like sound bites, can provide authenticity, humanity, and explanation to a story.

But obviously print is different from broadcast, because it lacks the layers of sound and moving pictures that provide the news audience the sense of immediacy and presence at a news event. Broadcast news stories can put the audience at the scene of the news; print stories can only re-create the scene through words and still pictures. But print's advantage over broadcast is its ability to devote more space to a story. The best use of that space comes in explaining complexity and context. More background information and more quotes can provide that complexity and context.

Broadcast news is constrained by the limited number of minutes and seconds in a newscast and the difficulty, if not complete inability, of viewers to return to a story after hearing it or watching it. While newspapers have limited numbers of pages to put stories, the space within those pages allows for more stories and for stories with more depth than can be aired on television or radio. But that additional space carries added responsibility to fill that space with information that is meaningful to the reading audience. Explaining complexity and context are the additional layers that print news must provide to its audience if it is to remain relevant. But to add that complexity and context to a news story you must add complexity and context to your reporting. And that means doing more to address the how and the why of a story, seeking out not just the hard pros and cons of a story but the middle ground. It involves getting the small details that illustrate the larger points.

Print journalists must go after those nuances in order to take advantage of their medium's unique strengths. But the skills needed to get those nuances can serve good journalism in any medium: newspapers, magazines, radio, television, and online. These skills may seem to be more of necessity for newspaper and magazine journalists, but they can mean the difference between mediocre and extraordinary news stories on television or online.

Print stories also must provide more description to compensate for the lack of sound and pictures. That requires more attention to detail and more diligence at noting the sights, sounds, smells, feel, even taste of the people, places, or things needed to tell a news story with depth and context. While a camera and an audio recorder may be necessities for a broadcast reporter, they also can be useful tools for print reporters in the gathering of the details. These technologies can support and reinforce notes and impressions. The ability to think visually that is so vital to broadcast stories can be important for setting the scene and the tone in print stories. In print, the words paint a picture.

Producing stories for print requires writing that has more subtlety. If broadcast writing often emphasizes stark contrasts, the black and white of a situation, print writing can present more of the grays. The leads and the organization of print stories allow for flexibility and variation in writing. In broadcast, the sound and the pictures intermix with the words to provide much of that variation. Print has to rely on the words. The detail and context expected in print stories should compensate for the lack of sound and limited availability and use of pictures or graphics.

Capturing the necessary description and context for print stories requires expanding and adjusting news-gathering skills. Stories that demand more depth of information require more sources, more layers, and more time. Learning to dig deeper for print stories helps develop stronger, more creative reporting for stories in any medium.

Part of that digging involves numbers. Statistics and financial data pervade all types of news. As such, all journalists need to understand how to use numbers, even in a limited capacity, in relaying information to their audiences. Stories involving numbers and statistics often need reflection and dissection. Newspapers and magazines can provide that to their audiences more easily than broadcast.

To better use the strengths of print as part of using convergence to reach news audiences, we look at news writing and news reporting for a print audience.

PRINT LEADS: VARIATIONS ON A THEME

No matter what format you are using to tell a news story—radio, television, Web, newspaper, or magazine—you want to start out strong. You want your story to get people's attention while providing them key information. Your lead (also spelled "lede" to differentiate it from the hot metal lead used by old printing presses) is the key. It either opens the door to your story or slams it shut in your audience's face. Writing coach Chip Scanlan breaks leads into two categories: tell me the news and tell me the story. Veteran writing and reporting educator Melvin Mencher refers to them another way: direct and delayed leads. In chapter 5, they were called hard and soft leads.

In writing basic broadcast news stories, hard leads give the news; they provide new information that is direct and concise, in one sentence. The same rules can also apply to a basic print news story, but with some stylistic variations. Understanding these variations of leads helps in both print and broadcast storytelling.

Hard Leads: Tell the News, Be Direct

Three kinds of hard leads are the summary lead, the umbrella or shotgun lead, and the delayed identification or blind lead.

Most news stories that aim to quickly get out the latest, best information use summary leads. Summary leads include most, but not necessarily all, of the five Ws and H (who, what, when, where, why, and how). "Readers" in broadcast media often used a summary lead. For example: "President Bush is promising to veto any legislation that would loosen federal limits on embryonic stem cell research."

An umbrella or shotgun lead groups two or three related stories together under one overall topic. For example: "Car bombs in three central Iraqi cities leave as many as 10 people dead and dozens injured, as the new government plans new antiterrorism measures."

A delayed identification or a blind lead often leaves out a detail, such as a specific name or location, to avoid making the lead too wordy or difficult to follow. For example: "Medical researchers discover that the chicken pox vaccine may work to prevent painful shingles." Another example: "Two Bridgewater women die after their car slammed into the guardrail of Interstate 95 early Tuesday."

All of the examples of hard news leads were written in broadcast style, but they could also work as the lead in a print story. But because of the nature of a print story—it can be read and reread, and it needs detail and context—the writing and the stylistic rules governing that writing are different from those for broadcast.

Print leads differ from broadcast leads in that they can be longer, even two or three sentences. But they still must be short; as a general rule about twenty-five words or less.

Print news stories differ from broadcast in that they do not and really cannot emphasize immediacy; they are often written and read after the news has happened. Because of that, print leads can include yesterday and should be written in the past tense.

Unlike broadcast, print leads can have abbreviations, and names in the lead can include initials. Partial quotes can be used, because quote marks can be read. And attribution can come at the end of a sentence, particularly if the person speaking is not as important as what they are saying.

So the three leads above would be a bit different if they were appearing in print. The summary lead might read: "In a direct challenge to Congress, President Bush said yesterday he would veto legislation that loosens federal limits on stem cell research. The veto would be the first in Mr. Bush's presidency and would set up a showdown with Congress to override it."

The shotgun or umbrella lead could read: "As car bombs killed as many as 10 people yesterday, the new central government met to find new ways to put an end to the terror attacks. The central government is exploring plans to increase police patrols and expand roadside checkpoints."

The delayed identification lead would put details in the second sentence or paragraph. "An experimental chicken pox vaccine may have a beneficial new use—the prevention of shingles in older adults, according to findings released yesterday.

"Doctors in 22 Veterans Administration hospitals along with 38,000 patients tested the vaccine and found it to effectively cut the number of cases of shingles by 51 percent."

In the lead about the car accident, the names of the two people killed would be in the second paragraph.

Notice that attribution in two of the three preceding leads came at the end. The delayed identification lead used the term "according to" for attribution, a phrase several news organizations, print and broadcast, dislike and avoid, but it can be used in moderation.

Each print lead is specific about the time element of the story: yesterday. The length of each lead is counted in words, not seconds, and all of them would exceed the five-to-eight-second time frame of a broadcast lead, if read aloud. Print leads can allow for an explanatory clause, such as the ones used in the summary lead ("In a direct challenge . . .") and the umbrella lead ("As car bombs killed 10 . . ."). Most explanatory clauses can begin with a preposition (for, from, in, on, at). Notice also that the hard print leads have the opportunity to focus on the specific, such as "51 percent" in the shingles vaccine story. In broadcast, it may be tightened to merely "half."

Print leads for hard news stories still tell the news. They still are direct in providing the information. But they have more space in which to tell it; they can use more words to add a bit more context and detail without being overstuffed with information. Although print leads have the freedom and flexibility to be longer, good print leads use that freedom and flexibility judiciously. Just because you *can* use more words in a print lead does not mean you *should* use them. A print lead should be short enough to be read aloud without having to take a breath. Again, twenty-five words or less is a good rule of thumb. Print leads should use more words to provide context that clarifies, not confuses the reader about the focus of the story.

For example, in the umbrella lead about bombings in Iraq and government responses, the focus of the lead was on what the government was doing as opposed to the bombings. The bombings helped provide a context as to the situation the government was facing. Too much detail about the bombings—where they were, how many people were killed and injured, or who may have set them off—provides context, but all that additional information detracts from the story's focus: government action against terror attacks.

The temptation to get wordy in a print lead often stems from being unsure about what should be the focus of the story. This problem can crop up in stories about meetings or speeches. If the school board approves several items, it might be difficult to choose the best one. Or if a prominent person delivers a speech, it might be hard to pick the most important point presented. You can then submit to temptation and try to write an umbrella lead that has too much information in it.

For example: "The school board voted last night to increase high school activity fees, cut back on media center purchases, require paper instead of polyurethane plates in the cafeteria, and honor the swim team for its third-place showing in the regional swim meet."

This lead really should be considered a "suitcase" lead, because everything is being stuffed into it. The story then has a problem as to where it should go from there. The best approach to this story might be an umbrella lead, but focusing on the two key budget items—activity fees and media purchases—to open with a cohesive theme on efforts to balance the district's budget and avoid seeking a tax increase.

Print leads also can suffer from the so-what factor. For example: "The school board met last night and approved a host of budget items that aim to improve the education of the school system's 5,200 pupils." That lead may not be wordy, but it does not provide any pertinent information either. It reflects the failure to figure out the story focus.

A lead that gets to the point works better. For example: "High school students will be paying more for after-school activities but the libraries will be spending less in the budget approved last night by the Board of Education." This lead focuses more on the impact of the budget decision rather than on just the decision itself.

In organizing a print story, the format for more than a century has been the inverted pyramid. At the top, the widest part of the pyramid, you present the most important information, then you add detail, less important information, then more detail, until the story winds down. This style originated in the days of hot type, so that if a story ran longer than the space allotted to it, the story could be cut from the bottom without losing the most important information. A variation of the inverted pyramid can be found on many news websites, in which news stories are written in chunks, with the widest or biggest chunk at the top, followed by smaller chunks of detail, less important information. That style is a bit different from broadcast, which usually requires a wrap-up, a conclusion. But the basic thinking about news leads applies to any medium.

Some of the techniques that help ensure that broadcast stories make sense can and should be applied to print leads and stories: Read a lead aloud to tell if the words are easy to follow. Know the story to tell the story. Do your homework and understand what you are writing about before you write. Do not be afraid to rework a lead and a story.

Every story lead relies on news judgment to determine what is relevant or has the greatest impact for readers and what is the most unusual or provides the most tension or conflict. A print lead requires news judgment. It demands accurate, fast, and interesting writing.

Soft Leads: Tell a Story, Delay the Punchline

Print leads that tell a story use narrative devices to entice the reader. These leads sprinkle bits and pieces of information until the point or focus on the story is revealed in the "nut graph." The nut graph can be a sentence or a paragraph that should leave the reader thinking, "Aha! I see where we're going with this." The beginnings of these stories delay the key or nut of the story for a few sentences or paragraphs, which is why they are also called delayed leads. Although these leads generally work best with feature stories, they can be used in hard news reporting as well. And while they relate to print stories, these narrative devices are often applied in broadcast writing as well.

Four kinds of soft leads are the anecdotal lead, the example lead, the scene-setting lead, and the mystery or suspense lead.

An anecdotal lead begins with a short story or an anecdote that gives the reader a sense of a person, an event, or a situation. When the *New York Times* opened its series on class in America on May 16, 2005, the first story began with three anecdotes describing how three people from three different social classes had a heart attack. The nut graph followed and explained that their common experience of a heart attack led to widely different treatments because of their social class. The rest of the story went into detail on the three individuals, their treatment, and the effect of social class on their treatment and recovery, weaving in statistics that showed how these individuals represent a larger trend.

Broadcast news stories use anecdotal leads often when reporting on consumer issues. A story on interest-only mortgages might begin with the anecdote of one couple that could not afford a house with a conventional thirty-year mortgage loan but could when this new loan option was made available to them. The story would then explain the pros and cons of an interest-only mortgage. This particular anecdotal lead might also be considered an example lead, in which one couple's anecdote serves as an example to illustrate a larger trend. This same type of storytelling format can apply to print stories as well.

A scene-setting lead begins with a description of a place, event, or situation to give the reader a sense of being there and to set the stage for what the story is all about. It is the print equivalent of an opening wide shot or a bit of ambient or natural sound. When the *Providence Journal* profiled the comeback of former child country singer Billy Gilman, reporter Rick Massimo began the story by describing what Gilman was doing during the filming of a new music video. The description is used to set up the reader for a story about the singer who is no longer a child phenomenon.

Broadcast feature stories often use scene-setting leads. The story of a female football place kicker opens by setting the scene with the natural sounds and pictures of a football team running and tearing a banner at the start of a football game. In print, the reporter uses words to set up the scene, giving the reader a sense of what the story will be examining.

A mystery or suspense lead often describes a person or situation in such a way that it leaves the reader guessing as to how to solve an unasked question along the way. Each sentence of a mystery or suspense lead drops clues until the nut graph or sentence provides the

BOX 6.1

Example of a Scene-Setting Lead

"Cameras, lights and crew members are packed into Perks and Corks, a coffee shop–bar with dark beams and pastel walls in downtown Westerly, to shoot a short scene in Billy Gilman's *Everything and More* video. The goal here is a flashback sequence starring Gilman and his love interest in the video, played by 17-year-old Christine Perkins . . .

"Billy Gilman chasing after a girl? Sitting at a bar? Even if he's only drinking coffee? Heck, Billy Gilman drinking coffee?

"It's been a few years since Billy, who lives in Hope Valley and turns 17 in three weeks, was the boy wonder of Nashville, with a slew of youngest-ever accomplishments, a Grammy nomination and 2 million albums sold. Now Gilman, a skinny teenager with big blue eyes, is looking to be, literally, the Comeback Kid."

Rick Massimo, "Billy Gilman's New Pitch," *Providence Journal*, May 1, 2005.

BOX 6.2

Print versus Broadcast

Like many newspaper writers who are confronted with making the transition to broadcast writing, I thought the two styles could never mix. I had assumed that my news judgment but not my writing style could be transferred. I was wrong.

It was not until years later, as I looked back on some of my clips as education writer for the *Plain Dealer* in Cleveland, that I found a news feature story that could almost pass for a broadcast package script because it opened with a scene-setting description.

Here is the lead:

> The four-foot-high open letter to pupils on the wall of Room 107 said it all:
>
> "Dear Students:
>
> Your job is to learn to READ, WRITE, COMPUTE and THINK. My job is to help you learn.
>
> Sincerely, Your Teacher"

This description of a classroom on the first day of school sets up the story of a longtime school administrator who returned to teaching, taking a pay cut in the process. It takes a look at the first day of the school year by telling her story of her first day back in front of a chalkboard in a junior high school.

A television script would have opened with a shot of the open letter and a voice-over saying that first sentence.

I wrote that lead in 1984 and thought nothing of it until I was challenged by my students seventeen years later to prove that print and broadcast are not mutually exclusive. The message, not necessarily the medium, was at the heart of that story.

answer, the punch line. These leads are not question leads, but they do leave readers wondering exactly who or what the story is about.

For example: "Many of them make more money than a Cleveland school teacher, and some of them even make more than principals.

"They can open school and close it.

"Last Monday, Cleveland's custodial employees showed Cleveland they could keep children cold, in the dark or without water when 119 of them called in sick.

"Thus began the latest battle in contract negotiations . . ."[1]

Some of the suspense is dealt with in the second sentence about who really has the power, and then it is fully outlined in the nut graph about the opening of contract talks and issues on each side of the table. The story further cites payroll figures to outline the problems. The purpose of any delayed lead is to intrigue readers and draw them into the story.

Notice that the nut graph in the custodians' contract story was the third paragraph. A lot of news writing relies on the rhythm of threes. In broadcast, a sound bite often works well after the third sentence of a story. A list of three items works well in a summary lead. Using the third paragraph as a nut graph also takes advantage of the rhythm or rule of threes. Another writing technique is the rhythm of yin-yang or opposites, such as: "They can open a school and close it." Reading stories aloud aids in hearing that rhythm.

A lead that tells a story can also be a lead that tells the news. In fact, many news stories in newspapers these days do a little of both. Carl Sessions Stepp refers to this combination of news with narrative as "news plus."[2] These leads aim to focus a story on the context or trend while relating the news and information. An anecdotal or scene-setting lead can be used for a news-plus lead.

John Ellement of the *Boston Globe* wrote what could be considered a news-plus lead:

"PLYMOUTH—When Todd Carruthers tumbled out of a small rowboat and into Duxbury Harbor early Saturday evening, Scott C. Kirby knew immediately that his friend of some 30 years was in deep trouble.

"Carruthers, Kirby knew, could not swim. But what Kirby allegedly did next is one reason Plymouth County prosecutors and state Environmental Police are charging Kirby with the boating equivalent of drunken driving homicide."[3]

Ellement's story goes on to explain the case and outlines other efforts to prosecute deadly boating incidents. Although Ellement does not fall into the trap, some soft leads get so caught up in crafting a story that the news gets left behind or misplaced. It is what has been called "jell-o journalism," and it has been a problem for some twenty-five years, as narrative writing became admired in print. Jerry Lanson and Mitchell Stephens, who wrote about the problem back in 1982, note that "A feature lead on a news story *does* have the advantage of bailing out a confused reporter who can't figure out what the news story is."[4] As a result, a story can be a good read but have no point.

ADDING VOICE AND TONE FOR PRINT

One way to avoid jell-o journalism and to develop the right type of lead for a story involves determining the voice and tone of a news story. The lead sets the tone and introduces the voice in which a news story is told. In broadcast, the reporter or the anchor who is reading the track delivers the voice and tone of the story. In broadcast, you can make your delivery of the words fit the tone of the story. Voice and tone in a broadcast story comes from the words as well as the expression of the words. In print, you have to rely on just the words of the story to establish voice and tone.

Donald Fry has been quoted as defining the voice of a story as "the sum of all the strategies used by the author to create the illusion that the writer is speaking directly to the reader from the page."[5] Print has to "create the illusion" of speaking to the audience, while broadcast can deliver it directly. The voice of a news story is the manner or the style of expression in a story. Actors are keenly aware that the expression of a single word in a single sentence can change the meaning of what they are saying. By changing the manner in which the word is expressed, they can change the voice and tone. When using words alone, the reader may add the emphasis, but it may not be in the place you want it. When writing for print, you need

FIGURE 6.1. This Mike Luckovich cartoon, in the wake of the September 11 attacks, conveys a somber tone rather than the usual satirical tone of editorial cartoons. (By permission of Mike Luckovich and Creators Syndicate, Inc.)

to be very clear in determining the tone or attitude you want to portray toward the subject of a story and toward your audience reading the story. Your words have to ensure that your audience grasps the tone you want them to hear in your story.

In any newspaper you can find a spectrum of tones. On the op-ed page or in letters to the editor, you might find a tone of indignation or contempt. A political cartoon often can have a tone that is funny, sarcastic, poignant, or pointed. Mike Luckovich's cartoon of Lady Liberty crying, with the burning World Trade Center towers reflected in her eyes, is one example of poignant.

In a consumer technology column, you might find a somewhat promotional tone, encouraging readers to explore the new technologies listed in the column or explaining the benefits of a new technology. (Note that touting one product to the exclusion of others would be ethically suspect, if not prohibited.) When a 2003 Dan Gillmor tech column in the *San Jose Mercury News* addressed Voice over Internet Protocol (VoIP) technology, Gillmor wrote, "Two factors make VoIP virtually unstoppable: cost and the continuing evolution of communications technology."[6]

Op-ed column writers often take on different tones to make their point. *New York Times* columnist Thomas L. Friedman often uses a promotional tone when writing about globalization and the need for Americans and its leaders to address this new world economic order. "On foreign policy President Bush has offered a big idea: the expansion of freedom, particularly in the Arab-Muslim world, where its absence was one of the forces propelling 9/11. That is a big, bold and compelling idea—worthy of a presidency and America's long-term interests," Friedman wrote in an April 29, 2005, column. Friedman then chastised the Bush administration on globalization by writing, "on the home front, this team has no big idea—certainly none that relates to the biggest challenge and opportunity facing us today: the flattening of the global economic playing field in a way that is allowing more people from more places to compete and collaborate with your kids and mine than ever before."[7]

Veteran Boston reporter and editor Mark Leccese, in introducing print writing to his students, notes that news stories should take on a tone that is straightforward, serious, and authoritative. The voice of news writing, he adds, is clear, concise, and simple. The June 1, 2005, revelation that a top FBI official was the confidential source for Carl Bernstein and Bob Woodward's Watergate stories in 1974 and 1975 provides a solid example of the voice and tone of news stories versus editorials and analyses.

Here are two news story leads: "Three decades after he helped unravel the Watergate scandal that forced President Nixon to resign, former FBI official W. Mark Felt was identified Tuesday as the legendary source 'Deep Throat'" (*USA Today*, June 1, 2005).

"The mystery surrounding one of America's most durable journalistic secrets was solved yesterday with the unmasking of an aging, retired FBI official as the anonymous Watergate-era source known as 'Deep Throat'" (*Baltimore Sun*, June 1, 2005).

Here are two leads to editorials on the subject: "One of the best-kept secrets of journalism and government is finally out, in time to give a longtime FBI executive a jolt of celebrity and gratitude in his 91st year" (*Denver Post*, June 1, 2005 editorial, "Deep Throat Did the Right Thing").

"Mark Felt, the former no. 2 official at the FBI who became a famous news source, proved the tremendous value of one individual who breaks rules to reveal an important truth" (*Seattle Times*, June 2, 2005 editorial, "The Ultimate Source, Deep and Historic").

Each of the two editorials began with a statement of admiration, a point of view in favor of Felt's revelation. The voice and the tone of the editorials are different from the news stories because they are presenting an argument. Notice how the voice and tone changes in the following lead about the Watergate reporters, Woodward and Bernstein.

"It was like Simon sitting down with Garfunkel or Sonny returning to Cher. Woodward and Bernstein were sitting side by side, openly discussing the identity of Deep Throat. Starting on *Today* and wending their way from *Good Morning America* to *Larry King Live*, the two Watergate reporters basked in the relief and reflected glory of giving name to their anonymous source at long last."[8]

This story has a more entertaining, breezy tone to it. The opening paragraph provides the attitude, and it is carried through the entire article. It is not a hard news story about the revelation but a sidebar feature about the two journalists who became famous together thirty years ago and were famously together again in June 2005. The reference to a pop musical duo and the description of two guys sitting "side by side" provides that sense of lightness.

The words chosen to explain a situation by an impartial observer are different than those used by someone passionately involved. A news story is written with the voice of an impartial observer but uses quotes and words of sources who may be passionately involved. For example, a *Boston Globe* story about outrage over the early closing of a Catholic school quoted the mayor as saying, "Don't they care about the human factor?"

But the lead of the story set out a straightforward tone: "The Catholic Archdiocese of Boston, seeking to head off the possible occupation of a closing Catholic school by angry parents, yesterday abruptly changed the locks, canceled graduation ceremonies for children as young as 3, and canceled the final two days of classes."[9]

In a feature story, sometimes the voice of a key character may provide the voice, the point of view, for the lead of a story. That was the case for Gerald Carbone, at the *Providence Journal*, in writing a story about a graveside reunion of Vietnam soldiers. He wrote in an in-house column examining writing, called "Power of Words," that he decided that the voice of a story about an Army veteran who died in Vietnam would be that of his friend Richard Edgell.[10]

Here is his lead: "Rich Edgell steered his car slowly through the cemetery and, through the open windows, the tombstones on either side of the road seemed to whisper.

"His car was one of many in a long caravan wending its way through St. Ann's Cemetery yesterday, snaking toward the grave of Peter Frank Fegatelli.

"Edgell was the closest man to Fegatelli when he called 'I'm hit!' 33 years ago yesterday in a jungle in Vietnam. Those were Fegatelli's dying words. A helicopter carried him to an evacuation hospital, his first stop on the way to burial in St. Ann's.

"The men of Fegatelli's unit, Company D (RANGER), 151st Infantry of the Indiana Army National Guard, never got to see him again. And so they came to see him yesterday, more than three decades after their 19-year-old comrade fell."[11]

Carbone used a point of view to determine his voice in telling the story, as well as the tone in his example of a scene-setting, delayed lead. The nut graph is the fourth one, providing the center for the rest of the story.

Leads establish the voice and tone of a news story, but the entire story needs to maintain it. In print stories, the choice of language provides the tone. In the story about the Vietnam vets, the words chosen were reverential and somber. The word "whisper" in the lead provided the quiet tone that Carbone needed to carry through the story. The details Carbone used to describe the scene shaped the tone of the story.

Note that the lead lets the audience "see" Edgell and see what he sees. As such, this story could translate into a broadcast story, if a camera, or even an audio recorder, had captured what Carbone did in his notes. The mindset of convergence journalism notes the narrative similarities in delivering news and information as opposed to its differences. Good storytelling is good storytelling.

PRINT REPORTING: ADDING CONTEXT AND DETAILS

To capture details and nuances, reporters need to know how to look for them and find them. Good preparation—good background research and good observation skills—come in handy. If you have the background information about a person or an event you are covering, you can devote more of your limited reporting time gathering details and context. When gathering details and context, look for what is different or unusual in the scene or situation, to avoid the "vacuum-cleaner" mentality and waste time gathering extraneous information.[12]

For print stories, reporters need to dig deeper into the background information for a story if they expect to provide context. The better the background information, the better the reporting. Better backgrounding leads to more direct questions in interviews, more direct focus in observations, and better mental sorting of source information, comments, and perspectives. Good background information opens up a path for reporting that goes beneath the surface; it seeks the context of the news.

The background information gathered to report a story can then be passed on to readers to give them the context, the background, of the news. Print stories have more space to pass on that context.

For example, a story about a rally of motorcyclists at the statehouse advocating a loosening of helmet laws could begin and end with what people at the rally are saying and what information they are providing. But the story would have more context if you knew whether and when the state legislature would be voting on a helmet law bill, what is in the bill, if there is a counter effort to tighten helmet laws and who is affiliated with it, who are major proponents of loosening the law, and how prevalent motorcycle deaths and injuries are in the state with the current helmet law. Digging into public records, such as state highway department accident records, into past news stories, and into the websites of helmet law supporters and proponents before the rally adds depth and understanding to the reporting. Good backgrounding opens up more possibilities for good reporting, and good reporting leads to better stories.

Good backgrounding explains why beat reporters in newspapers often have an edge over their broadcast counterparts, who are often general assignment reporters without a specialty coverage area. Every story a beat reporter writes in his or her area of expertise becomes part of the background knowledge that informs the next story the reporter will do. Each time the transportation reporter has to write a story about a highway project's construction delays, the research she did for the last story on the project will help in formulating the reporting for the next story.

Reporters who are new to a topic need to do enough background research to feel competent to check, verify, and even expand on the initial information provided at a speech, meeting,

BOX 6.3

Legal Education

As the education reporter for the *Plain Dealer* in Cleveland, I sometimes spent more time covering the law than covering the schools. The school system was involved in a federal court action to desegregate its schools, and state education laws often opened up litigation. In writing about the Cleveland Public Schools' legal entanglements, I could get the court documents and comments from lawyers from all parties about legal precedents and various interpretations of the law. But I quickly learned that I could do a better story if I knew exactly what the laws that the lawyers were interpreting really said. I could ask better questions and avoid being misled or confused. I could avoid superficial reporting.

news conference, rally, or protest. They also should try to do enough background research to feel competent enough to uncover unreported or underreported areas on a beat.

Good backgrounding can help focus on-the-scene observation. More focused observation leads to better detail in stories. Curtis MacDougall, who wrote the standard journalism text, *Interpretative Reporting*, notes that careful observation begets good detail and description. He writes that "careful description means noting features that escape the untrained spectator."[13] A corollary might be that careful description means noting features that would reveal an aspect that your audience might find interesting.

Julie Sullivan, an award-winning reporter for the *Portland Oregonian*, has been quoted as saying that the details she chooses for a story are ones that she remembers from an interview or event, without referring to her notes first.[14] In writing about a tattoo school, Sullivan points out two items in the classroom that takes the room from ordinary to interesting. Here is part of her story:

"To understand how far tattoos and body piercing have traveled into the mainstream, enter Captain Jack's Tattoo and Body Piercing School on Southeast Hawthorne Boulevard. There, under posters of Marilyn Monroe and a prosthetic captain's hook, the licensed career school graduates tattoo artists after 210 hours of theory, 150 hours of practice and 50 tattoos."[15]

Notice that Sullivan did not go into a long-winded description of the room but mentioned just two items—the Marilyn Monroe poster and the prosthetic captain's hook—to give the reader an insight, a revelation, into how offbeat the school is. She also used a description that served the purpose of reinforcing the theme of her story: a tattoo school is joining the mainstream of vocational education. It is a good bet that those two items in the tattoo school classroom would not be found in a more traditional classroom. That twist helps readers picture the school and lures them into wanting to read more.

One of the more memorable stories among hundreds in the *New York Times* in the wake of the September 11, 2001, World Trade Center attacks was one by Jim Dwyer about the survival of six people in an elevator. Dwyer focused on a window washer's squeegee that the men in the elevator used to cut through Sheetrock and escape from the building before it collapsed. Here he uses detail about the men's grave situation:

"At that moment—8:48 a.m.—1 World Trade Center had entered the final 100 minutes of its existence. No one knew the clock was running, least of all the men trapped inside Car 69-A; they were as cut off 500 feet in the sky as if they had been trapped 500 feet underwater. They did not know their lives would depend on a simple tool."[16] The squeegee became the focus, the hero of the story.

In both Dwyer's and Sullivan's reporting, they found details that revealed an added dimension to their stories. Dwyer's detail came from attentive listening in interviewing the people in the elevator about their experiences. Sullivan's came during attentive viewing while visiting the school. Notice too that Dwyer and Sullivan used details that provided authority, such as the number of minutes left before the tower collapsed or the number of hours of study by the tattoo students. Those details elevated their print news stories to a level that made reading them more memorable.

Details come not just from observation but from interviewing and from interviewing a variety of people. It is easy to find two opposing viewpoints, and that stark conflict can make for a story with great tension. It is also easy to find people of similar viewpoints, such as most of those people at the helmet law rally. But that may not be the whole story. A story can be inaccurate if pertinent facts or perspectives are omitted or disregarded. Because newspaper and magazine stories have more space, newspaper and magazine reporters need to devote more time to getting more perspectives from more sources. Good background research and observation can lead reporters to both.

At that helmet law rally, good background about helmet legislation and motorcycle deaths and injuries could help focus questions posed to the rally's participants. But good observation at the rally itself, of people watching as well as those participating in it, might add another perspective. The people on the sidelines also have a perspective that may be worth reporting. The only way to know is to be observant and then act on those observations by asking questions.

Good background and observation, essential in any news story, can be critical in a profile, a news feature that highlights one person. Howard Bryant, a sportswriter and columnist for the *Boston Herald*, says he digs hard to find out an obscure but telling bit of information that he will use to connect with a pro football or basketball player who is the subject of a profile. Bryant says that that tidbit of background information can be just the icebreaker to get someone talking. "If you have something to open up, it tells them you did your homework."[17]

That crucial bit of detail found in background research opens up avenues for anecdotes that can reveal the essence of a person at the center of a profile. But background research is not limited to secondary sources. Friends, family, coworkers, teachers, classmates, and neighbors can provide information, or what could be considered third-party perspective. The obituary section of a newspaper has become fertile ground for profiles. The notion of an obituary has evolved from a story marking a death to a story celebrating a life in many news organizations.

The *New York Times* demonstrated that philosophy in a series of short profiles entitled "Portraits of Grief," about the more than 2,200 victims of the World Trade Center attacks in 2001. Each portrait was 200 to 250 words long, and captured a person's character and personality, but also a sense of loss in the community.

The *CBS Evening News* has been offering a broadcast equivalent in 2004 and 2005 in a segment called, "Fallen Heroes" on U.S. soldiers who have died in Iraq and Afghanistan. The segments run about twenty-five seconds and feature insights into each man or woman killed, such as their hobbies and personality traits, or their sense of duty to serve in the military and in a war zone.

The *Times* and the CBS stories, although short, focus on what made a person unique. The stories examine either a turning point in a life, a challenge or obstacle overcome, or an aspiration met or unfulfilled. They rely on third-party perspectives—family, friends, and comrades—to explain the individual. The *Times* also provided each person greater dimension by placing them in their work setting—the World Trade Center towers—and in another setting, such as at home, enjoying a hobby, or relaxing with friends. CBS also provides the work setting—the military—and the personal perspective in its stories about military war dead.

Although using different media to deliver these compact profiles, the *Times* and CBS use similar storytelling devices to make their stories compelling. Both news organizations have placed these profiles online, where they can be searched and updated, using the strengths of the Internet to expand the audience for the stories.[18]

DOTTING THE I'S AND CROSSING THE T'S

When words substitute for pictures, the words need to be precise. Attention to detail in producing news stories for print means precision in facts, spelling, grammar, and punctuation. While a misspelling can lead to a mispronunciation in broadcast, a misspelling can lead to angry calls and letters, even a lawsuit, in print. Sloppy grammar generates more of an outcry in print than in broadcast, because audiences more readily notice grammatical mistakes in text than in speech. Bad punctuation in a broadcast script may affect its rhythm and its sound, but bad punctuation in a print story affects a story's credibility.

Corrections columns in newspapers are filled with examples of tiny errors—the wrong date for a deadline, the wrong identities of two boys in a picture, an extra zero in a number, and a wife's name missing from an obituary are some errors that have appeared in corrections columns. To avoid these kinds of errors, print journalists need to be alert and to double-check for facts, spelling, grammar, and punctuation. That double-checking comes both during reporting and during writing.

In reporting, that may mean asking for the information again, or checking it with a second or even a third source. In writing, that may mean doing without some information if it cannot be verified. An old editor's line applies: "When in doubt, leave it out."

Precision with Quotes

Perhaps the trickiest area for precision in print is the use of quotation marks. Both sound bites and quotes lend authenticity to a story. With sound on tape in radio and television, the words that someone said are right there; the audience hears the person delivering them. In print, quotes are a re-creation of the actual utterances. To best evoke authenticity, the words inside quotation marks must represent the exact words spoken; anything else is deceptive. Problems with quotes plague print reporters, as sources claim they were misquoted or their quotes were taken out of context. Journalists have more trouble with the use of quote marks than any other punctuation.

Problems within the quotation marks arise when writers "clean up" some of the words spoken for sake of clarity. If someone speaks in fits and starts, adds "ums" and "ahs" to the sentence, makes a grammatical error such as mixing up verb tenses, print writers sometimes eliminate such verbal hiccups. But if the quote is so altered that it distorts the speaker's meaning, then the writer can be accused of misrepresentation.

Kansas City Star ombudsman Derek Donovan received complaints from readers questioning if the Washington reporter had altered President George W. Bush's language, when it quoted Bush as saying, "People that had been trained in some instances to disassemble—that means not tell the truth." Donovan notes it was a verbal hitch, explaining that the newspaper tries to follow the rule of never changing quotes.[19] Audio recorders can help in double-checking exact quotes, to help in discerning similar-sounding words that may mean something completely different. The *Associated Press Stylebook* states that ellipses (. . .) can be used to fix "casual minor tongue slips . . . but even that should be done with extreme caution."[20]

BOX 6.4

Quotation Rules

Print stories can deal with people's words in three ways:

- Direct quote, using a person's exact words: "I did not have sexual relations with that woman, Ms. Lewinsky," said President Bill Clinton in his first direct comments on the Monica Lewinsky scandal.
- Direct quote with ellipsis, using exact words but denoting areas where words have been omitted: "I did not urge anyone to say anything that was untrue," the president said, adding, "that's my statement to you. . . . And beyond that, I think it's very important that we let the investigation take its course."
- Paraphrase, using the essence of a person's words, not the exact words; no quotation marks are used: President Clinton denied any sexual relationship with former intern Monica Lewinsky.
- Partial quote, using a few exact words: President Clinton said he did not have "sexual relations" with Monica Lewinsky.

Note that punctuation, such as commas, goes within quote marks.

When ellipses are used within quotation marks, they alert readers that a portion of the comment has been edited out, either to make the quote clearer or to shorten it because of space limitation. What may be edited out could be a long-winded explanation or a section from a document with lengthy examples. The key to using ellipses is to use them to clarify and simplify but not to distort.

Print stories have the flexibility to use more quotes than broadcast stories, but they should be used to illustrate more context and subtlety, not to add density. Quotes should be used in the same way that detailed description is used in print stories: to reveal information and insight. Using too many quotes or using quotes that ramble on ends up filling space, but they may do little to tell the audience any interesting or useful information. Quotes must have a point. They should give the reader another voice in the story, provided that voice can explain, describe, enlighten, show, or evoke.

Precision in Fact

Newspaper style requires precise detail in identifiers, such as the names of people or businesses, the location of a building or a house, and the time of day when an event happened. Some general rules: Proper names of people often use middle initials: Capt. Phillip T. Esposito. Legislators' districts or states and party affiliations are included with a name: Rep. Bob Barr, R-Ga., or Sen. Kent Conrad, D-N.D. Full names of businesses are used: Microsoft Corp. Dates are spelled out if older than a week: September 11, 2001. Titles of agencies, officials, and experts are often not shortened: Dr. Michael Charness, chief of staff of the VA Boston Healthcare System. Numbers can be exact: $243.1 million budget.

Seemingly small errors can carry big repercussions. Referring to a gas leak on Peachtree Road instead of Peachtree Drive in Atlanta could lead to unnecessary panic and concern. Sloppiness in small details undermines readers' trust that journalists can get information right in bigger, weightier matters. National Public Radio ombudsman Jeffrey Dvorkin devoted a column to NPR errors, noting how people notice when the Department of Veteran Affairs gets called the Veterans Administration, or when Key Bridge in Washington is referred to as the Key Bridge.[21]

Precision with Words: Spelling and Meaning

Nothing offends a person more than having his or her name misspelled, and nothing shoots down the veracity of a story more than the wrong word. Smith and Smythe may be pronounced the same, but the print reporter needs to know and note the difference. A wrong middle initial or misspelling of the name of someone charged with murder (Jon H. Smith versus John T. Smith) can lead to a libel lawsuit. The *Associated Press Stylebook* includes common

BOX 6.5

Corrections

Many news organizations have policies and procedures for handling corrections. Most newspapers run corrections in a box or column on page 2 of the paper. When I was a reporter at the *Plain Dealer*, if you made a mistake that required a write-up in the corrections column, you had to write a memo explaining how and why the mistake happened and what you would do to ensure it would not happen again. It was a tedious exercise and one more reason, in addition to professionalism and credibility, that I would check and recheck my stories.

misspelled and misused words, and good reporters refer to it and to a dictionary to ensure precision in the words they use.

Here are a few common errors in word choice: uninterested (not interested) vs. disinterested (impartial); allude to (hint at) vs. refer to (note it); comprises (contains, includes) vs. composes (puts together). And computerized spelling programs do not help in determining the correct usage of a word; they only find spelling errors, not usage errors.

Political polarization and political correctness also make attention to word choice crucial. Even labels such as "liberal" and "conservative" elicit readers' questions as to journalists' biases and adherence to fairness.

News audiences may raise issues of precision more in relation to newspaper and magazine stories because of the permanency of the printed word. But sloppiness in any news outlet tarnishes the trust relationship between journalists and their audiences.

FOLLOW THE MONEY AND DO THE MATH

"Follow the money." It is the most memorable piece of advice about journalism, uttered in perhaps the most famous movie about journalism, *All the President's Men*. The line, from Deep Throat, the secret, unnamed source for Bob Woodward and Carl Bernstein, helped guide the pair's investigation into the 1970s Watergate scandal that forced the resignation of President Richard Nixon. The money the reporting pair followed involved presidential campaign contributions, and it tied a group of burglars to the Oval Office. By following the money, Woodward and Bernstein unearthed one of the biggest stories in journalism in a half-century.

Following the money may not bring you fame or fortune, as it did for Woodward and Bernstein, but it can bring story ideas. So too will a corollary statement: Follow the numbers.

To do either, you have to be willing to do the math. Money and numbers go hand in hand. The days are long gone when a journalist can demur and not do simple calculations to double-check a report or a source's statistical assertions. In the era of spin and manipulation, a reporter who uses information relating to numbers without checking it can develop a huge credibility problem. This is especially true for numbers taken from other stories that are accessed via the Web. In these cases, you are trusting the writer of the story to get the numbers right, and you are trusting the original source of the numbers, whether a report or a person, to get the numbers right. The old adage "Figures don't lie but liars can figure" reinforces the need for every journalist to be equipped with some basic math along with their notebook and digital camera.

It is not hard to think about the correlation of math and money in reporting about governmental spending, taxes, jobs, politics, technology, business, and finance. That is obvious. And every sports fan or rotisserie league player uses numbers and statistics all the time. But entertainment, health, medicine, and even lifestyle stories can also involve math. From box office receipts to trends in music, figures can inspire a story or make one better.

While journalists may be more adept in verbal than math skills, they are often called upon to translate numbers and mathematical concepts into useful information. The first mistake journalists make with numbers is to avoid them altogether. The second is to merely throw out a bunch of numbers without helping audiences understand them or relate to them. In either case, audiences are left confused and frustrated.

For example, a story about electrical rates going up might include information about the percent increase the power company wants the public utility commission to approve and the amount of revenue that increase will generate. So a lead might read: "Kilowatt Power is seeking a 4 percent increase, in an effort to generate $20 million in revenue over the next three years. The company plans to use the new revenue to upgrade its power grid which would lead to a 6 percent increase in monthly electric distribution, generating an additional 3.4 million kilowatts per day."

After reading all that, readers still have no answer to their main question: How much more will I pay? It helps the reader if you have a sentence that says, "An average homeowner who pays $200 a month in the peak summer months for electricity will be paying about $8 more each month, or nearly an additional $100 annually."

Consider how to help an audience relate to just how rich Microsoft's Bill Gates really is. In the past few years, his net worth has been hovering around $50 billion. Since a Hummer costs between $50,000 and $60,000, it is easier for people to grasp his wealth if they read that Bill Gates could buy a Hummer for every man, woman, and child in the town of Amarillo, Texas. It is also easier for people to understand the magnitude of his feat when Bob Beamon jumped twenty-nine feet, two and a half inches, in 1968 if they know that it was the equivalent of jumping two car lengths.

The *New York Times* had a little fun with a story about a twenty-by-fifteen-foot pothole. With graphic illustration and text, it was determined that the hole would fit a Hummer or eighty-six people and would rent for about $2,500 a month.[22]

When print journalists have only words to tell a story, they need to use imagery to help their audiences visualize abstractions such as billions of dollars and thirty-foot leaps.

Percents

Entertainment reporters in the summer of 2005 began focusing on whether the summer movie season was going to be a good one, based on a three-month slump in box office numbers. But which numbers really told the story: the amount of money being spent overall at the box office, the number of tickets sold, or both? And what decrease in percentage would be considered troublesome? Several news stories focused on the continuing box office slump, noting a drop-off of money spent each week in 2005 compared to 2004. So how big of a drop was there during the Memorial Day weekend? A simple percentage calculation comes in handy for that story.

To figure out the box office percentage decrease, apply these formulas:

Decrease: 2004 number ($238 million) minus 2005 number ($225 million) = difference this year from last: 238 – 225 = 13 million = difference

Divide the difference by the starting number, 238: 13/238 = 0.05 = 5% decrease

But what if the box office numbers increase next year? What would that look like?

Increase: 2006 number ($250 million) minus 2005 number ($225 million) = difference: 250 – 225 = 25; 25/225 = 0.02 = 2%

BOX 6.6

Percentage

A percent equals 1/100 of a whole. So the percentage equals the part divided by the whole.

Part / Whole = Percent (%) = Percent (.??)

6/10 = 60% = .06

25/125 = 20% = .02

BOX 6.7

Percentage Increase and Decrease

A percentage change equals the difference in the old and new number divided by the starting number.

Increase: New – Old = Difference, or 100 – 75 = 25
Difference / New = Percentage, or 25/100 = .25 = 25%
Decrease: Old – New = Difference, or 75 – 50 = 25
Difference / Old = Percentage, or 25/75 = .33 = 33%

And what if you wanted to know how much of the decrease in the box office receipts of *Star Wars Episode III* was between its first weekend opening and the third weekend? The same calculation would do the trick. (Here are the numbers to try it: $108.44 million = first weekend, $25.09 million = third weekend.)

Another use of the percentage formula can be used to determine how much an amount equals in comparison to the whole. Say you want to demonstrate how much of the Memorial Day weekend box office was produced by *Star Wars Episode III*. In this calculation, you do not need to worry about the subtraction part of the increase/decrease formula, just the simple division.

So let's see the impact of *Star Wars* on the Memorial Day weekend box office. *Star Wars* earned a little more than $70 million of the $225 million taken in by theaters over the four-day weekend. Part / Whole = 70/ 225 = 0.31 = 31%.

But what if you are an entertainment reporter who just got a press release from Fox, the company distributing *Star Wars*, bragging that their new movie's opening weekend box office receipts represents 40 percent or nearly half of the box office for the first three weeks it has been showing. How can you check if their percentage is right? First, you would have to add total box office receipts for the three weeks ($127 million + $225 million + $158 million = $510 million) and of *Star Wars* receipts ($25 million + $70 million + $108 million = $203 million): 203/510 = 0.40 = 40%.

One final point to remember: A percentage is different from a percentage point. Journalists are notorious for confusing the two and for confusing their audiences. When the *Star Wars*' share of the box office from its opening weekend of 70 percent dropped the next weekend to 30 percent, it dropped 40 percentage points, not 40 percent.

So if you wanted to point out how the movie public's interest in the movie is waning by showing how its percentage in the weekend box office receipts is falling, you would be wrong

BOX 6.8

Percentage Point Increase and Decrease

Percentage Point Increase = New – Old (10% – 7% = 3 percentage point increase)
Percentage Point Decrease = Old – New (7% – 5% = 2 percentage point decrease)
Percent Increase / Decrease = Difference / Starting Number (3/10 = 30% increase)
(2/7 = 28.5% increase)

to say that the movie's box office receipts dropped 40 percent. To determine the percent decrease, you would have to go back to our earlier formula and divide the difference (in this case 40 percent) by the starting number (in this case 70 percent).

Poll Problems

Confusion over percentage point increases and decreases and percent increases and decreases often develops when reporting on polls. You cannot escape polls when it comes to politics, but you can escape the manipulation and spin often accompanying them by political opponents with a double-check of the math. Polls contain myriad traps for the journalist, and percent change versus percentage point change is just one. Here are two more to be concerned about: margin of error and poll characteristics.

Any poll story should include the margin of error, which amounts to the range in which the poll sample numbers could vary from what might be results for an entire population. Say a poll of a thousand people about a city council race finds that 52 percent of those surveyed say they would vote for Jo Jones, while 48 percent favor Sam Smith, and the poll's margin of error is plus or minus 5 percentage points. That means that Jones could have support from as little as 47 percent to as much as 57 percent, while Smith could have support from as little as 43 percent to as much as 53 percent.

BOX 6.9

Margin of Error

1,000 people polled +/– 5% margin of error
Jo Jones 52% = range 47% to 57%
Sam Smith 48% = range 43% to 53%

Is Jones ahead of Smith in the polls? Not really. The margin of error means that Jones could have as little as 47 percent support and Smith as much as 53 percent. It could be a tie. In fact, during much of the polling leading up to the 2004 presidential election, numerous public opinion polls showed Senator John Kerry and President George Bush in a "statistical dead heat" because the margin of error was as small as two percentage points and the poll numbers remained tight, varying between 46 to 48 percent for the two men.

Note that polls are not foolproof. A journalist needs to remember that a public opinion poll only reflects what the public's opinion is at a certain time. A poll of likely voters two months before an election cannot truly reveal the election winner. And both sides in a political battle use poll results to put their candidate in the best light.

Here are some questions and issues to look at with public opinion polls: How random and how big is the sample? Who is being polled? How are the questions phrased? Is the phrasing aimed at getting a particular answer? Are the questions "tilted?" Who is behind the poll? Do pollsters have an agenda that might figure in the polling questions, its timing, and its interpretation?

Like public opinion political polls, scientific surveys and medical research studies also have math problems relating to percentages, margins of error, sample size, and sponsorship. Every day, a new medical or scientific report comes out that provides insight into a treatment for a debilitating disease or a warning about the harm of certain foods or the advantage of a lifestyle change. For example, the journalist who reports on a study that says that drinking a cup of pickle brine daily will cut the risk of developing colon cancer in half needs to ask questions about how this conclusion was reached. If a national pickle growers group sponsored the study of a group of ten people in their twenties, then those warning signals should lead journalists to doubt the overall usefulness and validity of that study.

Victor Cohn, the late science writer for the *Washington Post*, in his book with Lewis Cope, *News and Numbers*, suggests several questions that journalists can ask to check on the validity and usefulness of research findings. Not only should reporters ask questions about the research similar to questions asked about opinion polls (who is in the group of patients being studied and who did it or sponsored it) but also what the researchers did to ensure that their results would be statistically true and verifiable. That involves checking out survey questions to see if they are biased. (For example: Would you favor eliminating unnecessary federal handouts if it would cut taxes? or Would you favor eliminating federal welfare programs if it would cut taxes?) That also means asking about other explanations for the results and the measurements used to determine improvement or benefit.[23]

Another trap for journalists with scientific surveys and studies involves confusing correlation with causation. A correlation means a link has been found between two things, like bicycle riding and skinned knees. (For example: More children with skinned knees have been found to ride bicycles than ride pedal cars.) A causation links one action or item as creating or causing the other. (Riding bicycles will give children skinned knees.) The trouble begins

BOX 6.10

Mean versus Median

Mean or average = sum of numbers / number of numbers
Median = number at the midpoint of a list of numbers
Home Values:

House 1 = $5 million
House 2 = $5 million
House 3 = $4 million
House 4 = $3.5 million
House 5 = $2 million
House 6= $2 million
House 7 = $1 million

Total home values = $23.5 million – House 1 + 2 + 3 + 4 + 5 + 6 + 7
Mean = $23.5 million / 7 = $3.2 million
Median = $3.5 million

when journalists, in translating studies, simplify findings so much that they erroneously interpret a correlation to be a cause and effect. This problem can crop up when reading someone else's summary of the study without going to the original source.

Public records can be fertile ground for stories based on numbers, but they can be full of mathematical misunderstandings as well. Information about home sales, property values, and residents' incomes can provide insight into the financial well-being of individual communities. Understanding how to compute the mean or average versus the median can help provide that insight.

Say a block in the town you cover is full of huge houses and could be considered the most expensive block in town. How would you know? You could go to the city's property tax records and check out the assessed value of all seven homes on the block, add them together, and divide by seven to get the average value of the homes. But looking at the values of the homes, you see two very highly valued homes and several bunched at the lower end. The median value would be the value of the home falling in the middle of the list.

The mean or the average is useful when a list of numbers do not deviate from each other very much. But when a list of numbers has some extremes, the median works better. In computing the average annual salary of a school district employee, you would include the part-time cafeteria worker making $7,000 and the superintendent of schools making $75,000. The median salary might be a better measurement, and it would tell you that about half the district's employees make more than the median, $45,000, and half make less.

These simple math formulae come in handy on daily stories and major projects. Consider a story about the most dangerous neighborhoods in your town. If you pull the statistics on crimes filed by the FBI, will you have an accurate picture of the dangers in each neighborhood? How would you know? You could look at the numbers, compute the percentages, but is that enough? In 1998, the *Philadelphia Inquirer* wrote about the manipulation of police crime data when the numbers about the decline in rapes in the city did not quite "add up." The paper found that some major crimes were reported as minor ones, or were not reported at all, in a widespread effort to show a decline in city crime. Computer-assisted reporting, using a database on a computer spreadsheet, helped uncover that story.

One final area of numbers involves budgets. Governmental budgets can be a gold mine of story ideas, but it takes knowledge, creativity, and some hard work to find the mother lode. Budgets almost always involve change and conflict, two topics that always make for a good story. But budgets also contain lots of numbers and most people, when confronted with numbers, would rather avoid them than dig deeper into them. So a top challenge for journalists doing stories about budgets is to find the change and the conflict without overwhelming their audience, or themselves, with numbing numbers.

Every year, school superintendents, mayors, city managers, governors, and even the president of the United States are required to develop reports on the money expected to be coming into the treasury and plans for the money going out. A budget, at its simplest, is revenues, money coming in, and expenditures, money going out. School boards, town councils, state legislatures, county commissions, and even the U.S. Congress have to approve a budget or else government services do not get done. So another challenge of journalists is to explain to the audience how the budget affects them and their children or neighborhood. Budget stories involve impact, not just numbers.

When the Rhode Island governor announced his new budget in 2004, the *Providence Journal* devoted two-thirds of its front page and five pages inside the paper to stories and graphics to help readers follow how their tax dollars would be spent. Most useful was a section on the front page of "blurbs" and pictures on key budget provisions with major impact: cell phone fees for improving the 911 system, college tuition increases, and a cigarette tax.

With convergence, some news organizations are using multimedia storytelling to help in budget storytelling. The *Seattle Times* created "The Ax and Tax: A Budget Balancing Exercise" in 2003 which gave users the chance to give pay raises, trim higher education funding, and close foreign trade offices. The *Herald* newspaper in Everett, Washington, created an interactive map to help residents look at four plans for economic development along the city's waterfront and determine costs and benefits.

Numbers, like details, can help add veracity and depth to a news story. The print media tend to be where audiences turn to get further explanations about the government and their world. Understanding how to ensure that numbers provide that explanation gives print journalism relevancy and enhances reporting in any medium.

SUMMARY

News stories in print must use nuance and detail to add context. Print stories add context to make up for the lack of immediacy that broadcast can provide with sound and pictures. Print stories use more background and quotes to add context.

Leads to print stories that tell the news are hard or direct leads. Leads that are more narrative and tell a story are soft or delayed leads. Direct lead types are summary, umbrella, and delayed identification. Narrative lead types are anecdotal, example, scene-setting, and mystery.

The inverted pyramid is the most common story organization for news stories, putting the most important information first and funneling down from there. Stories that use soft or narrative leads include a nut graph that encapsulates the focus of the story.

Print stories can include direct quotes, which contain the spoken words verbatim, partial quotes, which contain a key phrase verbatim, or paraphrases.

Knowledge of numbers comes in handy for adding detail to stories. Stories about polls, surveys, scientific studies, and budgets involve some understanding of math.

LEARNING THE LINGO

Anecdotal lead
Ellipsis
Margin of error
Mean or average
Median
Mystery or suspense lead
Nut graph
Percent and percentage points
Scene-setting lead
Voice and tone

NOTES

1. Janet Kolodzy, "City School Custodians Clean Up in Overtime," *Cleveland Plain Dealer*, December 12, 1983, A1.

2. Carl Sessions Stepp, *Writing as Craft and Magic* (Lincolnwood, IL: NTC/Contemporary Publishing Group, 2000), 93.

3. John Ellement, "Boater Charged with Homicide in Drowning," *Boston Globe*, June 14, 2005, A1.

4. Jerry Lanson and Mitchell Stephens, "Jell-o Journalism: Why Reporters Have Gone Soft in Their Leads," *Washington Journalism Review*, April 1982, 21.

5. Roy Peter Clark and Don Fry, *Coaching Writers: Editors and Reporters Working Together Across Media Platforms* (New York: Bedford/St. Martin's, 2003), 154.

6. Dan Gillmor, "Dan Gillmor Column," *San Jose Mercury News*, June 8, 2003.

7. Thomas L. Friedman, "As the world flattens, America's at a loss for big ideas," *New York Times*, April 29, 2005, B11.

8. Alessandra Stanley, "Woodward and Bernstein, Dynamic Duo, Together Again," *New York Times*, June 3, 2005, A16.

9. Michael Paulson, "School shuts to ward off parents, Archdiocese says it tries to avert an occupation," *Boston Globe*, June 9, 2005, A1.

10. "The Power of Words: Deciding on a Deadline: The Point of View," June 19, 2002, at www.projo.com/words/tp061902.htm (accessed December 4, 2005).

11. Gerald M. Carbone, "Their R.I. Brother," May 11, 2002, at www.projo.com/words/st061902.htm (accessed December 4, 2005).

12. Melvin Mencher, *News Reporting and Writing*, 9th ed. (New York: McGraw-Hill, 2003), 269.

13. Curtis MacDougall and Robert D. Reid, *Interpretative Reporting*, 9th ed. (New York: Macmillan, 1987), 177.

14. Carole Rich, *Writing and Reporting News*, 4th ed. (Belmont, CA: Wadsworth, 2003), 501.

15. Julie Sullivan, "Tattoo U. A storefront in southeast Portland is an offbeat 'college' where students learn the art of decorating human real estate," *Portland Oregonian*, June 12, 2005, L1.

16. Jim Dwyer, "Fighting for Life 50 Floors Up, with One Tool and Ingenuity," *New York Times*, October 9, 2001, B1.

17. Howard Bryant, presentation to Emerson College journalism students, Fall 2003.

18. www.nytimes.com/pages/national/portraits/index.html (accessed December 4, 2005).

19. Derek Donovan, "Quirks of Spoken Language Make for Tough Calls," *Kansas City Star*, June 5, 2005, B8.

20. *Associated Press Stylebook* (New York: Basic Books, 2004), 207.

21. Jeffrey Dvorkin, "A Rash of Errors on NPR," June 14, 2005, at www.npr.org/templates/story/story.php?storyId=4702972 (accessed December 4, 2005).

22. Anahad Connor, "A Hole So Deep and Wide, People Stopped and Stared," *New York Times*, June 21, 2005, A19.

23. Victor Cohn and Lewis Cope, *News and Numbers*, 2nd ed. (Ames: Iowa State University Press, 2001), 63.

SEVEN

Online Basics: Tying It All Together

BEFORE WE CAN address how to go about reporting and producing news for the Web, we need to define online journalism. Just as the term "convergence" has taken on a variety of meanings as it relates to the world of journalism, the term "online news" has come to mean different things to different people. News for the Web could be defined by what has been published on the Internet so far, particularly by traditional mainstream media. (Note that while the World Wide Web and the Internet are distinct entities, many people use the terms interchangeably. The Internet is the connected network of millions of computers, while the Web is the collection of information accessible via the Internet.) But that definition may be too limiting, as newspapers, magazines, and radio and television stations have been inconsistent in devoting extensive resources or showing avid interest in extensive online news. News for the Web could also be defined by its potential, by the hints of innovation seen in special projects or presentations, including anything that delivers information to a browsing public, from e-mails to Web logs to discussion boards. That definition might be too scattered. To determine how to do news for the Web, you must understand both the reality of today's online news offerings and the potential of organizing news and information for the Web, an ideal that rarely gets fulfilled.

Much of what traditional news media have placed on their websites falls into two categories: timely, succinct news reports, and in-depth, explanatory, multimedia interactive projects and presentations. In that sense, online news has followed the pattern that newspapers, news radio, and television stations have previously set in providing a mix of short, updated daily news reporting and long, more thoughtful special projects reporting.

Publishing the latest news on the Web reflects news organizations' understanding of the Internet's key strengths of immediacy. People at work may have easier access to a computer than to a radio or television and seek up-to-the-minute news by checking online. Wireless technology allows for an extension of online news onto devices such as cell phones and personal digital assistants (PDAs). News compilers like Yahoo!News and Google News update their links to news stories constantly, although a large number of these stories may be wire service stories listed in different online news sites, like those affiliated with ABC News or Britain's *Guardian* newspaper. Traditional news organizations often rely on wire services for updating or refreshing their online news content. A University of Texas examination of thirty newspaper websites found that a little more than a third were constantly updating their home pages from sixty to two hundred times a day during the period studied. Those news organizations aim to take advantage of the Internet's strength of providing new and immediate information to its browsing audience.[1]

As new technologies have emerged, this updating of the news with stories initially generated for a newspaper, newscast, or by a wire service has become more automated. As a result, the emphasis of work for online journalism can and should move away from people "shoveling" news stories onto websites. While "shovelware," the derisive term for repurposing news content, has been the most used and visible form of journalism online, it fails to utilize all the strengths of the Internet in informing the public. The difference between online news and its print and broadcast siblings is that it can be interactive, it can be linked and searched, and it can be multimedia. Playing to those strengths requires a different mindset about the journalistic process, which is only just now undergoing exploration.

Online journalism takes the notion of convergence and puts it in one physical space and place: the computer. Online journalism, or what also has been called digital storytelling, embodies the mindset of convergence because it allows news consumers to be active, not passive; it puts the audience, or users, not the news organization, in control. Said another way, traditional news stories are told, while digital news stories are experienced. Journalists in the online world are no longer the "sage on the stage," a phrase used to describe the way professors used to lecture from a podium, aloof and separate from their students. Journalists are being asked to be more the "the guide on the side," a phrase used in education circles to define more collaborative and interactive learning. Online journalism has the potential to do more guiding as well as more telling.

In fact, journalism today is going through the same dramatic change in style that education has been struggling with for at least a generation. Being the guide on the side still requires the same kind of preparation, research, and collection of information that was needed to deliver pearls of wisdom from the lofty podium on the stage. The same holds true for journalism on the Web. The same accuracy, multiple sourcing, interviewing, and gathering of information and elements needed for news in newspapers, in radio, and on television apply to news on the Internet.

Whether lecturer or guide, guiding as well as telling requires more than just a slight adjustment. So too in journalism; a website with streaming video of television packages or e-mail addresses beneath newspaper bylines does not go far enough in capturing the strengths of news on the Web. Doing journalism on the Internet requires thinking more collaboratively. Online journalism requires teamwork with the audience as well as with journalists who have different storytelling skills and abilities.

Teamwork provides an apt framework for examining the unique nature and features of online news: interactivity, searchability, and multimedia. In producing news for the Internet, news organizations are beginning to realize that few people can be great text writers and editors, reporters, layout designers, graphic artists, videographers or photographers, *and* Web page coders. Just as the initial notion of a convergent journalist as a jack-of-all-trades and master of none has evolved into the idea of a journalist with an understanding of multiple media and a willingness to use their strengths, online news reporting and producing is evolving into multimedia, interactive, team-produced news.

The *Providence Journal*, like many other newspapers, has been using its online site, projo.com, to present the daily news as reported by its newspaper staff. But it also expands its journalism with special presentations. It tries to take advantage of the strength of immediacy of online, plus the interactivity and multimedia aspects of it.

The shooting death of veteran police detective James Allen on April 17, 2005, at the Providence police headquarters became on opportunity for reporting both the immediate story in the hours and days after the shooting and a more detailed presentation of pictures, slide shows, audio clips, maps, and a "guestbook" for the community to post comments in the aftermath. Weeks after the shooting, visitors to projo.com could still read the initial reporting on the shooting, view video reports of the detective's funeral, get profile information on both the slain detective and the man accused of shooting him, as well as follow the investigation and legal action in the case. But the website visitors could also add something to the online coverage: their comments, remembrances, and concerns that the shooting evoked.

The detective shooting story relied on the teamwork between the paper's and the website's staff, and between the journalists and the audience for the website. It required thinking about the teaming of storytelling elements—words, pictures, sound—in the news-gathering as well as in the news producing. It also teamed different media to tell different parts of the story: video clips on the funeral, a graphic map of the police chase of the suspect, text files on the filing of charges, and the suspect's court appearances. It was multimedia.

Projo.com also offered links and archives that allowed the audience to search for information and to be interactive in choosing what part of the story they wanted to explore. It gave the audience a place to be a part of the story via the guestbook.

Although online news has these new aspects of interactivity, searchability, and multimedia, most of its practitioners believe they must adhere to the tried-and-true basic journalistic values of accuracy, fairness, sourcing, independence, community, and transparency. Credibility is the calling card of all journalists, and online news is no different. Online journalism is built upon the basic foundation of journalism values, with the addition of common journalistic skills such as reporting, writing, organizing, synthesizing, and using visuals. It is topped off when these basic values and skills are affixed to the new storytelling and story-making opportunities created by new technologies. Online journalism ties it all together: the old values with the new technologies, traditional skills with innovative production, and journalists with their audiences.

Nora Paul, head of the New Media Studies Center at the University of Minnesota, notes that in the ten years since online news emerged, not all the promises of this new outlet for journalism have been realized. Online news, especially that produced by traditional media like newspapers, is still working on the balance between giving audiences short, quick spurts of the latest news and providing them with other tools and content so they can become immersed in a subject. The dialogue between journalists and their audiences is beginning to emerge through the growth of Web logs or what are commonly called blogs. "New methods for crafting and delivering compelling news stories online are still a long way from being fully developed," Paul writes.[2] But they are being developed.

This chapter looks at some basic skills and thinking about producing news on the Web. That look addresses breaking, continuously updated news, which might be considered "short-form" online news, and more extensive developed projects that could be considered "long form." Both can involve various levels of multimedia and interactivity. However, resources of time, technology, and people often determine the extent of their use.

Some of the basic ideas of using words, pictures, sound, and interaction in the daily online news offerings provide the foundation for their use in more elaborate special projects. Some aspects of what is presented online today are based in print and broadcast news. Writing and page design have print underpinnings, while the mixing of video, audio, and graphics on the Web has a broadcast foundation. However, online news is adapting those formats to fit its unique platform; it is taking old skills and giving them new applications.

This chapter begins with some basic writing tips for the Web. We look at how people look at and look for news and information on the Web to determine how we should be writing that material. We see how some of the earlier lessons about writing for print and for broadcast can apply to some of the writing done for online. We also explore the organization of writing that is unique to online because of the unique way people interact and confront a computer screen.

We examine interactivity, and how to plan and organize the news and information being put on the Web for news audiences to best use it. From links to polls to timelines, from databases to discussion boards, the Web can provide various avenues for news audiences to not merely get the news, but to experience it. To provide those experiences, we need to think about and determine which interactive and multimedia experiences have news value for audiences.

Because online has the capacity to present news in dozens of different ways, this chapter delves a bit further into how to approach a story to address online's unique storytelling aspects: interactivity and multimedia. This chapter looks at the presentation of visual elements in providing news and information online and how to determine when and where they fit. That involves ways to expand story planning strategies to ensure that interactivity and multimedia are not just gimmicks but vital aspects of relaying the information to the public.

Writing, visuals, and interactivity can come together when doing news online. Online news represents yet another way for journalists to help people and communities get informed. It puts the audience back as the focus for news.

WRITING ONLINE NEWS

When you log on to your computer to get news, you might go to Google News or Yahoo! News. You would find a home page or opening page to the site, with a column along the left side that serves as a index, multiple headlines in the center section of the page, maybe a picture or two, and maybe a short blurb of one or two sentences summarizing a main or top news story. When you go to a news site like MSNBC.com or CNN.com, you also find the left-side index, with a prominent picture at the top center, maybe a blurb or two on some major story, and lots of headline links.

When you go to a home page, you do not do a lot of reading on that page; you scan and skim. Even if home pages were designed differently, with fewer stories and more information on those stories, you would probably still do a lot of scanning and not a lot of reading. That is the nature of online.

When you do read text online, you probably have a limit as to how much you will read before abandoning the story. Will you scroll down through a page or click on to a continuation of the story on another page? How many pages are you willing to click through to stay with the story? You might decide to print out a long story rather than read it from the computer screen. That, too, is the nature of online.

Web habits, like the Web itself, have their roots in traditional media but have been adapted to fit the strengths and weaknesses of this new media platform. Users usually scan and search the Web rather than stay in one place very long. Their only loyalty may be with the page where they start their interaction. They may set a home page on their browser and bookmark a favorite site. But rarely do Web users start and end their sessions on the Web in the same place. Users stick with one site as long as it delivers what they are looking for. When it does not, they go looking elsewhere on the Web until they find what they want. When journalists produce news for the Web, it is produced for browsers, not readers or viewers.

If you put yourself in the seat of a person looking for news as opposed to someone providing it, you can get a better idea of how to produce news and information for the Web. Jakob Nielsen has been doing just that since the 1990s. Nielsen conducts what has become known as Web usability studies. During the first decade of widespread Web use, a few key differences emerged in how audiences consume information presented via a computer. People scan rather than read online, a quality Nielsen has examined extensively. He also found out that people read online text differently than text printed on paper. Nielsen and John Morkes note that people read slower online, about 25 percent slower than when reading printed text. To address these unique features of online use, Nielsen provides several tips to make Web work more user-friendly:

- Write tight. Keep your text short.
- Write with the idea that your audience is scanning, not reading. Nielsen calls this "scannability."
- Split up long pieces of information into blocks using hypertext links to take browsers to other areas of the page for more information.
- Use graphic bullets to break up lists of materials.
- Use plain language.
- Write in chunks and use the inverted pyramid (see chapter 6) in writing these chunks.[3]

Some of Nielsen's tips may sound familiar because they apply to news writing in other media. Print and broadcast news rely on short, simple, direct sentences, with few adjectives and adverbs. In straight news stories, the lead sentence or lead paragraph states a main point of the story, with more elaboration and detail following. Writing straight or hard news stories for the Web requires the same straightforward, no-nonsense writing. State the action, reaction, and outcome. Use simple narrative. Denote and define the conflict that makes the story news.

Because the vast majority of online news users look to the Web for news between 9:00 a.m. and 5:00 p.m., while they are at work and in front of a computer, much online news writing and producing in that time frame involves breaking news and updates. When the 9/11 Commission opened its hearings on the terrorist attacks on March 23, 2004, the producers at MSNBC.com focused on updating the cover or home page of the website to ensure that the latest information from the hearings was out front. To do that, Steve Johnson, an interactive producer, wrote and rewrote the headline and one-sentence blurb link that appeared superimposed over an image slightly left of center near the top of the page. That was one of many stories that Johnson updated throughout the morning. At the same time, David Friedman, a

FIGURE 7.1. Multimedia editor David Friedman coordinates various visuals—graphics, animation, video, and still pictures—for stories at MSNBC.com. (Photo by the author)

multimedia producer, was capturing still photos from the hearing video that was airing live on the MSNBC cable channel. If Friedman chose a picture of the burning twin towers, Johnson had to write a different headline and blurb than when Friedman opted for a wide shot of the commission at the hearing. Friedman also monitored the hearing so he could produce video clips of the hearing to be used on the site. Both men needed to keep updating and refreshing the offerings to users on the home page of the MSNBC.com news site.

Andrea Panciera, editor of the *Providence Journal*'s website, projo.com, finds that writing for the daily breaking news cycle for the website is similar to writing for a wire service. "It's a building story . . . but in the old days the public may not have seen the information coming through that way and now the public sees how the story builds as it happens."[4]

While the basic news writing form works for the latest "headline" news, the presentation of that writing online must be different because of the scannability factor of online news. Unless they have digital recording devices like TiVo, news consumers cannot skip around in a broadcast story. And they may not be compelled to do so with a newspaper story. Those stories are produced and written so that the viewer and the reader go from information point A to point B and so on. But with online news, a Web user can move within a story and even out of it. As a result, writing has to be organized in chunks, with guideposts. Links can serve that role in an online story. They are guides or markers to alert browsers as to where they can find information.

Notice that most stories online have spaces between paragraphs and that the paragraphs are no more than two or three sentences long. Again, that text organization follows the rules of simplicity that guide print. Those spaces set off scannable chunks of information. And often a lead paragraph in online might resemble the lead paragraph of a broadcast story: a short, one-sentence summary.

Yet those chunks of information connect and flow together; they are not just scattered pieces or strings of information. Writing for online, just like writing for print and broadcast, requires the journalist to make the connections between these scattered pieces of information. This may be even more important online, as users jump around within a story. Notice the careful, limited use of pronouns in online stories. A "he" or "she" in an online story needs to be in close proximity of the named person being referred to. For example, a May 19, 2005, MSNBC.com story on a battle between Republican and Democratic senators over judicial nominees did not use any pronouns to make it easier for users to follow exactly who was talking or taking action.

Headlines and Links

Online news sites use guideposts such as subheads and links to help users navigate to the information they want most. These guideposts can either be highlighted within the text of a story or grouped together as a list alongside or beneath a story. They can be short headlines scattered throughout the text. They can be pictures or words and pictures. They can use different typefaces and different sizes. They will add space between blocks. The aim of the guideposts is to provide information options for users. So writing headlines and determining links adds more layers or elements in the storytelling process. This layer of links separates online from print and broadcast.

A headline that works on the printed page of a newspaper may not necessarily work online. But for many news websites that are tied to newspapers, the headlines often do not stray far from what was in the paper.

Deb Bloom, news editor for the *Christian Science Monitor*'s website, csmonitor.com, is responsible for reworking or massaging the stories from the paper for the website. Since *Monitor* stories often are aimed at providing more context, or the story behind the story of major news events, part of Bloom's job is to set up links to the hard news stories on the website's Latest Briefs section. She also may have to tighten the caption of a photo accompanying the story. Bloom says that while newspaper headline writing style might serve as a good template for

TERRORISM & SECURITY
A DAILY UPDATE

Lack of funds slows Iraqi reconstruction

Key projects 'grinding to a halt' as funds diverted to increased security needs.

Yahoo, Chinese police, and a jailed journalist

Rights groups are trying to raise the case of Shi Tao at a China Internet summit this weekend.

Readers Vote: Should Yahoo have given Chinese officials information that led to the jailing of a journalist?

As Israel leaves Gaza, will militants lay down their guns?

President Abbas is faced with a growing challenge as Palestinian militants vie for influence.

Dragging economy pushes Germans to polls

Monitor correspondent Andreas Tzortzis explains the implications, who's ahead, and why the elections are early.

Koizumi presses bid to reshape politics

Japan votes Sunday in a snap election called by the prime minister over his economic reforms.

Andy Nelson - Staff

Four years later: A vision for ground zero takes hold

A grand master plan is in place, complete with a soaring Freedom Tower and a memorial for those lost on 9/11.

HURRICANE KATRINA

Where do gas prices go next?

A few critical factors will govern how far they fall from record levels.

A native son takes charge

If Katrina is the new 9/11, First Army Lt. Gen. Russel Honoré is the new Rudy Giuliani.

Partisan bickering over Katrina escalates - to peril of both sides

Unlike 9/11, when Americans came together, the hurricane's aftermath has intensified polarization.

- **How you can help**

News updates: AP's The Wire

NFL contenders seek perfect balance

The Patriots have proven that winning in the new century is a blue-collar business that spreads the wealth.

- Agassi proves he's still a contender
- This game puts a new spin on golf

Caught in a jam

'Moe' is a jam band at the center of a thriving subculture where community is as important as music.

Movies

Robert Redford finds 'Life' after stardom

In 'An Unfinished Life,' the actor delivers an Oscar-worthy performance.

More reviews

- Green Street Hooligans
- The Man
- Separate Lives
- Monitor movie guide

Orchestral music, with passion *fortissimo*

'Music From the Inside Out' is a behind-the-scenes look at the Philadelphia Orchestra.

- **All of today's headlines**
- **Past five editions**
- **Corrections**

SUPPORT THE MONITOR

→ **Help the Monitor.** Donate now to support independent journalism.

→ **Free sample issue**

Apparel
Buy Shoes
Business Resources
Business Cards
Search Engine Optimization, Inc.
Financial
Car Insurance
Gifts
Engagement Rings
Italian Charms Sale!
Send Flowers - Florists
Graphic Design
Logo Design - LogoBee
Home & Garden
Home Furniture Sale
Find Great Furniture
Furniture Store
Legal Services
Find A Lawyer
Real Estate
Home Foreclosures
Home Loans
Moving
Moving Companies
Mortgage Calculator
Real Estate
Services
Wedding Favors
Weddings
Travel
City Hotels
Discount Hotel Rooms
Hotels
Hotel Reviews
Web Services
Cheap Web Hosting
Dedicated Servers
Email Hosting
Web Hosting
Web Hosting Reviews

The Monitor's View

US-European freedom train

Opinion

American crisis of confidence

Generosity's place on a dark and stormy night

An activist for moderation

Web columns & blogs

BLOG VERBAL ENERGY

Double-jointed words in our language

Clay Bennett cartoon

→ **Today's cartoon | Previous**

FIGURE 7.2. *Christian Science Monitor* Web page, September 10, 2005. (Reproduced with permission from the *Christian Science Monitor*. All rights reserved.)

headline writing online, the *Monitor* site requires headlines to serve as blurbs of a story and not just be a title or clever phrase.[5]

Cyberjournalist.net columnist Jonathan Dube notes that several studies show that online users prefer straightforward, informative headlines over clever or cute ones that may mask the story's focus.[6] Headlines, of course, are just one type of link used online. Online stories often include links to other stories, websites, or online activities. Both headlines and links within stories should be aimed at giving online users choices about the information they want to seek out.

Bob Stepno, who teaches online journalism, comments that "writing for the Web should offer choices—a choice of short and long versions of a story, a choice of 'entry points' or a choice of media. To interact with these choices, links should be obvious and easy to follow . . . clear and informative."[7] Few people are willing to venture into a totally dark alley, and confusing links are the online equivalent of a dark alley. For example, a link about a court ruling on a law to ban gay marriage that says simply "Details" does not give a user much insight. A better link might be, "Marriage Ban Upheld." Steve Krug called his book on Web usability "Don't Make Me Think!" to drive home the point that Web users want simple, clear information both in Web writing and Web design.

Remember that list of bullet points from Nielsen about online writing? In a textbook, all you have is the list. On a website, you might want to make each bullet point a link. On the Web, if you click on the bullet point about scannability, you could be sent to another point in the text that explains scannability in more depth. You click on that link because you choose to learn more about scannability. Links should take users exactly where they want to go.

Not only do links themselves need to be clear to help guide the user, online news sites should also know what their users will get when they click to outside websites. Journalists need to think of a link as an element of an online news story. As such, they must often decide if a link is reliable and accurate, just as they do with a quote from an interview or details from a source. A news website that links to whitehouse.com (a pornography site) instead of whitehouse.gov (the U.S. president's site) is playing a losing game with its credibility. News links also can frustrate users if they are sent to a story or website that is not informative or useful.

While headlines and links are viable online guideposts, the organization and placement of guideposts also helps the Web user. Over the past ten years, there have been three "eye-tracking" studies, aimed at measuring how people look at Web news, and they have yet to come up with the perfect formula for putting news and information out online. But research is providing more clues about how news consumers connect with the news and information on a Web page.

FIGURE 7.3. A "heat zone" map from the Eyetrack III study showing how people look at a Web page and how long they might stay on a certain section of the page. (By permission)

The latest eyetrack study used innovative technology to follow users' eye movements on a Web page. And it found that people:

- notice and scan headlines especially on the top left side of a page;
- read text blocks, if they are short and use smaller type;
- can seem indifferent about pictures, but will notice bigger pictures rather than smaller ones;
- check out the first two to three words of a headline or a text to see if it grabs their attention.[8]

Many tips about Web writing can be found on websites in news organizations that pursue and promote coordination and convergence among media outlets. A visit to the *Christian Science Monitor* website, csmonitor.com, reveals a prominent picture slightly to the left of center with lots of short linking headlines and one-sentence summaries on columns to the left and to the right of the picture.

In writing those headlines and summaries, Web writers have to walk a fine line between telling too much and too little of the story. Broadcast tease writers have the same problem: providing just enough information to tell what the story is about, but not too much that the audience is unwilling to stay with the story to find out more. A good Web headline, like a good broadcast tease, needs to be understandable to someone who is interested in the story.

For example, a May 13, 2005, story on csmonitor.com about the impact of *Star Wars* director George Lucas had the headline, "Why the Force Is Still with Him." It provided just enough information to attract interest without giving away too much of the story. The headline makes reference to the twenty-seven-year span of *Star Wars* movies without ever mentioning *Star Wars*. Anyone who knows what the Force is would probably be interested in George Lucas, the man behind the *Star Wars* story. The summary sentence, "George Lucas's influence on pop culture broadens with the final 'Star Wars' episode," also gives Web users enough information to determine if they want to go further.

The broadcast tease style, like the print headline style, relies on active voice and present tense. A headline on CNN.com about military base closings reads, "Towns vow to fight base closings plan." The lead story on NWCN.com, the website for Northwest Cable News in Seattle, also has a headline that uses active voice and present tense: "Base supporters prepare to fight for jobs." The one-sentence summary, "Though Washington was spared, Oregon will lose two in the latest base closure round," follows the pattern of giving enough detail to allow users to determine if they want to click on the story and find out more about the towns in the region affected.

The difference between a broadcast tease and a Web headline, however, is that Web users may expect a headline to tell them just enough of the story for them to understand it, giving them the option about going further. A tease is not designed to allow opting out. Web users expect choices.

HTML

Chunks, links, headlines, and lists of bullet points have proven to be some of the tried and true ways to organize text to take advantage of the Web's strengths. How to create those chunks, links, headlines, and lists on the Web requires some knowledge and understanding of HTML or hypertext markup language. Most Web pages are embedded with HTML, which is the code or tags that help computers translate text and images to look the way they do on the Web.

Most Web pages are simply text files. They consist of text and HTML coding or tags that control the way the page appears on a Web browser like Internet Explorer, Netscape, or Mozilla Firefox. A Web page is a file that ends in either "htm" or "html." Websites have a URL or uniform resource locator, the Web address that tells servers and browsers where to find it. The URLs also list the domains or hosts for the Web page to help locate them.

Here are common top-level domains in the United States:

.com = commercial or business sites
.edu = educational sites for schools and universities
.gov = government sites
.net = network sites
.org = organization sites

BOX 7.1

Finding HTML

On any Web page, like espn.com or ljworld.com, you can find HTML in three easy steps.

1. Click onto the Web page.
2. Click on the View menu in the top toolbar.
3. Click on Page Source or Source, and a window into the world of HTML will open up.

The first HTML tag you will find is one that says HTML and a title. If there is a picture at the top, you will find a code for the size, location, and placement of that image. If there is a headline, you will find HTML for the size, font, and type for the letters in that headline. When there is text, like a caption to a picture, you will find HTML about indentation, breaks, font, size, and location.

Sites in other countries may have a domain to indicate the country, like .ca for Canada and .ru for Russia.

Any page created by word processing software can be a Web page by hand coding the HTML. To create a Web page this way, you begin with the HTML of HTML. Your page should begin with an <html> tag and end with an </html> tag. Your page should also have a title that looks like this: <title>your title</title>. After that, there are tags for formatting text, tags for displaying pictures, and tags for links. Dozens of books and thousands of websites have information about writing HTML. The key to all HTML is that its information is contained in brackets <>. Every tag begins with <>, such as <title>, and every tag ends with </>, such as </title>.

Software like Dreamweaver or FrontPage automatically create this code and tags. In the waning days of the twentieth century, HTML was hand-coded. Some news producers still pre-

FIGURE 7.4. MSNBC .com's Steve Johnson and Elizabeth Wollman work with a Web publishing tool to post items on the website. (Photo by the author)

fer to hand-code Web pages. But many, like Steve Johnson and Elizabeth Wollman at MSNBC.com, use content management systems to publish on the Web. Their job is to update the home page and the front pages of the website's news sections. Rather than starting the page from scratch, the content management system provides blocks and templates that producers fill with content. One template would be for the headline that is superimposed over the main home page picture. Another would be a template for the headline links. Another is the template for the home page's menu. Johnson, who worked in newspapers and television before online news, says that much of the headline writing and editing resembles what is being done in newspapers. But thanks to the publishing tool, headlines can be rewritten, their order on the page can be rearranged, and the cover page can be updated as often as necessary.

Links

Links make the Web different from any other medium. You can link to another website or another Web page or even to e-mail. You can embed a link in text or in an image. Links on a Web page are called hypertext. They are highlighted or underlined. When you click on hypertext, the Web browser brings up another Web page.

To link to another page, all you have to do is include the URL or address of another Web page, starting with the code <a href>. A link to CNN.com would look like this:<a href= http://www.cnn.com>cnn home page. The words "cnn home page" acts as a caption. A link to another page on your website points to the name of that page. For example <a href= urge2converge.html>book title page would be a link to the title page of this book.

Learning some basic HTML tags can help journalists overcome technophobia when dealing with the Web. Part of the job of a journalist is to translate information so a wide variety of people can understand it, and that information is becoming more technically oriented. "Competent reporting in today's society . . . demands reporters who are able to understand a potentially numbing variety of data, studies and documents," writes Robert Niles, editor of *Online Journalism Review*. Eliminating fear of technical jargon can help reporters in that translation so they do not become what Niles calls "easy marks" for people who take advantage of journalists' lack of knowledge to spin a technical story.[9]

All sorts of books have been written with details about the intricacies of HTML. But the development of content management systems has rendered extensive knowledge of HTML less necessary for many journalists to work online.

Writing for the Web taps only a portion of the Web's capabilities. It represents a venture into exploiting the Web's interactivity but does not expand the story experience for the user. Visuals, audio, and animation are some ways to do that. Chat rooms, blogs, interactive graphics, and quizzes and surveys can enrich an online news package

BOX 7.2

The Geometry of News Writing

Three types of geometric shapes may help in visualizing how news can be written to fit the platform—print, broadcast, online—and to fit the type of news story—hard news, news feature, breaking news.

The pyramid, or the inverted pyramid, has been a staple of news writing for more than a century. The information is organized from most important to least important, from the broadest context to the narrowest. This geometric shape for news has worked best in breaking news and in print.

▲ or ▼

The circle is a common reference point in organizing a broadcast story. Broadcast stories require a beginning, middle, and end, with the end referring back to the beginning idea. A broadcast story completes a circle of information. Unlike a print story, it cannot wind down; it has to wrap up. This wrap-up information usually refers to what may be the likely next step or outcome of the action mentioned in the lead. This way, the story is a complete circle.

○

The rectangle or block has become the shape of choice with online writing because people scan for chunks of information. But those rectangular chunks may be organized with a summary chunk or rectangle at the top. So online may be best represented by a rectangle, but those rectangles may be arranged in a pyramid pattern.

■

Another shape, albeit not a geometric one, used in storytelling is the hourglass. This is more often used in doing feature stories. It usually starts with an anecdote or information that sets out the major point of the story, then narrows to provide more details, and then expands again. Both print and broadcast use this shape in organizing some stories.

⌛

INTERACTIVITY

The ability for the online news audience to talk back to the people who produce and distribute the news as well as to take part in the production of the news separates online journalism from traditional media. News is no longer linear, a one-way monologue. It is now a conversation, with many voices and many choices. It is interactive.

In the decade since the World Wide Web revolutionized the way people communicate, shop, play, and are entertained, digital interaction has evolved. Part of the job of the online journalist is to determine the type of interactivity that the audience will find useful and that is best suited to the story. Journalists also weigh the benefits of interactivity against the amount of time and energy needed to produce these interactive features. More extensive Web news projects tend to have more layers of multimedia interactivity. Multimedia projects take a lot of planning, effort and coordination.

Take a look at interactive features on CNN's website, cnn.com, for a typical national or international news story versus one of the network's most ambitious convergence projects, its Cold War series. A story about the decline of gas prices on the morning of May 23, 2005, viewed about one hour after it was posted, has text, a picture, one link to a related story about oil prices, and "story tool" links to print, e-mail, or save the item. The Cold War series offers maps, timelines, message boards, interview clips, and interactive games among the myriad of online activities paired with the twenty-four-part series that aired on CNN in 1998 and 1999.

The range of interactive features online is expanding as new technologies and ideas develop. New types of interactivity are being tried on almost a daily basis. They range from the simple, like links within a story, to the complex, like incorporating searchable databases and games. They range from having the audience provide tips and comments about a story to having the audience determine the parts of the story they want to know and use.

Feedback, Talk-Back

Audience feedback to news has been around since letters to the editor were first printed. But with the Web, feedback can take several different forms and can create a conversation, making news organizations seem less detached from the people they are trying to reach. Feedback and talk-back can involve the following:

BYLINE LINKS Click on the byline and an e-mail link opens up that allows a user to send comments or tips to the reporter. Problems can arise with abusive e-mails or too many e-mails for reporters to sort through on a daily basis.

COMMENT LINKS These provide opportunities for readers to send information and reaction back to the newsroom. Many of these links are grouped in a "story tools" section at the bottom or in a box alongside the main story.

POLLS Readers can vote on a question about a story or topic of the day. ESPN.com always runs a sports poll that gets tens of thousands of responses each day. TBO.com, which is the website for the converged *Tampa Tribune* and WFLA television station, also runs an online poll with questions that may deal with serious topics or entertaining ones.

FORUMS OR DISCUSSION BOARDS These are places on the website that serve as hosts for a community conversation. The negative aspect of this citizen dialogue comes when a forum becomes a home for hate-filled rants and requires "netiquette" monitoring. In some cases, the forums or boards have been taken down because of the amount of time and energy spent policing them. The *Ventura Star* in California removed their discussion board for a week in May 2005 until it was able to mount better control through an online registration system. Discussion boards are like e-mail in which people are having conversations but not in the same time frame. These chats are "asynchronous," the term for communication between different people at different times.

CHAT ROOMS Chat rooms allow for synchronous or live communication. Discussions are more or less synchronized. Chat rooms could be considered instant messaging for a group of people. News organizations have put reporters as well as news subjects online in chat rooms. The question-and-answer, back-and-forth of the discussion can be informative and newsworthy. It can be a simple way for the person with information—reporter or news maker—to explain and clarify events and activities. But chat rooms are usually open for only a short period of time and once that is over, people cannot continue the conversation.

PHOTO GALLERY FORUMS Several online news organizations allow users to submit pictures for a communal look rather than a communal talk. It resembles a community photo album. In Lawrence, Kansas, ljworld.com, created a place for people to submit pictures from their senior proms, an important rite of passage in many communities that rarely makes its way into newscasts or newspaper pages. The site also carries a section for pictures from local soldiers in Iraq and Afghanistan. Several news websites do the same.

Clickable Interactives

Cyberjournalist Jonathan Dube describes clickable interactives as interactive versions of newspaper and television graphics. They can include animation, audio, video, maps, and graphics.[10]

CHARTS AND MAPS The *Orange County Register*'s website used a chart of pictures of various types of candy as a guide about lead-tainted candies for its users. The chart was part of an investigative series in 2004 on the problem of lead poisoning in common foods. The paper's website also provided clickable graphics that allowed the user to get information about the sources of lead in candy and the testing being done.[11] When the *Christian Science Monitor* decided to look at the future of Amtrak in 2002, it created an interactive map of the various Amtrak rail routes so viewers could view details and statistics relating to their cost and use.[12] In both cases, users were in charge of determining exactly what they wanted to see. They could click through every section, and the sections could be examined in any order. The graphics allowed for exploration and explanation.

TIMELINES History buffs love timelines, and interactive timelines allow users to pick and choose the point in time to be examined. CNN used timelines to help mark the various ups and downs of diplomatic and military wrangling during the fifty-odd years of the Cold War, and the *New York Times* allowed users to move left to right with their scrollbar along a timeline to learn about key dates in the evolutionary history of Islam. Timelines provide a visual way to encapsulate a series of events. MSNBC put together a timeline of new developments in the rape accusations case of pro basketball star Kobe Bryant in 2003 and 2004 which was highlighted by a key development each month. The Public Broadcasting Service, PBS, does a lot of interactive activities as part of its educational mission. A series on teaching in the United States included an interactive timeline that explained different movements within American education and provided excerpts of the television series.

QUIZZES AND CALCULATORS Although not a site affiliated with a traditional news organization, WebMD.com, which supplies information about health and medical topics, allows users to take quizzes and use calculators to help determine health risks and conditions. Website visitors can administer a self-test of about five questions to determine diabetes risk. The site also supplies a calculator to help users determine if they can benefit from the new Medicare prescription drug benefits. PBS uses quizzes to accompany websites related to special shows. A 2000 *Frontline* documentary, "The Future of War," provided an interactive quiz to test knowledge about the size and operations of the U.S. Army. Calculators can tailor information to specific users. Quizzes can help users reinforce what they know or what they need to know, opening up further opportunities for journalists to provide information.

Interactivity in news aims to engage Web users in topics that are relevant to them and to their place in the community. When people engage in an activity, they remember it better. Educator Edgar Dale came to that conclusion nearly fifty years ago in examining how teachers can better help students develop skills that help them analyze, evaluate, and design.

Interactivity is another tool journalists can use to provide audiences with useful and relevant news and information.

MULTIMEDIA

The multimedia aspect of online journalism can provide an audience with a story or parts of a story that are not as effectively understood if told only with text or only with visuals. Multimedia often works in tandem with interactivity to present a challenging news experience. Like interactivity, it adds another dimension to reporting and presenting the news that is not available in print and broadcast.

Multimedia means simply using more than one communications instrument. It represents the converging of formerly separate information paths: the written word, the spoken word, the still picture or graphic, and the moving picture or graphic. The computer makes all sorts of multimedia combinations possible. But in the newsroom, limitations on resources like time, energy, and technology impact the type of multimedia news being offered online. Plus, the audience for online news relates to information, consumes information, and reacts to information differently. All those considerations, coupled with an understanding of the strengths of each medium being put together come into play in deciding how to use multimedia for news stories.

Cyberjournalist Jonathan Dube has written that multimedia can best be used to *show* information.[13] Sound and visuals have been used by broadcast journalists for decades to show the news, letting the audience see people and events for themselves. But putting sound and pictures online allows the audience the option of choosing how much to see and hear as well as when to see and hear it. So the use of sound and visuals online must acknowledge how people operate online in a different way than they operate with broadcast: People are active, not passive, online; people jump around in search of choices; people want chunks and bits.

During breaking news, multimedia may merely mean putting content on the website in a number of forms: text stories, blurbs, still pictures, and streaming video and audio clips. MSNBC.com multimedia producer David Friedman explained President George W. Bush's entire March 2004 speech on the first anniversary of the start of the war in Iraq, aired on the website as well as the cable channel. The website also posted key excerpts. Both the full speech and the excerpts were put online within minutes after the president finished.

Long-form multimedia storytelling, using sound and visuals, is evolving into something different than simply streaming a radio or television piece online. Multimedia storytelling, if using text and visuals, can be more than a caption and a photo. Slide shows, animation, games, and podcasting are new multimedia storytelling techniques.

Slide Shows

MSNBC.com's Friedman says thinking of the audience and what they could get from multimedia drove the picture stories he put together during the 2004 New Hampshire presidential primary campaign.[14] Rather than report the campaign speeches, Friedman carried a digital camera and a minidisc audio recorder to capture the thinking of Granite State residents. He weaved a multimedia story about a variety of New Hampshire voters, their values, and their concerns about the election. His "Voices of New Hampshire" featured New Hampshire residents, audio about their life and political opinions, and Friedman's pictures showing them and their surroundings.

Slide shows pull together a series of still pictures and text to tell a story. Sometimes they are organized linearly, requiring the user to view one picture after the other. The order helps complete the telling of the story. At other times, slide shows are organized to allow Web users to pick and choose what they want to see. Some have captions and explanations, while others use either natural sound or a narration. Slide shows have reinvigorated the photo essay as a form of journalistic storytelling. At many websites, they are among the most popular features.

Slide shows can also add transparency to news reporting. The *Pensacola News Journal* put together slide shows depicting the work of individual staff photographers' coverage of Hurricane Ivan, its aftermath, and its cleanup. Using Flash software to build the slide show, each photographer had a chance to talk about the photos they took, to tell a story about the picture and how it came about.

Animations

Medical, science, and technology reporting have been dramatically changed as animation has allowed complicated breakthroughs to be illustrated and demonstrated online. The key to using animation is to use it when video, audio, or stills cannot make the point. MSNBC.com ran an animation to show how scientists are decoding DNA. The website of the *Pensacola News Journal* in Florida put together a simple animation that showed how a storm surge is created and how it moves to explain the flooding damage inflicted on the community by Hurricane Ivan in September 2004. The *New York Times* website, NYTimes.com created a series of animations to explain the structure of the World Trade Center towers and how they fell after being hit by planes on September 11, 2001. None of these stories could be told as well using text or video, or even still graphics. The animation of the graphics can be used to re-create an event, such as the collapse of the World Trade towers, and can illustrate what is otherwise impossible to see, like DNA.

Webcasts and Podcasts

A webcast streams out live video and audio of an event over the Internet. The webcasts that have produced the most news over the past few years have not been done by traditional news outlets. For example, a website called OR-Live.com sponsored a series of webcasts of surgeries, from heart angioplasty to gastric bypass. A North Dakota hospital also aired laparoscopic kidney surgery on a webcast. Major League Baseball's website makes baseball games available online for a fee, so that Tampa Bay Devil Rays' fans can follow the action whether or not the game is televised. C-SPAN, which broadcasts live from the U.S. House of Representatives and the Senate when Congress is in session, also provides webcasts of those sessions. MSNBC.com has been adding interactivity to a webcast by linking users' e-mail questions to television news correspondents During the mourning period following the death of Pope John Paul II, Chris Jansing did a webcast from Rome in which she answered users' e-mail questions.

A podcast is similar to a webcast, except programs can be downloaded from a computer onto a portable digital audio device like an MP3 player or an iPod. *Newsweek* magazine produces a podcast, which it describes as "audio magazine subscriptions or portable on-demand radio shows."[15] ABC News is podcasting news shows such as *Good Morning America* and *Nightline*. One of the oldest black-oriented newspapers in the country, the *Chicago Defender*, has a podcast featuring interviews and other newspaper content in an audio form. Podcasting, like webcasting, was started outside of traditional news organizations, but several are trying it as another way to reach news audiences.

Radio stations have embraced podcasts and streaming audio as a way to expand their listening audience. Anyone who goes to the website of public radio station KQED in San Francisco can listen to the on-air programming. And two of its locally produced programs are podcast for listeners. Podcasts allow radio programs to be portable, so listeners do not have to tune in at a certain hour to catch their favorite show. They can download and listen to it whenever and wherever they want.

Interactive Multimedia

Any type of interactivity in online news can be created in multimedia. The *Providence Journal*'s projo.com's look at a young woman with Indian immigrant parents combined a multimedia slide show with text and description. Quizzes and surveys can be multimedia; each week Tampa's tbo.com website has an interactive news quiz that combines national, state, and local news questions. Multimedia and interactivity can mix, such as when MSNBC.com created a game in which the Web users could put themselves in the position of an airport security person scanning for contraband items in luggage.

COLLABORATION, COORDINATION, CONVERGENCE

Because the Web offers journalists so many new avenues to provide news and information, it can be easy to be either paralyzed by all the choices or hyperactive, jumping around from option to option. In addition to the normal choices journalists make about facts, sources, and relevant information, online news adds the dimensions of interactivity and multimedia to the mix. Interactivity and multimedia are new tools in the journalist's tool chest for providing information, but they need to fit the job. A plumber knows not to use a hammer when a wrench will do the trick, because he has assessed the job and determined a plan of action. Journalists have to assess the job and determine a plan of action for interactivity and multimedia. They need to decide when a poll is right, or if a discussion board might be better; if a slide show of pictures might work better than an edited video package; if a pie chart tells more than a list of percentages.

Thinking and planning online news may be the hardest yet most crucial job for journalists working in this new news outlet. And the hardest notion to resist in online journalism is the tendency to put together an interactive, multimedia project that has great "gee whiz" value but little news value. It is the online equivalent of the doing a live report on television just because it can be done, although the audience does not see much in the live shot that help it to understand the news story being told. The best rule of thumb is to put the audience at the center of the journalism.

Bob Stepno, a former print and online journalist who has worked with and researched online news from its inception, emphasizes the need to give audiences choices in putting news on the Web. In a book on media writing, Stepno notes, "on the Web, planning a story is not only a matter of deciding what to say but choosing the form, or forms, in which to say it. Writers and producers of online sites get to make their own choices about which medium works best for the story at hand: text, still or moving image, sound or a combination."[16]

Just as broadcast is a combination of elements or layers of storytelling (words, pictures, and sound), so too is online. But with online news, journalists are juggling more layers (words, pictures, sounds, interactivity, and multimedia). Jonathan Dube, of cyberjournalist.net, sums up the strengths of each online layer: "Use print to explain. Use multimedia to show. Use interactives to demonstrate and engage."[17]

Those three rules can apply to determining the way daily, breaking news is presented on the Web as well as how more extensive projects are produced. A lot of daily news on the Web is presented as text to quickly explain the latest weather development, government action, social advancement, legal ruling, or threatening situation. Then the layer of video or audio sound bites shows the online user who is talking and the demeanor of the person talking. It can show a tornado touching down or a verdict being delivered to give the audience a sense of being there as news happens. This is online taking advantage of the strength of broadcast.

During the 9/11 Commission hearings, for example, MSNBC.com uploaded quick text stories to summarize the testimony, but they also pulled the video of the sound bites from key witnesses to allow the audience to judge for themselves their believability. When former national security adviser Condoleezza Rice testified before the commission on April 8, 2004, MSNBC.com carried short video clips of her testimony as well as text excerpts. It also posted an interactive poll, in which users could vote on Rice's testimony to engage the audience in the story. Even before Rice spoke to the commission, MSNBC.com employed interactivity by asking users to submit questions they would ask Rice.

That three-pronged approach is used at MSNBC.com in planning more extensive projects that are usually tied to NBC news projects, such as several interactive activities that accompanied a *Dateline NBC* show in 2004 about racial profiling. One included a map of twelve cities that the user could check out for the demographics of tickets and arrests. Another was a video "ride-along" with police in Cincinnati, Ohio, in which users were asked questions about their judgment if placed in a similar situation.

"Instead of dealing with two-dimensional, we're dealing with three-dimensional," says MSNBC.com's Angela Clark. Online has so many options, Clark says, that the biggest challenge for online journalists "is being discerning and choosing which element we want to put the most energy toward. . . . We're only limited by time and our imagination."[18]

"Once you've got that grounding of understanding what the issues are for each medium, then you can get smart about making decisions about which is the best way to tell a given story and what your different options are if you are operating in different media," says Michael Silberman, MSNBC.com's former managing editor at its New Jersey office. As managing editor, Silberman coordinated both the television (NBC and MSNBC) and online. Silberman says that perhaps the most important piece of advice in reporting and producing news is to think about the audience and how they are going to relate to the story. [19]

Leah Gentry of Finberg-Gentry, a digital consultancy, has taken the subject of the online audience a step further. A former online editor for the *Chicago Tribune* and the *Los Angeles Times*, Gentry suggests deconstructing and then reconstructing the elements of a story for the Web.[20] Breaking down or deconstructing story elements provides an opportunity to look at connections other than linear ones, such as chronological connections, and to look at connections among visuals, topics, and actions that help explain the main focus.

To help in the reconstruction, or drawing new connections among story elements, several online experts recommend storyboarding or story mapping. Just as mapping can help visualize the focus and the essential parts for the reporting of a news story, it can also help organize the focus and determine the essential parts of a story being produced for the Web. Television and film directors have for years used storyboards to plan their projects. Storyboards are drawings of the sequences of a visual story. But storyboarding takes those sequences and organizes them to show connections. A storyboard is more or less a visual outline of a story.

For online stories, mapping and storyboarding can place the pieces of the news puzzle in front of you, so you can see how they fit together.

Several online experts recommend thinking about online news not just as a story but as a project in which a team of journalists work to put together several layers, shells, or segments. Part of storyboarding or mapping an online news project involves delineating those segments and figuring out how to group them. Even daily news stories include several layers.

The trial over the disputed gubernatorial election in Washington State provided the website of the *Seattle Times* newspaper and Northwest Cable News an opportunity to provide a layered approach to a story that required constant updating throughout the day. On the cable news site, which is also affiliated with the KING-TV, online news users could click on video reports, could check out the main headline and story summarizing the day's testimony with a picture of the key witness, and could click on an interactive timeline chronicling key points in the dispute. The *Seattle Times* also provided previous stories on the ballot dispute and links to election board documents relating to the situation. Both sites posted updates of key testimony throughout the day.

Among the layers were text postings of the latest news, links to related stories about the trial issues and the trial judge, links to documents related to the case, interactivity via a timeline, a slide show of pictures from the trial for the *Times*, and a television package for NWCN.

Jane Stevens, in writing about storyboarding for online news production, recommends deconstructing a story into such areas as focus, the people or characters, the main event or situation, the process, the history, related topics, and viewpoints or sides of the story. But she also recommends deconstructing in terms of media, breaking down what parts of the story work best in video, audio, text, pictures, maps, and/or interactivity.[21]

In looking at the layers of the daily coverage of that gubernatorial election trial, the *Seattle Times* used both pictures and text to depict the main event or situation and used a timeline as well as interactive links to previous stories to provide the history.

In the extensive series of reports done in the aftermath of the February 2003 nightclub fire that killed a hundred people in West Warwick, Rhode Island, the *Providence Journal* used a variety of online storytelling layers to examine the tragedy. From computer animation simulations to examine building evacuation scenarios, to video depicting the flammability of polyurethane foam to accompany a series of stories on the widely used material, the paper and its website allowed users to view the information in dozens of different ways, in dozens of different combinations, from dozens of different angles and perspectives. The news audience was ultimately in control of the layers of the story about the devastating fire. But the journalists—the editors, producers, writers, and designers—coordinated the layers for the audience to read, hear, see, and experience.

The man in charge of ESPN's website, Neal Scarborough, calls the Web, "the wheelhouse" that can "take radio and put it in another form and take the magazine and put it in another form or take video shoots that the magazine does and put that online." Scarborough sees the Web as part of ESPN's mission to be what he calls "the nation's sports section."[22] For Scarborough, the Web is the place where the technology can come together with the content to serve the sports fan, ESPN's audience. For news audiences, news organizations are aiming to do the same thing.

SUMMARY

Online's capabilities of interactivity and multimedia provide journalists with a challenge and an opportunity to provide information in new storytelling forms. Studies show that people scan and search online and do not read for long periods of time, so presenting information online needs to respond to those habits. Writing should be "chunked," or presented in tightly written blocks. Headlines need to be simple. Links are key to giving online audiences a chance to interact and gather information in nonlinear fashion.

Interactivity can be as simple as an e-mail link for users' comments to multimedia maps, timelines, and descriptive animation. Multimedia includes any mix of text, visuals, and audio. Storyboarding, or a graphic, visual story outline, can help organize and coordinate the elements or layers of information that can be presented on the Web.

LEARNING THE LINGO

Asynchronous
Chunks
Eyetracking
Home page
Hypertext
Interactivity
Links
Multimedia
Podcast
Scannability
Storyboarding

NOTES

1. Rosental Calmon Alves and Amy Schmitz Weiss, "Many Newspaper Sites Still Cling to Once-a-Day Publish Cycle," July 21, 2004, at ojr.org/ojr/workplace/1090395903.php (accessed December 4, 2005).

2. www.ojr.org/ojr/stories/050324paul/print.htm (March 24, 2005, accessed December 4, 2005).

3. Jakob Nielsen, *Designing Web Usability: The Practice of Simplicity* (Indianapolis: New Riders Publishing, 2000), 101.

4. Andrea Panciera, interview by author, March 4, 2004.
5. Deb Bloom, interview by author, February 2004.
6. Jonathan Dube, "A Dozen Tips for Writing News Online," November 10, 2000, at www.cyberjournalist.net/news/000118.php (accessed December 4, 2005).
7. Bob Stepno, "Bob Stepno's Other Journalism Weblog," at radio.weblogs.com/0106327/stories/2004/12/30/webWritingInJournalismClas.html (accessed June 2005).
8. www.poynterextra.org/eyetrack2004/main.htm (accessed December 4, 2005).
9. Robert Niles, "From the Teaching Trenches: Hardcoding Is Harder, but Results Are Worth It," January 13, 2005, at www.ojr.org/ojr/stories/050113niles (accessed December 4, 2005).
10. Jonathan Dube, "Online Storytelling Forms," July 10, 2000, at www.cyberjournalist.net/news/000117.php (accessed December 4, 2005).
11. www.ocregister.com/investigations/2004/lead/index.shtml (April 2004, accessed December 6, 2005).
12. csmonitor.com/specials/amtrak/lines.html (May 2002, accessed December 4, 2005).
13. Dube, "Online Storytelling."
14. David Friedman, interview by author, March 23, 2004.
15. "Newsweek on air podcast," March 31, 2005, at www.msnbc.msn.com/id/7350215/site/newsweek/ (accessed December 4, 2005).
16. Robert Hillard, *Writing for Television, Radio and New Media* (Belmont, CA: Wadsworth, 1999) 158.
17. Dube, "Online Storytelling."
18. Angela Clark, interview by author, April 12, 2004.
19. Michael Silberman, interview by author, March 23, 2004.
20. Mike Ward, *Journalism Online* (Oxford: Elsevier Science & Technology Books, 2000), 123.
21. Jane Stevens, "Storyboarding," at journalism.berkeley.edu/multimedia/course/storyboarding (accessed December 4, 2005).
22. Neal Scarborough, interview by author, May 6, 2004.

PART III

The Next Wave

EIGHT

Participatory Journalism: Convergence Plus

IF A TREE FALLS in the forest but no one is there to hear it, does it make a sound? Philosophers and scientists periodically trot out this riddle to get a discussion going about perception versus reality. But journalists might pose that question about news and information: If journalism is distributed in a community but no one pays attention to it, is it journalism? Can journalism exist without an audience?

Traditional news outlets, from newspapers to network news, have been losing audience. News audiences are seeking and demanding news from different outlets at different times of the day and in different ways. The audience for news has not disappeared, but it has dispersed. The idea of news organizations being convergent—using multiple media to deliver news and information to audiences whenever, wherever, and however they want it—is a strategy to get journalists to catch up with the reality that they are doing reporting for scattered audiences. But while journalists have been debating the merits of convergence and some have been reluctant to try it, their audiences have not. News audiences understand convergence and they are not afraid of it. They are blazing new trails in convergence, filling the vacuum left by many traditional news organizations,

If convergence is a strategy for traditional media to get back to its roots of serving news audiences, then participatory or citizen media is a convergence strategy that news audiences are using to get journalism back to its roots. Participatory, grassroots journalism has exploded with the development, dissemination, and usability of Web publishing software. In the 1990s, the Web changed news audiences from being passive consumers to being interactive consumers. In the first decade of the twenty-first century, the Web, combined with faster data transmission such as DSL (digital subscriber lines) and broadband as well as blogging tools, are changing interactive consumers to be interactive producers as well. Participatory journalism, a term that has come into vogue with the rise of the Web log, or blog, is the next logical outcome of what is clearly becoming the consumer age of journalism. The technology of the Web has enabled news audiences, the consumers, to be in control. Their search for community and interactivity led to what could be considered self-service journalism. Others are calling it "we media." It represents a clear challenge to the way journalism has operated for generations, yet it could reinvigorate journalism's public service role in the process.

Journalists have been skeptical about convergence because it brings together people from seemingly disparate disciplines with incompatible mindsets—print, broadcast, and online—to produce and distribute news. Convergence requires a team approach to news; it requires sharing. Participatory journalism takes convergence a step further and requires sharing between producers and consumers; it requires audiences to be part of the team, part of the conversation. And audiences are sometimes deciding to share among themselves, leaving traditional journalism out of the loop.

"Call it Interactive Journalism, Participatory Journalism, Citizens Journalism or Civic Journalism, Phase II," writes Jan Schaffer, director of J-Lab, the Institute for Interactive Journalism. "The hallmark of what's happening is the convergence of the content creators—professional and amateur. And I would assert that this trend is far more important than the convergence of delivery platforms."[1] Convergence among news organizations needs to include convergence with citizens, the public, as well.

The head of the Associated Press, Tom Curley, notes that the Web has brought about a shift in the balance of power from news producers to news consumers.[2] Journalists are no longer the elite with the information and the means to distribute it. And this shift, according to Pressthink blogger Jay Rosen, a New York University professor, "means that professional journalism is no longer sovereign over territory it once easily controlled." Rosen adds that that does not mean traditional journalism news organizations will go away but that their influence is not singular anymore.[3] They are not alone.

Curley, as well as Dan Gillmor, author of *We, the Media*, a book about grassroots citizen journalism, have argued that journalism is no longer a lecture but a conversation. Journalists can no longer view themselves as the sage on the stage; they must step back, step down, and team up. Journalists have to begin a new type of journalism, sometimes being the guide on the side of the civic conversation as well as the filter and gatekeeper. The Web is allowing new forms of interaction and conversation to take place in new, digital communities not bound by geographical boundaries. It allows anyone with a computer the opportunity to exercise directly their freedom of the press. It is journalism of the people, by the people, as well as for the people.[4]

Throughout the nineteenth and twentieth centuries, journalists in the United States served as representatives of the public in the sphere of government, politics, business, sports, entertainment, and so forth. Journalists went where the average Joe could not go. Not everyone has the time or opportunity to follow the Supreme Court when it hears arguments in a case, but journalists have been able to sit in and serve as the eyes and ears of those who want to know what is going on. News organizations and the individual journalists who represent them have cachet because they are the surrogates, representatives for their readers, listeners, and viewers. Consider it representative journalism, à la representative democracy. Not everyone is in Congress, but the idea is that each person is represented in Congress by their representative and senators. As a reporter, CNN's Bob Franken has said that he views himself as "a citizen of the world."[5] As a journalist, he serves and represents that citizenship.

However, representative journalism, like representative democracy, is an ideal that never quite fulfills its lofty promise. Journalism is a business, and the old A. J. Liebling line that "freedom of the press belongs to those who own one" encapsulates the reality that business concerns often overshadow public service concerns. The reduction of international news bureaus due to high costs represents just one example of where the owners of the press have limited the freedom of its reporting.

Today, however, thanks to the Web, anyone who owns a computer owns a press. As a result, the Web is turning journalism from merely a representative form of information exchange to a town hall meeting, where all the individuals in the community represent themselves.

Town meetings are still popular in pockets of New England, and they demonstrate democratic governance in its purest form. But town meetings are limited in their effectiveness. The loudest voices may not be the best voices for determining a plan of action. So, across the United States, a mix of the town hall and the representative legislature operate to govern communities. Town halls have not replaced representative government, but sometimes they have supplanted it or more often enhanced or informed that representation. Citizen journalism may serve a similar role.

Citizen journalism is just getting started, but it could be commonplace in a short time, thanks to the exponential advancement of new Web technologies. Web logs, or blogs, grew from just a handful in 1999 to more than four million by the end of 2004, a period of just five years. Technorati.com, which is considered the expert on tracking the blogosphere, or the blog arena, estimated in mid-2005 that a blog was being created every 7.4 seconds. That is the equivalent of 12,000 new blogs a day.

Hugh Hewitt, a radio talk show host, newspaper columnist, law professor, and blogger with a conservative bent, has referred to this challenge of blogs to traditional journalism as "the information reformation." He compares today's traditional news media to the Roman Catholic Church at the time of Martin Luther. Gutenberg's press fueled that Reformation by putting the Bible in the hands of ordinary people, thereby challenging the church's control. Hewitt has argued that the Web is fueling the information reformation, putting news in the hands of ordinary people, attacking the news media's control.[6] Hewitt has embraced convergence, getting his commentary out in print in the *Weekly Standard* and in books, on radio with a syndicated talk show on seventy-five stations, and with his blog.

The rise of participatory journalism, in the form of blogs, podcasts, and other Web-based reporting, aims to complement and supplement but not necessarily supplant traditional news media. Not all mainstream media have lost touch with the audiences they serve, and not all grassroots journalism represents an attack on traditional forms of journalism. It does represent a warning to what Pressthink's Jay Rosen has called "Big Journalism," which has lost touch with their audiences, the people they supposedly represent and serve. As an extension of convergence, participatory journalism provides an opportunity by the news media to reconnect with audiences and rejuvenate its purpose. It enables journalism to return to its roots of public service.

Citizen or participatory journalism is evolving and mutating. It can encompass blogs that represent commentary on the day's events or blogs that serve as community news postings. It can involve a wiki, in which a news item or commentary is posted and anyone can add to or edit it. It can be a podcast reviewing favorite groups on a local music scene. It can be a collaborative effort between a reporter and experts to write and report a story, or it can entail a niche group of people, such as office workers or homeless activists, who publish news, information, and insights about their world. Groups that might not warrant much attention by traditional news organizations can create journalism useful to their special-interest communities. Participatory journalism involves "a citizen or citizens playing an active role in the process of collecting, reporting, analyzing and disseminating news and information."[7]

BOX 8.1

We Media Types

The following are some examples of various types of participatory journalism:

- Internet discussion boards, listservs, and forums (see chapter 7)
- User-generated contents from feedback to photos (see chapter 7)
- Web logs, or blogs, produced by individuals, activists, communities, in conjunction with traditional media
- Mob logs (using mobile/cell phones) and vlogs (using video)
- Collaborative reporting and editing for the Web, including wikis created and edited by anyone
- Podcasts

Source: Bowman and Willis, "We Media."

With participatory journalism, the news media landscape has expanded once again, and this expansion affects how all journalists work. This chapter briefly explores a few select aspects in the burgeoning area of citizen media and participatory journalism.

LINKING AND THINKING: BLOGS AND JOURNALISM

What a difference a year makes, especially when that year was the presidential election year of 2004. Blogs grew from being the ninety-pound geek to the two-hundred-pound weight lifter, demonstrating their power against the likes of CBS News, CNN executive Eason Jordan, and the presidential candidates.

A search of the word "blog" on LexisNexis helps illustrate the blog media phenomenon. In all of 2003, around 440 stories emerged in major newspapers, magazines, and journals about blogs. In 2004, the number was close to 1,000. And those were stories *about* blogs; the numbers triple when looking at news stories that merely mention blogs. The term "blog" became part of the lexicon in 2003 but grew into an information force in 2004. By June 2005, more than 200 articles were written about blogs in that month alone, including weekly reports or blog watches recommending blogs to check out.

The Pew Internet and American Life Project found that when it first began looking at blogs, in June 2002, about 3 percent of Internet users said they had created a blog; by the end of 2004, that had more than doubled, to 7 percent. The rise in readership, and ultimately the impact of the blogosphere, rose more dramatically. The Pew project found 27 percent of Internet users reading blogs at the end of 2004, compared to 11 percent just eighteen months earlier.

Traditional news media began paying closer attention to blogs after witnessing their impact on the superheated 2004 political scene. Bloggers asked and got credentials to the Republican and Democratic national conventions and issued reports on convention activities. When the mainstream media failed to explore some political stories in 2004 , the blogs created the "buzz" needed to force national news organizations to take notice. When that buzz grew to be large and loud about a topic, a blog swarm emerged. It was the year the blog swarm attacked in politics.

Politically oriented blogs represent one corner of the blogosphere. In fact, the vast majority of blogs have very little to do with politics or the news media. But they have a lot to do with the notion of community being redefined on the Web.

A common form of blog serves as a diary or journal posted on the Web. Like its paper precursor, it contains individual thoughts and commentary, with new entries as often as the diarist or blogger writes one. With blogs, the latest entry is at the top, but earlier entries can be read as well. Unlike paper diaries, however, the entries can be available only for a select group of individuals or to anyone and everyone on the Web. They often solicit comment. Blogs allow for interactivity between the blogger and the audience. Additionally, some bloggers use their blogs to list links to other blogs or online articles they like or dislike. Blogs "are a powerful draw in that they enable the individual participant to play multiple roles simultaneously—publisher, commentator, moderator, writer, documentarian."[8]

Profgrrrl is a blogger who follows the diarist mode, with input from the blogosphere. Her blog has generated comments from her audience ranging from the right dress to wear to a holiday party to job survival tips. As she noted in a blog aimed at winning a trip to the BlogHer conference (a July 2005 conference for women bloggers), "I have no idea how many people read my blog. I still write it for myself, but also with the hope that maybe others will relate to bits and pieces of my life as I work it out."[9]

An October 2003 survey of some four million blogs by Perseus Development Corporation, a business survey and marketing feedback agency, found that "the typical blog is written by a teenage girl who uses it twice a month to update her friends and classmates on happenings in her life."[10] But that was then. By 2005, however, the types of blogs and the types of bloggers was expanding almost daily, with males slightly outnumbering females in creating blogs.[11] However, while thousands of blogs are created each month, thousands of other blogs wither and die for lack of care and tending.

Businesses and governmental agencies are looking at blogs as a way to develop communication between them and their publics. One example of a business blog: the review section for books on Amazon.com. It acts as a blog for customers to share their comments on a book with other possible customers. Politicians have started blogs to provide information to their constituents but also to post interviews and comments related to news items about themselves. Nonprofit groups are developing blogs to exchange information about issues and concerns that do not merit much notice in mainstream media. Some "fake" grassroots blogs, called "astroturf," have now entered the blogosphere. Astroturf may be a political group or business posing as a common blogger without revealing its true agenda.

In the realm of journalism, categorizing blogs gets tricky. Sometimes individual bloggers do journalism, and sometimes individual journalists blog, so the lines between journalism and blogging can get blurred. Some blogs, done either by individuals or by groups, are connected to traditional media. A news organization's website might host a blog or even edit it. Other blogs are completely independent, while still others link to traditional news sites. A January 2005 conference at Harvard University titled "Blogging, Journalism and Credibility" concluded that "while some blogging is journalism, much of it isn't and doesn't aim to be. Both serve different and valuable functions within the new evolving media ecosystem."[12]

Rebecca MacKinnon, a former CNN correspondent now with Harvard's Berkman Center for the Internet and Society, cautions against trying to sort and categorize blogs. Blogging is about conversations, she says, and they are organic. As such, they can be nearly impossible to categorize. One day a blog might consist of a personal account about a sick cat, the next it could be spreading photos and information about a community environmental hazard. The former would not be considered journalism. However, the latter most definitely could be; it could be considered what some in the blogosphere call a "random act of journalism." Blogging is not just one thing, MacKinnon says, "just like telephoning is not just one thing . . . it's a medium and then it's an issue of what you want to do with the medium."[13]

Blog software makes blogging the easiest and cheapest self-publishing mechanism around. Many Internet service providers offer platforms to host blogs, and some provide content management systems for bloggers. That content management program allows bloggers to upload their material, by filling in templates that establish the look and organization of their website. Bob Stepno, who teaches online journalism and has a blog related to journalism, calls it "edit this page" technology. He says that blogger.com, typepad.com, xanga.com, livejournal.com, and moveabletype.com make it possible for someone to add or edit a blog.

Many blogs also use RSS, which stands for really simple syndication or rich site summary. RSS allows bloggers to provide short blurbs with links to be fed to anyone who signs up and uses a news reader. Rather than having to check dozens of bookmarked blogs individually, RSS allows for aggregating or grouping of anyone's individual favorite sites. As a result, RSS is the path by which information can be disseminated in blog communities. MacKinnon says RSS "allows you to speed read the Web."[14]

RSS is not just for blogs. Many news organizations generate RSS feeds of their Web material. They send out headlines, story summaries, or even complete stories when they are updated to people who subscribe to an RSS feed from their site. RSS has become a primary tool for individualizing news and information.

For news organizations, MacKinnon says, the big questions revolve around how much intermingling there will be between traditional journalism and this form of citizen or grassroots media.

Journalists for traditional news organizations have also started blogs. Some, like Dan Gillmor, former *San Jose Mercury News* technology reporter, started a blog tied to his newspaper work to solicit comments and tips related to his beat. But while his blog at times included his newspaper work, it was not directly tied to the *Mercury News*. Gillmor, however, has left the newspaper to start up an independent community news blog called Bayosphere, "of, by and for the Bay Area" around San Francisco.

News organizations have started news blogs that mix postings from their staff members and from their audience. The *Guardian* newspaper in London posts a news blog that has its reporters and editors providing information on the news of the day. MSNBC.com has a section on its website that includes blogs from Keith Olbermann, who anchors an MSNBC show, and Glenn Reynolds, who also blogs as instapundit.com. Reporters and editors of the *News & Record* in Greensboro, North Carolina, produce blogs, and the paper also operates a blog for readers to contribute news. MSNBC and CNN publish photos and comments from nonprofessional journalists under a Citizen Journalist banner.

BOX 8.2

We Media Functions

"We Media," a 2003 report from the Media Center at the American Press Institute, outlines several functions of participatory journalism that blogs have come to use and follow:

- Commentary
- Filtering and editing
- Fact-checking
- Grassroots reporting
- Annotative reporting
- Open-source reporting and peer review

Groups and individuals in communities such as Watertown, Massachusetts, and Brattleboro, Vermont, have launched blogs about their towns. Northwestern University journalism students created a news blog for the Chicago suburb of Skokie. These community blogs include reporting on events often bypassed by local print and broadcast outlets, as well as comments and concerns about what is happening around town.

Whether individual or group, media-connected or independent, blogs provide a mix of several of the functions that add value and supplement the more traditional forms of journalism and journalism distribution. Blogs affect journalism in numerous ways, most notably in providing commentary or reporting, and often a mix of the two.

Media and Political Commentary

The blogs that have received the most press about their work have been those that comment on major political stories or events or aim to serve as media watchdogs, monitoring and commenting on how the media cover news and events. These blogs often take news and information reported by newspapers, television and radio stations, and magazines and provide commentary about the reporting and links to the news and information sources. These types of blogs have been compared to talk radio, except that they are online and not broadcast.

For example, on powerlineblog.com, a *USA Today* story about the value of the U.S. dollar prompted this post by one of the site's three bloggers, Paul Mirengoff:

> Remember the hand-wringing last year about the declining value of the dollar? For some, this phenomenon was evidence not only that President Bush's economic policies were a disaster, but that the more enlightened European economy was about to supplant ours

in the world pecking order. These days, the left isn't talking about the value of the dollar. That's because the dollar has been surging for months. As *USA Today* reports . . ."[15]

Glenn Reynolds, a University of Tennessee law professor who also blogs as instapundit.com, often links and quotes from traditional news sources, with a sentence or two of comment. Reynolds's instapundit and Markos Moulitsas Zúniga's dailykos.com operate their blogs independently of traditional news organizations.

Some of the most prominent commentator bloggers have had ties to the news business. Jeff Jarvis, who blogs as buzzmachine.com, served as creative director for Advance.net, which involved online development for Advance Publications (including such properties as *Vanity Fair* magazine and the *Plain Dealer* newspaper). Ana Marie Cox, the driving force behind the gossipy Washington politics site wonkette.com, also worked in print before blogging. Andrew Sullivan and his Daily Dish at andrewsullivan.com and Joshua Micah Marshall of talkingpoints.com supplement their political commentary in print media with their blogs.

Many bloggers who like to comment on the media often work at filtering, editing, and fact-checking what is being produced by traditional news organizations. The most reported example of fact-checking and editing involved the blog swarm over CBS News's *60 Minutes II* report on documents relating to President George W. Bush's National Guard service. The fact-checking began with bloggers questioning the authenticity of documents CBS used for the report, and powerlineblog.com was among the leaders. The fact-checking focused on the typing in the documents, noting that typed letters and spacing could have been generated by computer and not by typewriter, as would have had to be the case in 1972, the dates on memos cited by CBS. But in addition to the fact-checking and editing done by the blog swarm, much of the blog postings included politically charged commentary. A *Columbia Journalism Review* look at what it termed "blog-gate" called the fact-checking warped by flawed information or faulty logic. "Personal attacks passed for analysis."[16]

Patterico's Pontifications at patterico.com is a blog run by prosecuting attorney Patrick Frey critiquing the *Los Angeles Times*. In one posting, for example, Frey found fault with the paper's editorial on retiring Supreme Court Justice Sandra Day O'Connor. His problem: the number of five-to-four Supreme Court cases in 2005 that featured Justice Sandra Day O'Connor in the majority. He came up with a different number than what the *Times* quoted. Bloggers have developed the term "fisking" to describe a point-by-point critique or dissection of a story or column.

Cases of blogger fact-checking indicate public demand for greater transparency from news organizations about their work. The often unchallenged authority of news organizations is being questioned. While this constant reviewing might seem like hectoring to many journalists, *We the Media* author Dan Gillmor argues that it could lead to better journalism. He points to his own reporting as proof. He calls it open-source journalism.[17]

BOX 8.3

A Random Act of Journalism

A blog of various sessions reporting on the World Economic Forum turned Rony Abovitz, a medical technology entrepreneur, into a journalist of sorts. Abovitz "broke" the story on former CNN executive Eason Jordan's comments about journalists under fire by the U.S. military in Iraq. Abovitz posted his notes and recollections of Jordan's comments at a session entitled, "Will Democracy Survive the Media?" on the Economic Forum's blog. Abovitz's posting, "Do US Troops Target Journalists in Iraq?" contained no direct quotes and was posted hours after the session, when Abovitz discerned that other journalists at the session were not reporting it.

Abovitz wrote: "Eason Jordan asserted that he knew of twelve journalists who had not only been killed by U.S. troops in Iraq but they had in fact been targeted." That sentence got picked up by the blogosphere and news spread rapidly. Although Abovitz's post noted that Jordan "backpedaled" from that statement and others at the videotaped but off-the-record session, Jordan and CNN were attacked for the assertion. About a week after Abovitz's blog post, Jordan ended his twenty-three-year CNN career, resigning from the network and apologizing for the remark. In a statement, Jordan said, "I never meant to imply U.S. forces acted with ill intent when U.S. forces accidentally killed journalists, and I apologize to anyone who thought I said or believed otherwise."

Looking back at the media firestorm he created, Abovitz notes that the mainstream media was late on the story while "some of the blogging looked like a lynch mob." And questions remain as to what exactly was said. Neither a transcript nor tape of the session has been released.

Source: Neil Reisner, "The Accidental Blogger," *American Journalism Review*, April/May 2005, 10.

Gillmor put a chapter of his book on his blog for comment and review. He also has posted questions and topics for possible technology stories and columns and has received comments that made him revise and improve his work. "If my readers know more than I do (which I know they do), I can include them in the process of making my journalism better," he says.[18]

News organizations already do some of this when they post transcripts of interviews, or create links to documents that are the basis for their reporting. It is an effort to make the work and decisions behind the journalism more apparent to news audiences. And individual professional journalists use blogs to get tips for stories and about their stories. But using nonjournalist bloggers as part of the reporting process is an emerging aspect of participatory journalism; it mixes professionals and so-called amateurs. Rather than just showing news audiences the reporting to help them trust and understand it better, pro-am participatory journalism puts news audiences in the middle of the reporting.

Reporting

Blogs have opened up reporting opportunities for both professionals and amateurs. Traditional journalists are using blogs to supplement their work in traditional news outlets like newspapers and broadcast stations. Amateurs are using blogs to supplement news about their communities that they believe gets overlooked. And professionals and amateurs are working together on blogs to enrich traditional reporting of major news events.

TRADITIONAL JOURNALISTS AND BLOGS Tim Porter, who produces firstdraft.com, found several journalists who say that blogging helps with their reporting. Todd Bishop, who writes about Microsoft for the *Seattle Post-Intelligencer,* told Porter that his Web log "has increased the general awareness of the paper's Microsoft coverage." Bishop adds that some of his blog readers had no idea he worked for a newspaper. Another reporter-blogger, Gery Woelfel of the *Racine (WI) Journal Times*, told Porter that blogs are not the future of journalism, "I think they're the 'present' of journalism."[19]

Other reporters use their blogs like a reporter's notebook to provide insights, tidbits, and analyses of news events that often are not given enough space or time in a traditional news outlet, particularly a newspaper. These pieces of reporting and commentary may not "fit" into the regular format of a news story, so in the past they have been cobbled together into a reporter's notebook. Often these blogs are essays that encourage reader feedback.

Reporters in Asia and Africa for the *Christian Science Monitor* post reporter's notebooks online; one posting looked at the "second-rate" Live8 concert in Johannesburg, South Africa.[20] Tom Regan writes essays and observations about American life in his Web log on the *Monitor*'s website. Sheila Lennon, of the *Providence Journal*, used her blog to get reports and add comments on the deadly nightclub fire in February 2003. "The readers became the sources as a community pooled its knowledge," Lennon was quoted as saying in a 2003 study. She added that blogging "was the only way to handle that much incoming information in a way that invited readers to add what they knew—or found—to our common body of knowledge."[21]

Kevin Sites worked as a producer for CNN embedded with U.S. forces during the initial days of the incursion in Iraq in 2003. Although in many ways his blog represented the classic reporter's notebook genre, he did not "embed" his blog into the CNN.com site, and it was independent of the cable network's editorial control. Because CNN and Sites differed as to whether the blog reporting was taking him away from his CNN work, Sites and the network

BOX 8.4

Blog as Reporter's Notebook

Kevin Sites used his blog to report stories that did not necessarily fit into the format of a typical television story. They might have what he calls "the same germ of an idea, but usually the blog story is the story in front of the story or the story behind the story." He says his blog stories often reflected the experience of an individual—a Marine, an Iraqi—or the atmosphere of an event or operation.

Sites offers the example of the situation he encountered during a Marine raid at dawn in Tallafar during the Muslim holy period of Ramadan. He says that one minute the Marines are holding the Iraqi man on the ground with a gun to his neck, and later, when the raid turns up nothing, the man is released and offers his captors breakfast. It is a meal the Iraqi cannot eat because of Ramadan fasting from dawn to dusk.

"I probably wouldn't have the time to do that story for, say, the nightly news," Sites says, where it would have competed against bigger events, perhaps a suicide bombing. With his blog, "the war is the backdrop, and I'm looking for the small element."

You can read Sites's blog of this experience at www.kevinsites.net/2003_11_02_archive.html.

Source: Kevin Sites, interview by author, May 2005.

parted ways. NBC News and MSNBC, which host blogs via its website, MSNBC.com, hired Sites and allowed the blog to continue.

Sites's conflict at CNN was one of several disputes between traditional news organizations and their staffers when reporters' blogs appeared outside their sphere of influence. For traditional news organizations, the issue of editorial control and credibility remains a concern when using blogs created by staffers or others. The culture or nature of blogs often encourages publishing information first, then allowing the blogosphere to check, verify, and correct. That mindset runs counter to the journalistic standard of verification before publication. News organizations have had to contemplate this philosophical difference.

A complete lack of editorial control also opens up blogs for flaming, the posting of hostile, insulting, or specious comments, what has been described as the online equivalent of yelling. The openness of blogs makes them prey to trolls, people who post insulting or hostile comments to disrupt and/or control a conversation. Flaming and trolls have led sites to require registrations and even to eliminate open-comment blogs, discussion boards, and other innovative moves toward participatory Web activities. Despite these problems, some traditional news organizations are trying to share and pair the production of news and commentary with their public.

PRO-AM COLLABORATION On December 26, 2004, and again on July 7, 2005, people with cell phones, camera phones, digital cameras, and video cameras became some of the first people on the scene to report on two deadly events: the Asian tsunami and the coordinated London bombings. Some of them sent out their reports on individual blogs; others used blog sites set up by traditional news organizations. For the London bombings, some news organizations, such as the Guardian Unlimited website, decided to post a news blog, providing updated reports every few minutes as well as post reports from amateur journalists and comments from people around the world. The tsunami and bombing reports represent a new stream for journalism, in which journalists and their public work together to provide information about what is happening in the world.

FIGURE 8.1. The *Greensboro News & Record* promotes citizen journalism through Town Square on its website. (By permission of the *Greensboro News & Record*)

The *Pensacola News Journal*, which used community forums on its website to allow comments by residents related to Hurricane Ivan in September 2004, added staff blogs (one in English and one in Spanish) with updates on Hurricane Dennis when it hit in July 2005 and a weather blog from a graduate student hurricane expert.

In addition to the citizen-journalist blogs that post observations, information, and photos from amateurs, some news organizations have set up staff blogs for sharing of information between news organization and the news public.

The *Greensboro (NC) News & Record* newspaper has been developing several online avenues for sharing and pairing its staff with the public at large. The Town Square concept at the paper involves everything from more reporter blogs to local community news reports from readers and Web users. This initiative gained the paper national attention and a write-up in *Editor and Publisher* as one of "10 That Do It Right" in 2005. And it may serve to encourage other news organizations to develop their own responses to the participatory journalism movement.

"We intend to build a Web presence that invites readers in to share the news they know and engage in the civic discussion," said *News & Record* editor John Robinson, in announcing the paper's plans. "Readers will help drive the direction."[22] Readers even drove the creation of the Town Square initiative. Lex Alexander, a twenty-year veteran reporter and editor at the paper, drew up a final list of fifty suggestions for this virtual town square, gathering many of the ideas through his own newspaper-connected blog. Many of the suggestions focused on three areas pertinent to citizen journalism: community, interactivity, and transparency. Among them:

- Assign local bloggers to cover activities the newspaper cannot.
- Structure Letters to the Editor as a blog.
- "Get Me Rewrite" to allow readers to rewrite stories pointing out omissions or adding different emphases.
- Blog story budget and editorial board meetings.[23]

The number of staff blogs has exploded since the initial Town Square report came out. Robinson, who himself began blogging with readers in August 2004, sees blogs as a way for reporters to interact and connect with their audience. As of mid-2005, more than a dozen staff blogs appear on the paper's websites. Religion writer Nancy McLaughlin used her blog, "The Front Pew," to spark discussion on the use of the Koran versus a Bible in swearing in witnesses in court. Education reporter Jennifer Fernandez used "The Chalkboard" blog that she writes with Bruce Buchanan to provide a list of school construction projects on hold because of rising costs. The list did not make it into the print edition.

The paper has also added podcasts to its webpage that provide information from the paper's weekly arts and entertainment section. Another section, "Your News," by individuals listed as a "contributing readers," includes everything from essays about patriotism, community announcements about Amateur Radio Field Day, and real estate tips to a short story about a nursing student who graduated while fighting sickle cell anemia and news about the Greensboro Truth and Reconciliation Commission. In the meantime, the *News and Record* is recruiting community members to serve as contributing reporters.

While the paper is working on more professional-amateur collaborative reporting, independent bloggers in Greensboro have joined together on greensboro101.com. The site posts the first few sentences of individual blogs and then provides links to the whole blog. The posts of several newspaper staffers, such as that of columnist Ed Cone, appear on the greensboro101.com site. *News & Record* editor Robinson, however, has said he does not view greensboro101 as competition. "Both of us benefit from a dynamic and robust civic-oriented cyberpresence, and I suspect we will for a long time."[24] Robinson has even suggested that the two join forces on an environmental issue that surfaced on the website.

"The goal is what every journalist's goal is: to spread the news and to get people talking about stuff that's important and what's happening in their community," Robinson told *Editor and Publisher* magazine. "We want to help people make smart decisions for their life."[25]

The inspiration for some of the sharing-pairing citizen journalism ventures in the United States comes from South Korea and a blog site called OhmyNews. Oh Yeon-ho, a veteran journalist of Korea's alternative media who was dissatisfied with the limitations of Korea's predominantly conservative traditional media, started the project in 2000.[26] Oh argues that journalists "aren't some exotic species, they are everyone who has news stories and shares them with others."[27] The motto of OhmyNews is: "Every Citizen's a Reporter" (with some editing).

The news site began with 727 citizen reporters and 4 editors. Oh said that while citizens like to write their own articles, many also like to be edited by professional journalists. So OhmyNews combines "the merits of the blog and the merits of the newspaper" with articles, often from a distinct perspective, with comments.[28] Five years after it started, OhmyNews has some 38,000 citizen reporters.[29] About a dozen editors review articles, fact-check, and fix typographical errors. Although it has not been entirely free of hoaxes, OhmyNews tries to guard against problems by requiring citizen reporters to use real identities and to assume personal responsibility for their posts.

The website also uses a few dozen "traditional" reporters to cover the day's news. Many of the site's more traditional reporters came from its citizen reporter ranks. The traditional editing staff determines where to place the stories on the site's home page. Hard news from both traditional and citizen reporters might merit the top center spots on the front page, followed by softer features and comments. Headlines and story blurbs at the top trickle down to one-line, headline links at the bottom. In 2003, the front page was being updated three times during the day. By 2005, it added video to the site and citizen anchors.

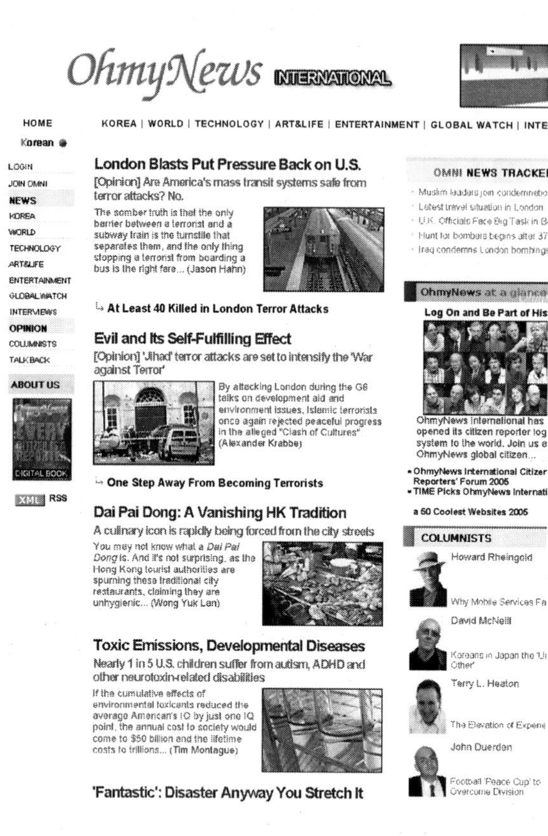
OhmyNews International Page 1 of 2

OhmyNews INTERNATIONAL

HOME KOREA | WORLD | TECHNOLOGY | ART&LIFE | ENTERTAINMENT | GLOBAL WATCH | INTE

Korean

LOGIN
JOIN OMNI
NEWS
KOREA
WORLD
TECHNOLOGY
ART&LIFE
ENTERTAINMENT
GLOBALWATCH
INTERVIEWS
OPINION
COLUMNISTS
TALKBACK
ABOUT US
DIGITAL BOOK
XML RSS

London Blasts Put Pressure Back on U.S.

[Opinion] Are America's mass transit systems safe from terror attacks? No.

The somber truth is that the only barrier between a terrorist and a subway train is the turnstile that separates them, and the only thing stopping a terrorist from boarding a bus is the right fare... (Jason Hahn)

↳ At Least 40 Killed in London Terror Attacks

Evil and Its Self-Fulfilling Effect

[Opinion] 'Jihad' terror attacks are set to intensify the 'War against Terror'

By attacking London during the G8 talks on development aid and environment issues, Islamic terrorists once again rejected peaceful progress in the alleged "Clash of Cultures" (Alexander Krabbe)

↳ One Step Away From Becoming Terrorists

Dai Pai Dong: A Vanishing HK Tradition

A culinary icon is rapidly being forced from the city streets

You may not know what a *Dai Pai Dong* is. And it's not surprising, as the Hong Kong tourist authorities are spurning these traditional city restaurants, claiming they are unhygienic... (Wong Yuk Len)

Toxic Emissions, Developmental Diseases

Nearly 1 in 5 U.S. children suffer from autism, ADHD and other neurotoxin-related disabilities

If the cumulative effects of environmental toxicants reduced the average American's IQ by just one IQ point, the annual cost to society would come to $50 billion and the lifetime costs to trillions... (Tim Montague)

'Fantastic': Disaster Anyway You Stretch It

OMNI NEWS TRACKE

OhmyNews at a glance

Log On and Be Part of His

OhmyNews International has opened its citizen reporter log system to the world. Join us a OhmyNews global citizen...

- OhmyNews International Citizen Reporters' Forum 2005
- TIME Picks OhmyNews Internati a 50 Coolest Websites 2005

COLUMNISTS

Howard Rheingold

David McNeill

Terry L. Heaton

John Duerden

FIGURE 8.2. OhmyNews.com, the South Korean website of citizen reporters, encourages reports from all over the globe. (By permission)

Oh admits he is not encouraging the nonprofessional citizen reporters to adopt a traditional news style of writing and reporting. "MyNews means you write your own news." In some sense, he says, OhmyNews represents the destruction of the concept of articles and reporters. "We do not regard objective reporting as a source of pride," he says in a 2004 interview with *Japan Media Review*. "Articles including both facts and opinions are acceptable when they are good."[30]

In choosing articles to put on the site, Oh says OhmyNews looks at how current and newsworthy a story might be, its impact, but also how lively the story is, how it might arouse interest and sympathy.[31] An example of the latter: "Netizen Debate over 'Dog Poop Girl.'" The story, which is a link off the home page, is about the Internet debate over the online publication of cell phone photos and comments about a dog owner who ignored the mess her dog made on a Seoul subway train. The story focuses on whether the woman's public online humiliation was exceedingly harsh and if "netizens" might have overreacted in an effort to address "antisocial" public activity. It raises questions about whether the reaction was an online witch-hunt or a new aspect of civic involvement.[32]

That give-and-take is the philosophy behind the website. "We make OhmyNews a public square and a playground for the citizen reporter and readers," Oh told an international newspaper group in 2004. "The traditional paper says 'I produce, you read' but we say, 'we produce and we read and we change the world together.'"[33]

OhmyNews reporters make some money with their articles. Top stories get a modest fee, between ten and twenty dollars. Site users can pay a "tip" to a particular story's citizen reporter if they like the story. Several citizen reporters have made a few thousand dollars, thanks to their contributions. OhmyNews, while popular in Korea, is moving beyond Koreans and its founder is now aiming to develop a worldwide network of citizen reporters to post on an English-language international edition.

INDEPENDENT COMMUNITY BLOGS While OhmyNews is going global, other participatory journalism endeavors are going local, hyperlocal. Hyperlocal news blogs aim to fill the gap left by traditional news media in suburbs and small towns by relying on nonprofessionals to supply information and commentary.

Lisa Williams, the driving force behind H2Otown-info.bryght.net, a blog on Watertown, Massachusetts, says she decided that the dozen or so pages devoted to her town of 32,000 by a weekly newspaper did not satisfy her need to know how things worked in this Boston suburb. So she launched H2Otown. In the blog's mission statement, Williams notes that "during the same time period this dramatic rise in my access to global news occurred, something else happened: it became harder to find out what was going on in my town and neighborhood. The economics of media made the life of independent local news services difficult or impossible. . . ."[34]

Williams, who had worked on a community newspaper briefly and for dot-coms in the 1990s, says she is not in competition with the weekly community newspaper. She is not looking for the big story, but is recording the increments of change and decision-making in the town. "I go where they're not reporting anything," she says. One example of a story that would not merit a notice in a traditional news outlet involved the fire at an unfinished furniture store. Another posting included a picture from a commercial real estate website that showed the inside of a Watertown watering hole up for sale. Browsers responded quickly with the name: The Spot. Williams also delivered more than a dozen short posts on city council meetings, from the $600,000 approved for playground upgrades to a vote on new voting equipment. Williams jokes that her motto might be "no story is too small." She says she considers her citizen journalism to be quite different from traditional news in that it is very clear that she has a "voice" projected in her posts, which she describes as "snarky" and smart, but not

FIGURE 8.3. The Backfence website seeks "hyperlocal" news from residents of suburban Washington, D.C., communities. (By permission of backfence.com)

mean. She uses the first-person voice in her reports and she admits she is a town booster. "I like my town and I want it to be better."

Backfence.com, a hyperlocal citizens media site in suburban Washington, wants to provide information but also thinks it could make money doing so. Mark Potts and Susan DeFife, who are behind backfence.com, say the site could make money with local advertising and online business listing. Backfence was operating in MacLean and Reston, Virginia, as of July 2005.

Backfence is set up to allow anyone in a community to register on the site and submit information to it by simply filling in an e-mail template. Backfence has rules that contributors must follow, but the website does not edit postings by individuals. It provides a community agreement, which is a list of rules that prohibits profane, obscene, libelous, or misleading content or material. Those who violate the agreement have their membership rescinded and are denied site access.

DeFife says that Backfence, like H2Otown, was started to fill a gap left by metropolitan daily newspapers that were stretching to cover the ever-expanding metropolitan area. Washington, D.C., alone has five- or six-dozen communities. "There's a huge gap in local information. You can get national news in many places, and very good national news. What is missing is that down-to-the-neighborhood level," DeFife says.[35] The Reston site, for example, included a short story on the Reston Community Center director leaving for a California job. On the MacLean site, a blog exchange discussed concerns about the area's hot real estate market and skyrocketing home prices. "It's like cable news for your neighborhood," Potts says.[36] But while backfence.com and H2Otown.com relate to geographically bound communities, political and social activists, business and technology groups, nonprofit organizations, and religious organizations have been creating community blogs within their circles of interests.

With so many blogs in the blogosphere, keeping track of them all has led to blog-rolling and tagging. Many of these groups, like the commentary bloggers, include a blog roll on their site, which is a list of other blogs they like or relate to. They also use tags, or subject categories, to group blogs on similar topics. Tags for the BlogHer conference on technorati.com include a list of related tags, such as blogging, bloggercon (a blogger conference), blogs, blog and women. Del.icio.us, which refers to itself as a social bookmarks manager, also provides tags for blogs.

Podcasts and blogs are developing into the next wave in citizen journalism. Podcasts are audio broadcasts via the Web. Several news organizations and journalists, particularly in traditional radio, produce podcasts that can be downloaded on iPods or MP3 players. But individuals with a microphone, digital recorder, and some software can produce podcasts. Anyone with software like iPodder can download podcasts for listening at any time or place. Vlogs are the video equivalent of podcasts and blogs. Steve Garfield has covered technology conferences and the Democratic National Convention in 2004 via his vlog. Each technological advance is expanding the possibilities of participatory journalism.

WIKIS: TOTALLY COLLABORATIVE NEWS

If this book were a wiki, anyone and everyone who reads it would have the opportunity to add, subtract, edit, reword, reorganize, or even delete its content. A wiki, which is derived from the Hawaiian term "wiki-wiki" meaning quick, refers to the software technology that is used on websites to allow anyone to revise or contribute content. While blogs allow for individuals to post content, they do not allow one person to change the content of another. Wikis do.

The first and most successful wiki so far is Wikipedia, an online collaborative encyclopedia with millions of entries and thousands of contributors that began in 2001. Wikipedians, people who contribute and use Wikipedia as a source of information, swear by the reliability

BOX 8.5

A Random Act of Journalism

During the London blasts, Adam Stacey's camera phone picture from inside the London Underground rail system was posted less than an hour after the first blast, making it one of the first images of the terrorism. Alfie Dennen posted the picture on his moblogUK, a mobile blog. For several minutes, and several postings, it was confusing as to what the picture represented. Then Dennen posted this:

"This image taken by Adam Stacey. He was on the northern line just past Kings Cross. Train suddenly stopped and filled with smoke. People in carriage smashed tube windows to get out and then were evacuated along the train tunnel. He's suffering from smoke inhalation but fine otherwise."

Within hours, news organizations from Sky News, the BBC, CNN, and the *New York Times* websites posted the picture. And wikinews used it in its stories on the bombings.

Dennen says he got Stacey's image from his girlfriend, who works in the same office as Stacey. He explains in an e-mail that he decided to post the image because "it was so arresting, I knew it needed to get out there." Dennen told the *Boston Globe*, "I think it's become one of the iconic images of the day."

Flickr.com, Yahoo's photo-sharing site, displayed Stacey's photo and hundreds more from nonprofessionals, as citizen journalism added to the overall reporting on the blasts.

FIGURE 8.4. Photo by Adam Stacey from London Underground bombings, July 7, 2005.

"It definitely can be true journalism," Dennen writes, allowing "that anyone in the right place at the right time can be a journo." But Dennen, who has a journalism degree, is cautious. "I think that the delineations between traditional journalism and 'citizen reporting' are necessarily strict; bloggers and the like are able to get the information out there fast, bypassing fact checking (perhaps) in order to get it out there, not needing to refer to editors and then are able to edit their work post reportage due to the malleable nature of the medium. Traditional journalists have a more vested responsibility and a lot more to lose."

Source: Alfie Dennen, interview by author, July 2005.

of its information. Researchers and librarians are not so convinced. Yet Wikipedia has developed a reputation, similar to that of Google, for being a useful tool or starting point for information searches. The news aspect of Wikipedia can be found in its current events section, in which major events or individuals connected to major events get a listing. For example, Wikipedia provided biographical information on Magdi el-Nashar, a man police linked to the London bombings, on the day his name was made public.

The success of Wikipedia spawned Wikinews in December 2004, applying the same collaborative concepts to news stories. In June 2005, the *Los Angeles Times* experimented with what it called a "wikitorial," or a collaborative Web editorial. The technology news website CNETNews.com also launched reader wikis on the future of Indian technology and on interactive television.

"We're sort of at a tipping point, or on the verge of a second phase in the development of the Internet as a communications medium," says Mike Yamamoto, executive editor of CNETNews.com.[37] Beginning in 2004, technology and social networks have been coming together to encourage grassroots communications on the Web. Wikis represent another aspect of that convergence.

Wikinews

For both the December 26, 2004, Asian tsunami and the July 7, 2005, London bombings, the beginnings of Wikinews articles appeared on the site within minutes of the events. Initial information was just a few sentences, but revisions were made every few minutes. In both instances, the history of the article could be followed to see just who was making changes and what changes were being made. Both stories listed hundreds of revisions, with some changes occurring days and even months later.

"Dan100" created the first story on the London attacks, opening with "London's Liverpool Street Station has been evacuated after an explosion inside at 8.49 a.m. local time."[38] The story listed no sources. Later, Dan100 would add dozens of revisions, as he gathered more information for the stories. Hundreds more revisions followed, including information from traditional news organizations such as the BBC. For the tsunami coverage, David Vasquez sparked the early coverage and links to everything from the U.S. Geological Survey website to other news articles, as the tsunami story unraveled on Wikinews.[39] The first stories had the feel of initial wire service reports on the events.

Wikinews, like Wikipedia, requires contributors to agree to certain policies. Unlike OhmyNews and indymedia, which also use and solicits articles, Wikinews asks each contributor to adopt a "neutral point of view" (NPOV). Rather than promoting an objective point of view, "the policy says that an article should *fairly represent* all, and not make an article state, imply or insinuate that any one side is correct."[40] Wikinews goes to great lengths to explain that the NPOV policy involves writing not to hide different points of view but to show their diversity. It also insists on using facts, a point illustrated in the editing history of the London bombing story, when an assertion was made and then edited with a caution to "please provide sources and avoid speculation. Report only confirmed information please."[41]

Other policies, which are developed by the consensus of registered Wikinews users, require writers to cite sources, be respectful, avoid copyright violations, and limit reverts (the wikis version of "undo") to three. The site has other information to help the contributing reporters—from suggesting writing style to defining of news and good content. But it operates under the premise of publishing first and then editing, albeit the editors are Wikinews users who become contributors. Some edits can involve punctuation, adding a subhead, or correcting spelling. Others add new information, such as the death toll updated by authorities during the London bombing or Prime Minister Tony Blair's statement.

In its first seven months, Wikinews boasted more than seven thousand articles in more than a dozen languages, and nearly four hundred Wikinews reporters.[42] However, many Wikinews stories rely on traditional news organizations' reports as source material, although the site is designed to point out original reporting by Wikinewsies. For example, a story about Hurricane Emily hitting the Caribbean island nation of Grenada contained comments to a Wikinews reporter from a local priest about recovering from 2004's Hurricane Ivan, as well as information from CNN and the *Guardian* about the storm. But Wikinews was considered by some to be more of a news aggregator than a news originator during its first few months of operation.[43]

Erik Moeller, chief research officer for the Wikimedia Foundation, has defended Wikinews's mix of original and syndicated news material in his periodic "state of the wiki" reports. "We are providing a service beyond collecting information content from various sources and putting it into our own words. We are *synthesizing* information content to give the reader a bigger picture: more information, less bias."[44]

In analyzing the first few months of Wikinews, Moeller adds that problems relating to libel, copyright violations, online vandalism, and bias have been infrequent. The bigger problem has been getting reporting participation in this brand of participatory journalism.

Wikitorial

That was not the case in the *Los Angeles Times*'s wikitorial experiment, which was shut down in less than two days because "a few readers were flooding the site with inappropriate material." Foul language and pornographic images led to the wikitorial's demise.

On June 17, 2005, the paper invited readers to rewrite the editorial, asking them to avoid hostile behavior and acknowledging that it "may lead straight into the dumpster of embarrassing failures."[45] The *Times* reported that "nearly 1,000 users registered to participate in the rewriting of Friday's lead editorial, called 'War and Consequences.'"[46]

Analysis of the experiment via blogs and news articles pointed out that the paper could have avoided some problems by setting up safeguards against anonymous postings, such as requiring registration and providing policing from wiki veterans.[47] Others argued that the wiki format encourages collaboration and consensus and an editorial does not.

Reader Wikis

While the *Los Angeles Times* attempted a wikitorial, CNETNews.com launched reader wikis about interactive television and India's technology industry. "We saw this new phenomenon emerging and although fraught with risk, if anybody should jump into this with both feet, it would have to be us," says executive editor Mike Yamamoto. "Whenever any of these new things come up, it's going to happen anyway . . . so rather than try and kill it, we try to ride with it."[48]

The success of the wiki, he says, depends on getting greater numbers of people to contribute and edit. Wikis depend on enough "good guys to correct anything done by bad guys." The format is still what Yamamoto calls "a work in progress."

For CNETNews' India wiki, readers were invited to "collaborate with other readers to predict the future of this nation's technology industry, collectively writing and editing your own chapter of this special report."[49] It was still up and running several weeks after CNET launched the experiment. The wiki accompanied a three-day series examining India and its technology industry. The reader wiki had more than a dozen "chapters," addressing such topics as competition from other countries and regions, such as Latin America, the next wave of new technology companies, cautions and concerns for tech businesses in India, and even information on the limited representation of the wiki audience.

This CNETNews wiki also carried a disclaimer noting that it bore no responsibility for the accuracy, integrity, or quality of the wiki's content.[50] Yamamoto says CNETNews staff

CNET News.com

CNET tech sites:

Product reviews
- Shop
- Tech news
- Downloads
- Site map

This page was last modified 01:53, 21 Jul 2005.
This page has been accessed 11330 times.

Search the wiki: SEARCH

India's Tech Renaissance: Reader Wiki Home page

Main Page

From India Tech Wiki

Welcome to CNET News.com's India Wiki. Here, you can collaborate with other readers to predict the future of this nation's technology industry, collectively writing and editing your own chapter of this special report. A few potential points to address: Can India realistically become a global tech powerhouse in the face of unprecedented competition? Has wage inflation made India a less desirable place to do business, in comparison to alternative countries such as Russia and China? Will India's steep poverty rate and other political concerns limit its growth potential? (Read the full special report here: "India's tech renaissance" (*http://news.com.com/Indias+renaissance+Move+over%2C+China/2009-1041_3-5751994.html*))

Please click the Edit button above and begin writing your story here:

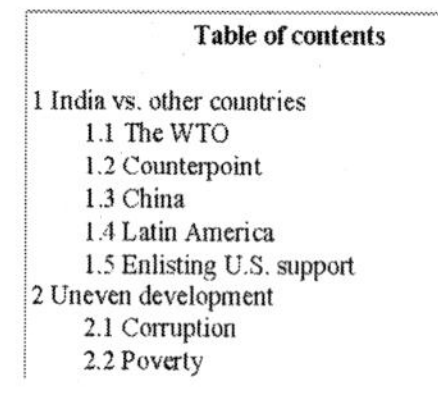

Table of contents

FIGURE 8.5. CNETNews.com's wiki reader. (By permission of CNETNews.com)

monitored the wiki, with some editing for spelling and style, but for the most part let the readers control it. Yamamoto says the new communications capabilities of the Internet require a new thinking about news. It requires embracing the concept that the story does not end with the publication of the news. A story begins when you publish material, Yamamoto notes, and continues when audiences respond. That interaction, once a dream of early Internet news advocates in the 1990s, is becoming a reality a decade later.

Blogs or wikis or podcasts, individual or group, independent or connected to news organizations—new technologies are opening up yet another avenue of convergence in which the news consumer joins in the producing of news. This type of participatory journalism poses new challenges to conventional, traditional news organizations and also to new consumers to be savvy in delineating news sources.

Steve Outing, who writes about media and technology for *Editor and Publisher* and Poynter Online, has tried to get a handle on the explosion of participatory journalism efforts on the

Internet. Outing suggests that traditional news organizations might want to look at establishing citizen editors, to not only recruit citizen journalists but help guide those nonprofessionals to write and report their stories as well as to monitor the site to avoid vandalism.[51] In June 2005, he listed eleven layers of citizen journalism that involve blogs, wikis, and other types of websites. His article generated e-mail comments outlining even more permutations. As Outing himself cautions, "Citizen journalism isn't one simple concept that can be applied universally by all news organizations. It's much more complex, with many potential variations."[52]

SUMMARY

Citizen or participatory journalism is another outgrowth of convergence, with news consumers themselves taking on the role of news producer as well. Blogs allow individuals to post essays, pictures, news items, and links to other blogs and websites through blogging software technology. Blogs can serve as personal diaries or journals, or they can be used to create community conversations. News organizations are setting up blogs to encourage members of the public to report on major news events. In the meantime, hyperlocal blogs have been created to provide neighborhood information often bypassed by traditional news organizations. Wikis, or collaborative Web activities, pose another outlet for individuals to provide information to a larger public.

Wikis and blogs defy simple categorization as they are being developed daily to meet different individual and community information needs.

LEARNING THE LINGO

Blog
Blog Roll
Blogosphere
Hyperlocal
RSS
Tag
Troll
Wiki

NOTES

1. Jan Schaffer, "Citizens and Convergence, Phase II," April 9, 2005, at www.jour.sc.edu/news/convergence/issue20.html (accessed December 4, 2005).

2. Tom Curley, keynote presentation to the Online News Association, November 12, 2004, at journalist.org/2004conference/archives/000079.php (accessed December 4, 2005).

3. Jay Rosen, "Bloggers vs. Journalists Is Over," January 15, 2005, at journalism.nyu.edu/pubzone/weblogs/pressthink/2005/01/15/berk_pprd.html (accessed December 4, 2005).

4. Dan Gillmor, *We the Media Grassroots Journalism: By the People for the People* (Sebastopol, CA: O'Reilly Press, 2004).

5. Alan Feuer, *Over There: From the Bronx to Baghdad* (New York: Counterpoint, 2005).

6. Hugh Hewitt, *Blog: Understanding the Information Reformation that's Changing Your World* (Nashville: Thomas Nelson, 2005), xvii.

7. Shayne Bowman and Chris Willis, "We Media: How audiences are shaping the future of news and information," September 21, 2003, at www.hypergene.net/wemedia/weblog.php?id=P3 (accessed December 5, 2005).

8. Bowman and Willis, "We Media," 25.

9. Playingschool.blogspot.com/2005/06/how-blogging-has-changed-my-life.html (June 19, 2005, accessed December 4, 2005).

10. Jeffrey Henning,"The Blogging Iceberg," May 2004, at www.perseus.com/blogsurvey/thebloggingiceberg.html (accessed December 5, 2005).

11. Lee Rainie, "The State of Blogging," January 2005, at www.pewinternet.org/pdfs/PIP_blogging_data.pdf (accessed December 4, 2005).

12. Rebecca MacKinnon, "Blogging, Journalism & Credibility: Battleground and Common Ground," January 21, 2005, at cyber.law.harvard.edu:8080/webcred/wp-content/CONFREPORT2.htm (accessed December 4, 2005).

13. Rebecca MacKinnon, interview by author, July 2005.

14. MacKinnon, interview.

15. Paul Mirengoff, "Another Pseudo-Crisis Passes," July 6, 2005, at www.powerlineblog.com/ (accessed July 6, 2005).

16. Corey Pein, "Blog-Gate," *Columbia Journalism Review*, January/February 2005, 30–35.

17. Gillmor, *We the Media*.

18. Gillmor, *We the Media*, 18.

19. Tim Porter, "Blogging the Beat," June 25, 2005, at www.timporter.com/firstdraft/archives/000461.html (accessed December 4, 2005).

20. "Jo'burg's second rate Live8 concert," July 6, 2005, at blogs.csmonitor.com/notebook_africa/2005/07/index.html#a0005479630 (accessed December 4, 2005).

21. Bowman and Willis, "We Media," 56.

22. John Robinson, "My Newspaper Column, January 15, 2005," at blog.news-record.com/staff/jrblog/archives/2005/01/my_newspaper_co_2.html (accessed December 4, 2005).

23. Lex Alexander, "News-Record.com as Public Square," January 4, 2005, at blog.news-record.com/staff/lexblog/archives/2005/01/newsrecordcom_a_1.html (accessed December 4, 2005).

24. John Robinson, "Greensboro101 and Competition," February 23, 2005, at blog.news-record.com/staff/jrblog/archives/2005/02/greensboro101_a.html (accessed December 4, 2005).

25. Jesse Oxfeld, "Letting the Blogs Out," *Editor and Publisher*, March 1, 2005, 39–42.

26. Leander Kahney, "Citizens Reporters Make the News," May 17, 2003, at www.wired.com/news/culture/0,1284,58856,00.html (accessed December 4, 2005).

27. Anna Fifield, "Korea's citizen reporters take on traditional media," *The Financial Times*, November 6, 2004, 9.

28. Jack Scofield, "Hacks of all trades: A South Korean website has let more than 30,000 citizens try their hand at journalism," *The Guardian*, July 22, 2004, 23.

29. Oh Yeon-ho, introduction to OhmyNews International Citizen Reporters' Forum, May 3, 2005, at english.ohmynews.com/articleview/article_view.asp?article_class=8&no=224341&rel_no=1 (accessed December 6, 2005).

30. Yu Yeon-Jung, "OhmyNews Makes Every Citizen a Reporter," September 17, 2003, at www.japanmediareview.com/japan/internet/1063672919.php (accessed December 4, 2005).

31. Yu Yeon-Jung, "OhmyNews."

32. Ronda Hauben, "Netizen Debate Ensues Over 'Dog Poop Girl'" July 10, 2005, at english.ohmynews.com/articleview/article_view.asp?menu=c10400&no=236643&rel_no=1 (accessed December 4, 2005).

33. Oh Yeon-ho, "The End of 20th Century Journalism," July 27, 2004, at english.ohmynews.com/articleview/article_view.asp?menu=c10400&no=169396&rel_no=1 (accessed December 7, 2005).

34. Lisa Williams, "The Blogger as Citizen Journalist," October 10, 2003, at www.cadence90.com/wp/index.php?p=1991 (accessed December 4, 2005).

35. Mark Potts and Susan DeFife, interview, May 2005, at www.pbs.org/newshour/media/newmedia/backfence.html (accessed December 4, 2005).

36. Pots and DeFife, interview.

37. Mike Yamamoto, interview by author, July 2005.

38. Dan100, "Coordinated Terrorist Attack Hits London," July 7, 2005, at en.wikinews.org/w/index.php?title=Coordinated_terrorist_attack_hits_London&diff=prev&oldid=96968 (accessed December 4, 2005).

39. David Vasquez, "Strongest Quake in 40 Years Hits Southeast Asia," December 26, 2004 at en.wikinews.org/w/index.php?title=Strongest_earthquake_in_40_years_hits_Southeast_Asia&diff=next&oldid=8999 (accessed December 4, 2005).

40. wikinews.org/wiki/Wikinews:Neutral_point_of_view (January 19, 2005, accessed December 4, 2005).

41. en.wikinews.org/w/index.php?title=Coordinated_terrorist_attack_hits_London&diff=97716&oldid=97713 (July 7, 2005, accessed December 4, 2005).

42. en.wikipedia.org/wikistats/wikinews/EN/ChartsWikipediaZZ.htm#2 (November 9, 2005, accessed December 4, 2005).

43. Simon Waldman, "Wikinews . . . dare I say what I think?," February 24, 2005, at www.simonwaldman.net/sssshhhh-wikinews-isnt-really-very-good (accessed December 4, 2005).

44. Erik Moeller, "State of the Wiki," April 28, 2005, at en.wikinews.org/wiki/User:Eloquence/State_of_the_Wiki (accessed December 4, 2005).

45. "A Wiki for Your Thoughts," June 17, 2005, at www.latimes.com/news/opinion/la-ed-wiki17jun17,0,4157492.story (accessed December 4, 2005).

46. James Rainey, "'Wikitorial' Pulled Due to Vandalism," *Los Angeles Times*, June 21, 2005, A15.

47. Jeff Jarvis, "Wiki Cooties and the Death of Editorials," June 21, 2005, at www.buzzmachine.com/archives/2005_06_21.html (accessed December 4, 2005).

48. Yamamoto, interview.

49. indiatechwiki.com/index.php/Main_Page (June 23, 2005, accessed December 6, 2005).

50. indiatechwiki.com/index.php/India_Tech_Wiki:General_disclaimer (June 23, 2005, accessed December 6, 2005).

51. Steve Outing, "New Desk in the Newsroom: The Citizen Editor's," May 25, 2005, at www.newmediamusings.com/blog/2005/05/new_newsroom_de.html (accessed December 4, 2005).

52. Steve Outing, "The 11 layers of citizen journalism," June 13, 2005, at poynter.org/content/content_view.asp?id=83126 (accessed December 4, 2005).

NINE

News for Kids: The Next Generation

CONVERGENCE MAY seem like a passing fad or experiment for many traditional news organizations and journalists, but it is routine for one sector of the news business: children's news. Interactive polls on websites? Every kids' news site, from *Nick News* to *Weekly Reader*, has several. Interactive maps and explanatory games? *Time For Kids* and *Scholastic* run a few. Multimedia projects? Participatory journalism? The British Broadcasting Corporation children's division, *Weekly Reader*, and *Time For Kids* have been using kid reporters for years. Print, online, and television cooperative ventures? *Weekly Reader* works with *Teen Kids News* produced by Alan Weiss Productions on a weekly newscast that is viewed in more than two hundred U.S. cities.

The news audiences of tomorrow are immersed in convergent news offerings today. If youngsters are interested in news when they are nine years old, then that interest might carry through to when they are nineteen or twenty-nine. In its marketing promotion, *Time For Kids* notes that by age ten, children have developed half of their consumer attitudes and skills. News organizations may need to consider how that development will affect news habits when children grow up. News designed for children in an era of camera phones, instant messaging, blogs, podcasts, and video games may have clues as to how news may need to be designed to captivate that audience so they can thrive in their complex adult world.

The people who say they are the most starved for time while being the most comfortable with using multimedia and multiple media are young adults. And if a 2005 survey of third through twelfth graders is any indication, that number will grow dramatically in the years ahead. A Kaiser Foundation survey found that "children and teens are spending an increasing amount of time using 'new media' like computers, the Internet and video games, without cutting back on the time they spend with 'old' media like TV, print and music."[1] The report found that young people are using media about six and a half hours each day and more than a quarter of those surveyed are using more than one medium at the same time, such as watching TV or listening to music while on the computer. The foundation, which conducted a similar survey in 1999, found that media multitasking jumped from 16 to 26 percent. And because of that multitasking, people under age eighteen are squeezing more than eight and a half hours of media consumption per day into that six and a half hours. And that is just media multitasking. A 2003 survey found that some 72 percent of people under eighteen said they do other things while watching television, an increase from 64 percent in 2001.[2]

The debate is now raging as to whether all that multitasking, and all that contact with popular culture, like video games and reality television, harms young people. Some people have argued that today's entertainment culture is rendering children incapable of exploring and engaging in complex ideas and issues. Steven Johnson, a science and technology writer, says it does not. In his book *Everything Bad Is Good for You*, Johnson argues that popular culture may be making people smarter. Johnson says that video games, reality television, and using the Internet require more complex thinking and problem-solving. He calls it collateral learning. "It's not what you're thinking when you're playing a game, it's the way you're thinking that matters."[3] Additionally, video games, reality television, and the Internet engage their audiences in the activities, Johnson writes. They require participation and interaction and decision-making.

If Johnson has a point, then news organizations that think young people shy away from complex issues because they are not entertaining enough may be underestimating their audience. If Johnson is right, then audiences who are increasingly entertaining themselves with complex interactive activities may expect news and information delivered in a different, interactive, perhaps convergent way.

David T. Z. Mindich also found that young people find news, particularly political and government news, less engaging and more passive. In his book *Tuned Out*, Mindich reports that people who do follow the news do so because their work and social conversations demand it, and they developed the habit when they were young.[4] He also finds that the response by most traditional news organizations to the challenge of engaging young audiences "range(s) from unimaginative to useless."[5] To engage young readers or viewers, he notes that traditional news outlets may resort to choosing stories that rely more on celebrity than substance. And Mindich indicates that may not be the right strategy. "In trying to make newspapers matter to young people, they make them matter to no one."[6] The same conclusion can be made for not just newspapers but for other news outlets.

For years, more than nine hundred U.S. newspapers have used Newspapers in Education programs as a way to reach youngsters by making copies of the daily newspaper available in the classroom, along with lesson plans for teachers to tie current events to their curriculum.

Hundreds of others provide a kids' news section in the paper. But a visit with some eighth graders at a Chicago middle school found few read newspapers, except in class and for class. Several of the students said they get their news of the world from parents or online aggregators like Google News and Yahoo! News. Several liked getting video and audio reports of news via the Internet. And many of them admitted knowing more celebrity news or sports news than world and national events.

GAMES

While news organizations may see their audiences as readers and viewers, the next wave are increasingly gamers, who like to explore, according to Shayne Bowman and Chris Willis, media design consultants. Bowman and Willis believe that news organizations can learn a lot about making news interactive by looking at games. "Media organizations don't realize that their job is connecting. They can no longer just be the 'big mouth,' they have to be the 'big ear,'" they said at a 2001 conference. "Today, news media organizations are story instigators. They start stories."[7]

Glenn Thomas, who is a designer and advocate of interactive games for news, noted in a 2002 speech that games in news can allow people to explore complex and difficult stories that they may not have the time or inclination to read about. "Games can become a tool, another tool in your arsenal to tell a story better" and inform people who do not read newspapers or watch television newscasts. "People who grew up playing games have a certain sense of exploration and sense of control that I think works against current traditional journalism of telling people what's right," Thomas said, "To some degree they expect to find out what's right."[8]

Several news outlets designed for children having been turning to convergence and interactivity, especially through games, in hopes of keeping their audiences engaged and informed. Education researchers say they have noticed that convergence is just a way of life for children, who "move between media seamlessly," so it makes sense that educational publications would be more convergent.[9] *Weekly Reader*, *Time For Kids*, and *Scholastic News* publish a series of grade-specific weekly news magazines that reach young audiences through school subscriptions. But they also provide students, teachers, and parents with numerous interactive online activities to complement and enhance the print materials. Many of the news for kids online sites have incorporated news quizzes and multimedia games to engage their audiences in news stories. The printed publications are oriented for classroom use by teachers and their students, while the websites are more often used by students when they are at home.

Suzanne Freeman, web editor for Scholastic.com, has found that children "expect a website to do something, not just read." As a result, they expect their news differently. She says they go online looking for games and information. "The challenge is making the website interactive and still giving them the content they need."[10]

TimeForKids.com, for example, has an interactive news game called Mag-o-matic that allows players to choose pictures and write headlines for a *Time for Kids* magazine cover. The children's BBC website has a game that tests players' news judgment with a variety of story headlines, asking players to determine which ones are newsworthy. Scholastic News has an interactive hangman game that has players spell out words related to news stories. Weekly Reader website visitors can play News Busters, which has the look and feel of the television game show *Jeopardy*.

All the sites also offer polls for online users. Poll questions ask about the latest Harry Potter book or what comic book would make a good film, whether adding vitamins to candy is a good idea or if users wear helmets when they ride their bikes. *Weekly Reader*'s Mia Toschi says television stations that air the weekly *Teen Kids News* shows get the poll results and some of those stations do reports on the polls. Each presidential election year, for example, *Weekly Reader* polls its audience on the race, and the polls' results have been good predictors of the final outcome.

While these news outlets have games, polls, and chats, they also have their share of hard news. For example, the website, bbc.co.uk/cbbcnews, published updated information in its section on the search for the July 21 London bombing suspects, just like its adult news page. The section posted the transit camera pictures of four suspects, just like the main BBC News home page. The website also streams a three-minute newscast that is tied to *Newsround*, the thirty-year-old BBC news program for young audiences. In addition to news updates, the site provided information to youngsters about handling their concerns and fears following the attack, with advice from child psychology experts.

Teen Kids News, a program linking *Weekly Reader* and hundreds of U.S. television stations, opens each of its half-hour television news magazine with the headlines of news from the week, from hurricanes to wildfires to the London bomb attacks. Then it presents longer reports on issues, ranging from home schooling from the perspective of the teens learning at home to autism and its effect on the siblings of autistic children. While the news is written in appropriate language and vocabulary for a younger audience, it does not shy away from tackling hard news that engages its audience. Both the BBC and *Teen Kids News* mix sports, lifestyle, and entertainment reports with news features of harder issues. For example, the release of the sixth installment of the Harry Potter book series warranted extensive coverage on the BBC site, while Teen News often profiles athletes and examines the problems of dating.

KID (CITIZEN) REPORTERS

The BBC for children has been pushing innovation in terms of participatory journalism through its Press Pack Reports. In this section of the website, the BBC provides games, instructions for producing stories, and information about the people and jobs associated with a newsroom. Then it provides blogs, reader news contributions to entice youngsters to join in the news producing process. One Press Pack contribution, from a twelve-year-old girl from

Edinburgh, examined a proposal by a teachers' group to no longer mark "fail" but "deferred success" when students do poorly on exams. In another part of the website, two students, one in Edinburgh and the other in London, blogged about their wait in line for the midnight release of *Harry Potter and the Half-Blood Prince*. And it is asking for its audience to contribute their podcasts and podcast recommendations to add to the website.

Weekly Reader, which has been providing news to children via the classroom for more than a hundred years, has teamed up with *Newsweek* in *Newsweek in the Classroom*. But its strongest convergence project may be *Teen Kids News*, with an estimated four million viewers in middle and high school to complement the nine million subscribers to the print publication. The program can be picked up by school systems on their public access channels or on regular broadcast channels. The scripts for the news show are also available on the show's website for teachers to use to work with students on public speaking and oral presentation skills.

Weekly Reader's Mia Toschi says the program was created with the dual goals of "teaching kids about the news so they can understand the world about them and to get them reading." The program dovetails with *Weekly Reader*'s *Current Events* publication. "Our program teaches kids about the news but we also teach kids to be reading." But rather than having adults or young adults report and anchor the weekly news show, teens are behind the anchor desk and putting together video reports. "It's not patronizing to kids because it's kids talking to kids in their language," says Toschi. She adds that the hope is that when kids get news about the world in their language and from their peers, they will become more interested in the world around them and develop interest in more sophisticated news. If they know more about their world, Toschi said, they will make better choices.[11]

Martha Pickerill, editor of *Time For Kids* magazine, a competitor with *Scholastic News* and the *Weekly Reader* publications, says the increase of violent and explicit information in adult news offerings has opened up a need and a demand for kids' news. Toschi says that *Teen Kids News* can be used for family viewing because "we don't have anything embarrassing" like Viagra commercials or extremely violent imagery. "We don't shy away from tough issues, but it's being done in a sensitive way." Pickerill also says her magazine provides a "combo platter of things" to its more than four million student readers. "They see that we cover the whole world and the things that they are inherently interested in."[12]

They also see news reported by children like themselves. The kid reporters for *Scholastic News* also did television reports on NBC and MSNBC during the 2004 presidential election campaign. Kid reporters have covered the Super Bowl and the presidential inauguration, interviewed members of President Bush's Cabinet and celebrities, and have provided reports on news from their area. Kids' news editors say their young audiences are telling them they feel respected and valued when they see other kids in professional roles as reporters and presenters. Scholastic.com's Freeman adds that current events might seem to be a turn-off for kids and teens "but a fresh look at it from their peers works well."[13]

Teen Kids News reporters come from the New York area because the show is produced in New York but the program enlists kid reporters in special contests. One contest required participants to write their own news feature, with the winners appearing on the news show and having their story published. Another asked contestants to interview someone who was an eyewitness to history and write up their interview. Winning entries were posted online. The reporters program grew out of *Weekly Reader* field trips, which sent kid reporters to special events like the Super Bowl and National Basketball Association All-Star Game. During the 2004 presidential campaign, kid reporters covered the Democratic and Republican party conventions and the debates.

Kid reporters for *Time For Kids* participate in an annual national search that determines their selection. *Time For Kids* requires budding reporters to submit articles and interviews, and the finalists submit videos as well. *Time For Kids* reporters suggest story ideas, but magazine and web staff members determine the assignments. Some assignments include interviews with newsmakers, and editor Pickerill says the reporters "ask the tough questions."[14]

"Kids are on top of the convergent journalist," says Scholastic.com's Freeman, and Michael Cappetta is one of those kids. By age fourteen, he had reported on the national political scene for both print and television and is producing a cable show for a teen audience. "If I was a news professional now, I would want to be making relationships with the next generation of news consumers," Cappetta says. That generation, his generation, is very conscious of news and its biases, he says. Cappetta also notes that "the impression is that people my age are only watching MTV. They are, but they are also interested in hearing local news." But local news must reflect his generation, he adds, not what adults think reflects them. Cappetta says teens want news that can be accessed quickly and immediately.[15]

The kids of today are "going to expect news even faster," Freeman says, "to know more in less time."[16] They are already getting news in different formats as kids; they will be expecting more of that as they grow up. That will be the challenge facing the next wave of journalists in the new age of convergence and consumer-driven news. Understanding the strengths of different media and harnessing those strengths to get news to audiences is the challenge facing journalism today.

SUMMARY

The news consumers of tomorrow are entrenched in multimedia and convergence news choices today. Educational and news organizations that provide news for kids have been exploring convergence through use of games, polls, quizzes, and child reporters. Traditional classroom news publications have been expanding their reach with young audiences through websites and cooperative ventures in television.

LEARNING THE LINGO

Collateral learning

NOTES

1. "Media Multi-Tasking: Changing the Amount and Nature of Young People's Media Use," at www.kff.org/entmedia/entmedia030905nr.cfm (accessed December 1, 2005).

2. "How Children Use Media Technology" at www.knowledgenetworks.com/info/press/collateral/HCUT_2003_PressSummary.pdf (accessed December 1, 2005).

3. Steven Johnson, *Everything Bad Is Good for You* (New York: Riverhead Books, 2005), 40.

4. David T. Z. Mindich, *Tuned Out: Why Americans Under 40 Don't Follow the News* (New York: Oxford University Press, 2005), 73.

5. Mindich, *Tuned Out*, 112.

6. Mindich, *Tuned Out*, 113.

7. Shayne Bowman and Chris Willis, "What Can News Media Learn from Computer Games," November 3, 2001, at www.hypergene.net/ideas/playnews.html (accessed December 1, 2005).

8. Glenn Thomas, "What Can Computer Games Teach Journalists?" August 8, 2002, at www.pewcenter.org/doingcj/speeches/s_aejmcglennthomas.html (accessed December 1, 2005).

9. L. Plowman and C. Stephen, "A 'benign addition'? Research on ICT and pre-school children," 2003, at www.ioe.stir.ac.uk/docs/Lydia_JCAL_benign_addition.PDF (accessed December 1, 2005).

10. Suzanne Freeman, interview by author, January 2005.

11. Mia Toschi, interview by author, August 2005.

12. Martha Pickerill, interview by author, January 2005.

13. Freeman, interview.

14. Pickerill, interview.

15. Michael Cappetta, interview by author, January 2005.

16. Freeman, interview.

Index

Note: Page numbers in *italic* type refer to illustrations or figures.

About the Author

JANET KOLODZY considers herself a "consecutive convergent," having worked in newspapers and television as well as dabbling in online before joining the journalism faculty at Emerson College in 1998. During her nine years in newspapers, she was both a reporter and editor at the *Arkansas Democrat* and the *Cleveland Plain Dealer*, before moving to the Cable News Network. During her eleven years at CNN and CNN International, she worked as a writer, copyeditor, producer, and senior producer. She also spent one summer working at CNN.com.

As an educator, Kolodzy has been instrumental in the design and implementation of convergence-oriented undergraduate and graduate curricula at Emerson. She has developed and taught two key convergence skills courses: "The News-gathering Process" for undergraduates and "Writing and Reporting across the Media" for graduate students. She has written papers and made panel presentations about teaching convergence and convergence journalism practices at several national and regional conferences over the past three years.